The Challenge of Pluralism

Religious Forces in the Modern Political World
General Editor: Allen D. Hertzke, The Carl Albert Center,
University of Oklahoma at Norman

The Challenge of Pluralism

CHURCH AND STATE IN FIVE DEMOCRACIES

Stephen V. Monsma
J. Christopher Soper

ROWMAN & LITTLEFIELD PUBLISHERS, INC.
Lanham • New York • Boulder • Oxford

ROWMAN & LITTLEFIELD PUBLISHERS, INC.

Published in the United States of America
by Rowman & Littlefield Publishers, Inc.
4720 Boston Way, Lanham, Maryland 20706

12 Hid's Copse Road
Cummor Hill, Oxford, OX2 9JJ, England

British Library Cataloging in Publication Information Available.

Library of Congress Cataloging-in-Publication Data
Monsma, Stephen V., 1936–
    The challenge of pluralism : church and state in five democracies
/ by Stephen V. Monsma and J. Christopher Soper.
        p.   cm. — (Religious forces in the modern political world)
    Includes bibliographical references and index.
    ISBN 0-8476-8568-3 (cloth : alk. paper). — ISBN 0-8476-8569-1
(pbk. : alk. paper)
    1. Church and state—History—20th century.   2. Democracy-
-Religious aspects—Christianity—History—20th century.
3. Religious pluralism—Christianity—History—20th century.
I. Soper, J. Christopher.   II. Title.   III. Series.
BV630.2.M595   1997
322'.1'0904—dc21   97-9791
                                                    CIP

ISBN 0-8476-8568-3 (cloth : alk. paper)
ISBN 0-8476-8569-1 (pbk. : alk. paper)

Printed in the United States of America

∞ ™ The paper used in this publication meets the minimum requirements of
American National Standard for Information Sciences—Permanence of Paper
for Printed Library Materials, ANSI Z39.48–1984.

Dedicated to

Mary Carlisle Monsma
Martin Monsma
Kristin Monsma
Jane Woodwell
Katharine Soper
David Soper

Contents

Preface

*A*merican society continues to be deeply divided on the question of the proper relationship between the institutions of church and state. Almost every year the Supreme Court is marked by sharp divisions in the church-state cases that come before it, divisions that mirror the disagreements and controversies of the broader American society. It was while we were discussing church-state practice in the United States that it occurred to us that a comparative analysis of how other western pluralistic democracies resolve church-state tensions might shed new light on this enduring issue in American politics. This book, then, is a comparative study of church-state policy in the United States, the Netherlands, Australia, England, and Germany. We do not pretend that this book will resolve a political debate in the United States that is as abiding as it is frustrating to the groups and individuals involved in it, but it is our hope that it will provide a different perspective on it.

As we delved further into the study of these five countries, we were struck at how contemporary church-state practice had much to do with each nation's unique history and cultural assumptions about the proper place of religion in public life. This book is not an apology for the church-state practice in any one of these countries, but we have attempted to be sensitive to each nation's particular history in the story we have told. At the same time, our study has convinced us that sufficient similarities in the church-state experiences of the five countries exist that allow us to make some general conclusions that would apply to each. Democracies, we believe, can and should learn from each other.

The lessons these countries offer are particularly important now. Increasing levels of religious pluralism in the modern world raise tensions among religious groups and challenge the inherited church-state models of the nations in our study. In addition, the growth of the welfare state has led to an expansion of government involvement in almost all aspects of society, including religious life, and threatens to undermine past relations between religious and political institutions.

We are convinced that the answer to these growing conflicts is to be found in a church-state policy that is genuinely neutral among all religious groups and between religious and secular perspectives generally, and that accommodates and promotes the religious pluralism that is a natural feature of each nation. We do not believe that the state can attain genuine neutrality, or evenhandedness among religious and secular groups in society, with a church-state policy that supports only some religious groups and practices but not others, nor through a no-aid-to-religion standard that ends up favoring secular over religious perspectives. Either of these policies would violate the standard of government neutrality that we believe should lie at the heart of a country's church-state policy. It is to the extent that the five nations in our study fall short of this goal that we are critical of their practices, while it is to the degree to which each attains this evenhandedness that they serve as a model from which we hope to draw some lessons.

We have received assistance and cooperation from many people in our research for this book. We would like to thank the dozens of people whom we interviewed in each country for our study. They gave freely of their time and expertise, provided us with invaluable insight about the church-state practices of their countries, and were a constant source of support with the hospitality they extended to us. We also owe a considerable debt to the following people who read portions of the manuscript and gave numerous suggestions that helped us avoid errors and generally strengthened the book: J.P. Balkenende, Sophie van Bijsterveld, Gary Bouma, Stanley Carlson-Thies, Lothar Coenen, Michael Hogan, Cees Klop, Frans Koopmans, George Moyser, Jorgen Rasmussen, Gerhard Robbers, and Jerry Waltman. We also would like to thank Lothar Coenen for his help in arranging for many of the interviews in Germany. The blame for any remaining errors of fact or interpretation is, however, ours alone. Stephen Wrinn, our editor at Rowman & Littlefield, provided just the right combination of encouragement and suggestions to strengthen our manuscript, and he wisely selected an outside reviewer for the book who read the entire manuscript carefully and made very helpful comments. We would also like to thank the American Politican Science Association and Pepperdine University for providing us with grant money for travel to each of these countries.

Finally, we would like to thank our families for their constant love, moral support, patience, and interest in our work: our wives, Jane and Mary, and our children, Katharine and David, and Martin and Kristin. They all richly deserve the dedication of this book.

Chapter 1

INTRODUCTION

*F*rom Plato's discussion of religion in the *Laws,* to the conflict between Pope Gregory VII and King Henry IV in the Middle Ages, to present-day debates about the proper role of religious groups in the making of public policy, the world has seen no lack of debate and discussion about how two of the most powerful and longest lasting of human institutions—the church and the state—are to relate to each other.[1] Religion is such a pervasive, deeply ingrained aspect of human existence that few, if any, examples can be found of human societies in which religion does not play a prominent role. Similarly, government is such an omnipresent feature of human societies that again few, if any, examples can be found of human societies with no political or governmental frameworks. As a result of the enduring presence and power of both the church and the state in virtually all human societies, one of the perpetual issues with which all societies have to struggle is how these two spheres of human endeavor should relate to each other.

This book explores how five western liberal democracies—the United States, the Netherlands, Australia, England, and Germany—have sought to deal with this issue. All five are successful, stable, democratic nations, yet they have approached the question of church-state relations in somewhat different ways. Especially in the United States church-state issues have remained on the front burner of discussion and debate. There are interest groups committed to one side or the other of church-state questions, Congress struggles each year with constitutional amendments that seek to change the ground rules of church-state relations, issues such as prayer in public schools regularly enter into presidential campaigns, and almost every year the Supreme Court decides church-state cases marked by closely divided decisions and at times embarrassingly vitriolic opinions. In the other democracies considered here, new church-state issues are being raised by changing immigration patterns that have recently brought sizable numbers of nonwestern, non-Christian immi-

1

grants into them, creating significantly greater religious pluralism. Three of them are experiencing new church-state issues because of new human rights standards being raised by the European Union. This book compares the approaches these five western democracies are pursuing in church-state relations. Our goal is to give new guidance to all democracies and to the United States in particular in their attempts to relate church and state to each other in a manner that is supportive of their citizens' religious freedoms and the role religion plays in them.

Exploring the issue of church-state relations in these countries has taken on a new importance because there is increasing talk of devolving certain activities and programs previously run by government agencies to private, usually nonprofit organizations, many of which have a religious history or orientation. As western governments look to private, often religiously based organizations to play larger roles in society, questions of church and state are bound to be magnified. If programs and activities that were previously run by government agencies are to devolve on private religiously based agencies, usually with accompanying governmental funds, are their religious orientations likely to be toned down or eclipsed? Should they be? If religiously based agencies are excluded from governmental funding programs—as is largely done in the United States in the case of elementary and secondary schools—is that a form of discrimination against religious agencies? These questions are not new. What is new is that if governments are to move in the direction of public policies that depend more and more heavily on private agencies for education, welfare, health, and other services, these questions will come to be written much larger than they have been in even the recent past.

In this introductory chapter we set the context for our study by first considering three basic church-state questions that repeatedly arise in democratic polities. In subsequent chapters we explore how each of the five countries has responded to these questions. The next section sets out a basic religious liberty goal that we will use as a standard against which to evaluate the strengths and weaknesses of the five countries' approaches to church-state issues. The third section describes three models of church-state relationships, and the final section explains why we selected these five democracies for this study.

Three Questions

Questions of church and state have often proven contentious even in stable, successful democracies. More specifically, there are three very basic questions that at various points in history, and today as well, have confronted democratic societies. One question is: *How far can a democratic polity go in permitting religiously motivated behavior that is contrary to societal welfare or norms?* There is general agreement that when the exercise of religious freedom by one group has the effect of endangering the health or safety of others or of significantly disrupting the smooth functioning of life lived in society, the claims of religious freedom must yield to the welfare of the broader society. On this basis, most western democracies require, for example, religious burial practices to meet normal health standards and require religious processions on public streets to obtain the normal permits regulating the timing and size of such processions. But this leaves many questions. How serious must the threat to public health and safety be before the government insists that even religiously motivated practices must be curtailed? How significant must the disruption to the normal functioning of society be before government has a right to limit or forbid a religiously motivated practice?

There is also the matter of religious groups violating deeply held societal norms. Modern democracies—no matter how committed to religious pluralism—would not allow human sacrifice, even if it were part of a group's sincere religious beliefs. Allowing human sacrifice would so violate such deeply held norms as respect for human life that society would be torn apart, if it were allowed in the name of religious freedom. Democratic societies that are fully committed to freedom of religion have decided there are certain norms or values so fundamental to human existence and so deeply held that religion cannot be used as a basis for their violation. In such cases religion must yield to the claims of the broader society and its values. When those values are violated by religious groups the force of law can be brought to bear on them. The political order sometimes outlaws and punishes certain religiously motivated practices.

Here also questions arise over where to draw the line between practices that are legally permissible and impermissible in the name of religion. Human sacrifice may be out, but what about polygamy—a burning issue in nineteenth-century America. Or today what about female circumcision? It is practiced by certain African cultures as a religious rite, but should it be allowed when their members are living in western societies? Or what is to happen when Muslim schools in western societies teach attitudes and values—such as those relating to the role of women in society—that are today rejected by those societies? These are not trivial questions. Religious freedom is a fundamental freedom. Many Americans, when referring to religious freedom as the "first freedom," have more than its location in their Bill of Rights in mind. The horrors of religious wars and of western societies burning religious heretics at the stake not that many years ago stand as vivid testimonies to the importance of religious freedom. Let no one take it for granted or look lightly on attempts even to nibble away at its fringes.

But societal unity and welfare are also of crucial importance. What makes a society into a society is much more than a conglomeration of persons occupying the same territory. Instead, a society is marked both by cooperative efforts promoting societal welfare that make possible life lived in a complex, interdependent society and by shared values, myths, and memories that lead persons to identify themselves as a people. It is as persons identify themselves as members of a common society that cooperative tasks, sacrifices for the larger good, and other basics of human civilization are made possible. When common values and beliefs of a fundamental nature are shattered, or when some persons' practices endanger and disrupt the lives of others, society is threatened with disintegration: at best, cooperation is made difficult and, at worst, barbarism and civil war result. Sarajevo stands as an end-of-the-twentieth-century symbol of the horror that can result when bonds of respect and civility are broken.

In addition, something more than societal unity may be at stake. Many theorists have contended that free, democratic government is finally dependent upon a populace with certain internalized values and habits of the mind. Clinton Rossiter once wrote, "It takes more than a perfect plan of government to pursue ordered liberty. Something else is needed, some moral principle diffused among the people to strengthen the urge to peaceful obedience and hold the community on an even keel. . . . [Democratic] government rests on a definite moral basis: a virtuous people."[2] If, in fact, a "virtuous people" is essential for a successfully functioning democracy, any movements—including religious ones—that work to build up a sense of virtue or morality among the public and that teach respect for the welfare of others become crucial for a healthy democracy, and any movements that undercut or subvert a sense of virtue, morality, and consideration for others pose a significant threat to democratic government. Does democratic self-preservation thereby mean religious movements that undercut a sense of public virtue and morality, or that subvert respect for the welfare of others, should not receive religious freedom protection?

In short, religious freedom, on the one hand, and shared values and beliefs and public health and safety, on the other hand, are enormously important. That fact raises the stakes in resolving the question of how far a polity can go in permitting behavior contrary to societal welfare and norms that is nevertheless justified on the basis of religious beliefs; it does not make resolving it easy.

This leads to the second basic question related to religion and society that confronts democratic polities today: *Should the state encourage and promote consensual religious beliefs and traditions in an attempt to support the common values and beliefs that bind a society together and make possible limited, democratic government?* This is the positive version of the first question just raised.

If certain shared values are crucial for societal unity and democratic governance, should government perhaps not only oppose those religious practices and movements that would undercut those values, but also encourage them in a positive manner through the promotion of certain consensual religious values and symbols? As we will see more fully later, in nineteenth-century America the common schools were seen as being extremely important precisely because they taught not only knowledge and skills but also values and beliefs. Horace Mann and his fellow New England school reformers saw the common school as the key device by which democracy would be safeguarded in the face of a rising tide of uneducated frontier farmers and millions of immigrants from foreign lands. Thus Bible reading, prayers, and moral lessons were an integral part of the common school. It was a consensual, civil religion that marked the common schools, but it was thought crucial that the state play an active role in supporting and propagating religion of this sort. In England today the established Church of England is often seen as important in inculcating a sense of national unity, honor, and morality that are crucial for free, democratic government. But when the state supports religion of this sort, does it perhaps violate the norm of religious freedom for all? After all, there are many people holding to distinctive, minority religious beliefs or to clearly secular worldviews who are left out of a consensual civil religion. They may very well see a state-supported consensual religion as undermining their own faith or secular worldview.

A third basic question emerges from a fundamental fact of life in all industrialized, urbanized western democracies: the expansion of the modern administrative state into almost all areas of life. Whether it is economic regulation and stimulation, health care, education (from preschool preparatory programs to postdoctoral fellowships), care for the elderly, land-use planning and zoning, radio and television licensing and regulation, preservation of historical sites, or regulation of abortion and other health services, the modern administrative state is active in regulating, supporting, and providing services. But almost all the areas just cited as examples of state activity are also areas in which religious communities have been and continue to be active. This leads to the question: *When religious groups and the state are both active in the same fields of endeavor, how can one ensure that the state does not advantage or disadvantage any one religious group or either religion or nonreligion over the other?* If the state, for example, collects taxes from the entire population in order to fund its own secular schools and to help fund the programs of the schools of the traditional, well-established religions, but does not fund the schools of newer, non-mainstream religions, is it not advantaging some religions and disadvantaging others? Or if the state funds its own secular social service programs and those of secularly based nonprofit agencies, but leaves religiously based groups involved in the same social service programs to struggle on without state help, is not religion clearly being disadvantaged? But if the state inserts religion into its own activities or funds the activities of religious groups, does it not run the risk of favoring one religious group over another or of favoring religion over secular belief structures? As the modern state has entered more and more areas to regulate, fund, or provide services, questions of evenhandedness among all religious groups and between secular and religious groups arise.

In the following chapters we will consider how each of the five countries whose church-state principles and practices we have chosen for analysis have responded to these three questions.

A Basic Goal

In discussing and at some points suggesting answers to the three questions raised in the prior section, we will hold to the basic ideal or goal of governmental neutrality on matters of religion. We define neutrality as government neither favoring nor burdening any particular religion, nor favoring or burdening religion as a whole or secular systems of belief as a whole. Governmental religious neutrality is attained when government does not influence its citizens' choices for or against certain religious or secular systems of belief, either by imposing burdens on them or by granting advantages to them. Instead, government is neutral when it is evenhanded toward people of all faiths and of none. This concept of state neutrality on matters of religion is what American legal scholar Douglas Laycock has termed substantive neutrality and what Stephen Monsma calls positive neutrality.[3] Laycock describes substantive neutrality as being achieved when the government minimizes "the extent to which it either encourages or discourages religious belief or disbelief, practice or nonpractice, observance or nonobservance."[4]

We believe this goal takes precedence over any specific theory or means that at one time or another and in one polity or another has been put forward to structure church-state relations, such as an established church, a multiple establishment, no aid at all for religion, a wall of separation between church and state, and financial support for a wide range of religious expressions. All these and more have been tried and implemented at one time or another in the five democracies considered here. But we believe none of them should be taken as ends or goals in themselves. The appropriate goal should be governmental neutrality toward all religious groups and toward religion as a whole and secular worldviews as a whole. That is the standard against which specific church-state principles and theories, or specific means to implement those principles and theories, should be judged. It is when this goal of neutrality is fully realized that the moving words of U. S. Supreme Court Justice Potter Stewart take on life and meaning: "What our Constitution indispensably protects is the freedom of each of us, be he Jew or Agnostic, Christian or Atheist, Buddhist or Freethinker, to believe or disbelieve, to worship or not worship, to pray or keep silent, according to his own conscience, uncoerced and unrestrained by government."[5]

This basic goal or ideal of governmental neutrality on matters of religious belief and nonbelief is largely in keeping with the liberal tradition within western society, yet differs in some important ways from that tradition. That tradition emerged on the western scene in the eighteenth-century Enlightenment, received a concrete manifestation in the French Revolution, was a strong social and political movement in the nineteenth century, and is a very active force down to today in all five democracies considered here.[6] In fact, in a generalized way one could say that virtually all of western society today is liberal. Individual rights are universally respected (in theory and usually in practice), inherited class distinctions are not seen as giving special political prerogatives, the one person-one vote principle is the norm, and selecting political leaders by free, competitive elections is fully accepted. In the sense of holding to principles such as these, all five of the countries included in this book are liberal democracies.

Liberalism can, however, also be seen as a more specific, philosophical theory or movement. Liberalism in this sense is often referred to as Enlightenment liberalism. It reacted with horror to the religious wars of the seventeenth century and to the often conservative nature of religious bodies that supported hereditary privileges and authoritarian government and opposed democratic reforms. Liberals placed great faith in human reason, believing that if people were freed from existing economic, political, and religious constraints they could, through the exercise of their reason, reach a consensus on the virtues and institutions needed for a free and prosperous society. Religion in its particular manifestations was seen as rooted in authority and superstitions and—when brought into the political arena—as a dangerous force, since it would work to divide society and become a basis for one group to use the political order to force its will onto others. On the other hand, basic, consensual religious beliefs were both discoverable by human reason and adequate to construct a free, prosperous society. Thus Enlightenment liberalism believed religion in its particular manifestations should be banned from the public realm as a dangerous, divisive force; it saw religion in its rational, consensual manifestation as potentially having a positive, unifying role to play in the public realm.

Thus Enlightenment liberals typically called for a strict separation of church and state. They believed such a separation would spare the state from the dangerous divisions particularistic religion posed, yet would not harm particularistic religion, since it would continue to flourish in the purely private realm. Religious belief was something that people would be free to express in their private lives, but was of no concern to the state. The state would thereby be neutral on matters of religion. It would neither help nor hinder any particular religion. The state would only support and identify with rational, consensual religious themes, such as duty, honesty, responsibility, and respect, on which all religions and even all reasonable nonreligious people agreed. It thereby equated government neutrality on matters of religion and strict church-state separation. This meant Enlightenment liberals also saw religious freedom as being wholly a negative freedom, that is, as consisting of the right to be free from government restrictions or restraints on one's exercise of religion. They, for the most part, did not see it as also containing an element of positive freedom, that is, as requiring certain positive governmental actions that would make it possible for people to live out their religious faiths. All that it felt was necessary for people to be fully free was for government to stay out of religious affairs.

Enlightenment liberalism was often at odds with the existing church authorities, since they—not surprisingly—resisted both the liberals' theoretical assumptions and the practical political consequences of those assumptions. This meant Enlightenment liberalism often had an anticlerical nature. Today it is sometimes forgotten that the French Revolution was as much a revolution against the organized church and social class privileges as it was a revolution against an authoritarian monarchy.

All five countries considered in this book had strong Enlightenment liberal movements, and the story of church-state relations in each of them is to a significant degree the story of the varied ways in which the conflict between the Enlightenment liberals and opposing movements played out. We will return to this issue in subsequent chapters.

The concept of governmental neutrality on matters of religion as defined earlier in this section is clearly in the tradition of liberalism as a generalized force in western societies, but differs in some important respects from the assumptions and beliefs of Enlightenment liberalism. Enlightenment liberalism rested on three interrelated assumptions: that particularistic religion could be safely assigned to the purely private sphere without infringing on the religious beliefs and practices of its adherents, that a public realm stripped of all religious elements would be a neutral zone among the various religious faiths and between faith and nonbelief, and that religious freedom would flourish in the absence of governmental restraints and with no need for positive governmental actions to equalize the advantages enjoyed by religious and nonreligious groups. On the basis of these assumptions the Enlightenment liberal perspective equates strict church-state separation and government religious neutrality.

These liberal assumptions, however, are coming under increasing attack in today's world. As Robert Bellah and his associates have written: "Yet religion, and certainly biblical religion, is concerned with the whole of life—with social, economic, and political matters as well as with private and personal ones. Not only has biblical language continued to be part of American public and political discourse, the churches have continuously exerted influence on public life right up to the present time."[7] As will become clear as this book progresses, the religious communities of all five countries considered in it are concerned with a wide range of public policy questions and are active in providing education, health care, and other social services. If indeed religion has a strong public facet to it and if religious groups, as well as government, are actively involved in education and other service activities, the Enlightenment liberal belief that limiting religion to the purely private realm leads to state neutrality on matters of religion is simply not accurate. If this is the case, removing all religious elements from the public sphere and seeing religious freedom as requiring no positive steps to recognize or support religion are, at the least, drawn into question. Thus earlier in this section we defined government neutrality not in terms of strict church-state separation or any other specific church-state arrangement, but in terms of an evenhandedness among people of all faiths and of none. We view neutrality in terms of government not influencing by its actions its citizens' choices for or against any particular religious or secular system of belief. It should neither advantage nor burden religion. We do not assume that withdrawing all government support for particularistic religion, extending government support for generalized, consensual religion, or merely removing all government restraints on the exercise of religion necessarily equates to neutrality.

Three Models

Even a cursory look at church-state relations in the five democracies to be considered reveals that they all have followed different church-state policies. In thinking more systematically about church-state relations in these countries and in organizing the mass of observations we will be making, it is helpful to think in terms of three basic models of church-state relations that modern, western democracies have followed. None of the five countries under review here follow any one of these models in a pure form, but starting out with these three models in mind will help to organize and focus the mass of observations we will be making.

One model is the strict church-state separation model. Under this model—which traces its roots to the Enlightenment liberal view of society and politics—religion and politics are seen as clearly distinct areas of human endeavor that should be kept separate from each other. Religion is seen as a personal, private matter, best left to the realm of personal choice and action. When religion and politics are mixed—with either the state dictating religious beliefs or practice or religion using the state to advance its cause—both religion and politics suffer. The state should be neutral on matters of religion and this neutrality is assumed to be achieved best by keeping religion and politics separate. Those who support this model point to the religious wars of the seventeenth century and present-day religious strife in Bosnia-Herzegovina and the Middle East as examples of what happens when religion and politics mix. Of the five countries under consideration here the United States comes the closest to following the strict separation model.

A second model—at the opposite end of the continuum from the church-state separation model—is the established church model. Under this model the state and the church form a partnership in advancing the cause of religion and the state. Church and state are seen as two pillars on which a stable, prosperous society rests. The state provides the church with recognition, accommodation, and often financial support; the church provides the state with an aura of legitimacy and tradition, recognition, and a sense of national unity and purpose. In present-day modern democracies it is usually seen more as a traditional, innocuous, but also helpful holdover from earlier times, when a church-state partnership was seen as crucial for both political stability and religious prosperity, than as a living, vibrant church-state model essential in today's world.

Religious establishment can take several different forms. It can, first, be either formal or informal. In formal church establishments the government recognizes and supports one particular church or denomination, and while other religions are tolerated, they clearly do not occupy the favored position the established church does. Religious establishment may also be more informal in nature. Here one particular church is favored by the state, and that church supports the existing political order, but both occur not because of formal, legal provisions, but because of certain informal forces such as those of tradition or the overwhelming numerical or cultural strength of one religion. Church establishment can also be marked either by only one particular established church or by a system of multiple church establishment. Under the latter system, the state seeks to favor and work with a number of favored religious bodies. Here the state usually promotes a generic "religion-in-general"[8] that is more of a civil religion, supportive of the state and its traditions, than a particularistic faith. Of the five countries considered in this study, England is the only one with a formally established church, although some observers would make the case that in Germany there is an informal multiple establishment.

The third church-state model is the pluralist or structural pluralist model.[9] Under this model "society is understood as made up of competing or perhaps complementary spheres."[10] Included among these spheres or realms of societal activities are education, business, the arts, and the family—and religion and government. These spheres have distinct activities or responsibilities, and they are to enjoy autonomy or freedom in their efforts to fulfill them. But it is crucial to note that the pluralist model sees religion not as a separate sphere with only limited relevance to the other spheres as the liberal strict separationists do, but as having a bearing on all of life. Pluralists also stress the existence of secular perspectives or worldviews that play a similar role to religion in society. "Pluralism is a matter of political respect by the state for the many world views held by the different kinds of institutions that fulfill the differentiated needs of a free society."[11] Government is not to takes sides among the plurality of religious and secular worldviews swirling about in society. It is to seek equal justice for all of them, with justice essentially defined as giving them all their freedom and neither advantaging or disadvantaging any of them. The Netherlands is probably the clearest example of a country that has self-consciously sought to follow this model. Germany—in addition to possessing some aspects of the multiple, informal establishment model—and Australia also possess some features of this model.

In the following chapters we describe church-state relations in the five countries and seek to classify the five countries in terms of these three models, even while recognizing that none of them will be pure examples of any of them.

Five Stable Democracies

As explained earlier in the chapter this book explores how five stable, western, liberal democratic countries have sought to respond to key questions posed by the intersection of those two great human institutions: the church and the state. We believe the five countries chosen for our study to be particularly well suited for our purposes for three basic reasons. First, they are all stable democracies whose successful commitment to religious freedom is generally recognized. Germany has the Nazi regime in its past and the eastern part of the country emerged from an oppressive communist past only recently, but for fifty years West Germany—into which East Germany was absorbed—has been recognized as part of the family of liberal western democracies. Thus the five countries selected fit our purpose of wishing to explore how polities recognized as mature, successful democracies have dealt with the issue of church-state relations.

Second, all five countries are religiously pluralistic, with predominantly Christian, Protestant traditions but also with sizable Catholic populations and many smaller religious minorities. In the case of Germany and the Netherlands Protestants and Catholics are today about numerically equal, but even in those countries Protestants have been dominant in a social and political sense through most of the modern era, and thus it was the Protestants that set the tone or played the dominant role in working through church-state issues. None of the five countries is either overwhelmingly Protestant, as is the case with the Scandinavian countries, or overwhelmingly Catholic, as is the case with Spain or Italy. In all five there is a religious pluralism, characterized by large numbers of both Catholics and Protestants and a variety of Protestant groups. Also, all five have come to be marked in recent years by sharply increasing numbers of adherents of non-Christian faiths and people of no religious faith. Religiously, all five nations are facing the challenge of pluralism.

A third characteristic of the five countries is that, despite their similar cultural heritages and similar religious composition, they have chosen distinctly different approaches to church-state issues. England has an officially established church; the United States has followed a route emphasizing strict church-state separation; Australia has constitutional provisions very similar to those found in the American Constitution but has interpreted and implemented them in a quite different manner; the Netherlands is known for following a self-conscious policy of religious pluralism; and Germany, although not having an officially established church, has a long history of close cooperation between the state and the church. Thus the five countries are not carbon copies of each other. They offer a rich texture of differences that make them excellent subjects for comparative study.

Each of the following five chapters deals with one of the five countries and follows the same basic outline. Each chapter first gives a brief description of some salient characteristics of the nation and next gives a historical summary of church-state relations in that country. Church-state relations have clearly been shaped by the unique history of each country, and this section seeks to explain these unique sets of circumstances and how they have led to certain theories, assumptions, and mindsets that have guided church-state relations in that nation. Each chapter then considers how—in light of its history and church-state theories and assumptions—the country has handled the issue of the free exercise of religion, especially for minority religious groups. Then the chapter considers how the country has dealt with the issue of state accommodation of and support for religion, with special attention being paid to public policies as they relate to issues of education and religiously based social service organizations. The final section of each chapter offers some concluding observations and evaluations of the country's church-state policies.

Notes

1. Throughout this book we will follow conventional American usage and use the term "church" to refer generically to religion in its various manifestations.

2. Clinton Rossiter, *Seedbed of the Republic* (New York: Harcourt, Brace &

World, 1953), 447. Also see James Q. Wilson, *The Moral Sense* (New York: Free Press, 1993).

3. See Douglas Laycock, "Formal, Substantive, and Disaggregated Neutrality Toward Religion," *DePaul Law Review* 39 (1990), 1001–6, Stephen V. Monsma, *Positive Neutrality* (Westport, Conn.: Greenwood, 1993), chap. 5, and Stephen V. Monsma, *When Sacred and Secular Mix: Religious Nonprofit Organizations and Public Money* (Lanham, Md.: Rowman & Littlefield, 1996), chap. 6. It should be noted that this goal of governmental religious neutrality is itself not neutral. It makes a choice in favor of a certain type of governmental religious neutrality and thereby reflects certain assumptions and values that differ from those, for example, of Erastian or Enlightenment liberal thinking.

4. Laycock, "Formal, Substantive, and Disaggregated Neutrality Toward Religion," 1001.

5. From Stewart's dissent in *Abington School District v. Schempp,* 374 US at 319–320 (1963).

6. On Enlightenment liberalism and its impact in western society see Peter Gay, *The Enlightenment: An Interpretation* (New York: Knopf, 1966), and Henry A. May, *The Enlightenment in America* (New York: Oxford University Press, 1976).

7. Robert Bellah, Richard Madsen, William M. Sullivan, Ann Swindler, and Steven M. Tipton, *Habits of the Heart* (New York: Harper & Row, Perennial Library, 1986), 220.

8. The term is Martin Marty's. See Martin Marty, *The New Shape of American Religion* (New York: Harper & Row, 1958), 2, 31–44.

9. On this model see Carl H. Esbeck, "A Typology of Church-State Relations in Current American Thought," in Luis Lugo, ed., *Religion, Public Life, and the American Polity* (Knoxville: University of Tennessee Press, 1994), 15–18 and Monsma, *Positive Neutrality,* 137–71.

10. John G. Francis, "The Evolving Regulatory Structure of European Church-State Relationships," *Journal of Church and State* 34 (1992), 782.

11. Esbeck, "A Typology of Church-State Relations," 15.

Chapter 2

THE UNITED STATES: STRICT SEPARATION

$\mathcal{I}$n 1947 the American Supreme Court declared in ringing words:

> No tax in any amount, large or small, can be levied to support any religious activities or institutions, whatever they may be called, or whatever form they may adopt to teach or practice religion. Neither a state nor the Federal government can, openly or secretly, participate in the affairs of any religious organizations or groups and *vice versa*. In the words of Jefferson, the clause against establishment of religion by law was intended to erect "a wall of separation between church and state."[1]

Later the Court went on to insist that the wall between church and state "must be kept high and impregnable."[2] There is, however, more than a little irony in the fact that the Court decided, after articulating these ringing words of strict—even absolute—church-state separation, that the First Amendment allows government to aid religiously based schools in the form of subsidies to transport children to them. As one of the dissenting justices complained, the Court's decision reminded him "of Julia who, according to Byron's reports, 'whispering "I will ne'er consent,"—consented.' "[3]

There is much in this early decision that typifies the Supreme Court's approach to church-state issues. It has usually supported strict church-state separation in theory and often insists on it in practice, yet at other times it finds means by which to relax the application of the strict separation principle. In so doing, it reflects the broader American society that usually supports church-state separation in principle, but often favors state accommodation of and support for religion in specific instances.[4] The result—many observers are convinced—is a muddled, confused body of law, marked by "contradictory principles, vaguely defined tests, and eccentric distinctions."[5]

15

This chapter explores the American approach to issues of church and state, noting the strong commitment to strict church-state separation, efforts in practice sometimes to hold firm to it and sometimes to modify it, and the resulting state of affairs. We do so in six sections. First, we give some relevant information on the American society and political system, next we give some necessary historical background. The next three sections consider free exercise theories and practices, establishment theories and practices as they relate to elementary and secondary education, and establishment theories and practices as they relate to other concerns. Finally, we make some concluding observations.

The Nation

With a population of 250 million drawn from most of the other nations of the world, the United States is by far the most populous and most diverse of the five countries considered in this book. It is also clearly a—and some would say the leading—stable democracy in today's world. The United States has the oldest written constitution in the world, and its religious freedom protections are thereby the oldest written constitutional protections of religion.

Two characteristics of the American people are especially relevant to this study and worth noting. The first of these is the great religious diversity of the American people, a diversity that is clearly greater than that of the other countries considered in this book. From the founding of the nation through the nineteenth century the United States was an overwhelmingly Protestant country. There was diversity within this Protestantism, but by the mid-nineteenth century the large mainline denominations—Methodists, Presbyterians, Congregationalists, Episcopalians, Baptists, and Lutherans—dominated the religious life of the nation. Since the nineteenth century much has changed. Both conservative, evangelical Protestants and Roman Catholics now challenge the dominance of mainline Protestantism—both in numbers and in cultural and political power. Numerically, survey research shows that approximately 22 percent of the population consider themselves white mainline Protestants, 23 percent white evangelical Protestants, and 20 percent white Catholics.[6] Black Christians make up 9 percent of the population. Equally important, the social and educational gap that once existed between Catholics and Protestants has closed. Two researchers have concluded, "White Catholics are now very much a part of the established American middle class and upper-middle class."[7] Similarly, the success of the highly conservative, evangelical political organization, the Christian Coalition, with 2 million members, demonstrates the growing political and social power of evangelical Protestants.

Adding to American religious diversity is the 2 percent of the population that is Jewish, the 2 percent that is Mormon, and the 0.5 percent that is Muslim.[8] Secularists—those without any religion commitment—now constitute about 11 percent of the population.[9] In addition, one finds many small faith groups in the United States, including Hinduism, Buddhism, Native American religion, New Age spirituality, and a variety of sects. It is no exaggeration to say that any religious group present in the world has its adherents in the United States. The end result of this religious diversity, and especially the combination of declining numbers among mainline Protestants and the rise of both Catholics and conservative, nonmainline Protestants, is that no one religious tradition is socially or politically dominant in the United States today. Christianity is, of course, the dominant religion but it is fractured into literally thousands of separate groups.

A second important characteristic is Americans' high rate of religious membership and activity, when compared to the people of other modern, industrialized countries. The results of a 1994 poll, for example, led its authors to conclude that "at the end of the 20th century, the wealthiest, most powerful and best educated country on Earth is still one of the most religious."[10] Forty-four percent of the American people in a recent poll reported attending religious services once a week or more, compared to 18 percent in the former West Germany, 14 percent in Britain, and 10 percent in France.[11] Eighty-two percent of Americans identified themselves as a religious person, compared to 55 percent in Britain, 54 percent in West Germany, and 48 percent in France. As one researcher has written, "By just about every measure that survey researchers have conceived and employed, the United States appears markedly more religious than its peers in the family of nations, the other industrial democracies."[12]

Politically, it is important to keep in mind the crucial role played by the American Supreme Court in constitutional interpretation. The nine life-appointed justices of the Supreme Court have the final word in interpreting the religious freedom language of the First Amendment. They can hold any act by any branch of the national, state, or local governments to be in violation of the First Amendment and therefore null and void. Thus the story of church-state relations in the United States is to a large degree a story of the Supreme Court's interpretations of the basic, simple—yet devilishly elusive—words of the First Amend-

ment: "Congress shall make no law respecting an establishment of religion, or prohibiting the free exercise thereof." Before we turn directly
to these struggles, it is important to consider some key elements of the
history of the development of church-state attitudes, practices, and principles.

Historical Background

American church-state theory and practice has gone through four
distinct stages during the past three hundred years. The first stage was
the establishment of religion during the colonial era of the seventeenth
and eighteenth centuries. When the American colonies were first settled,
most followed the prevailing European pattern of creating established
churches. The English Puritans in New England, the Dutch Reformed
in New Amsterdam, the Anglicans in Virginia, and other colonists elsewhere assumed that "the pattern of religious uniformity would of necessity be transplanted and perpetuated in the colonies."[13] The assumption
was that religious unity was essential for political unity. Thus the favored
churches were granted tax supports of different types, dissenters were
subjected to penalties of varying severity, and civil authorities exercised
control over certain ecclesiastical affairs.

The second half of the eighteenth century saw a major upheaval in
this system, when a movement to disestablish the churches emerged at
about the same time as the movement for independence from Britain.
This disestablishment was the result of two dissimilar movements that
came together in a "strange coalition."[14] The first of these movements
was the Great Awakening, a religious revival that swept through the
colonies in the 1740s and beyond. It is hard to exaggerate the breadth
and depth of this revival. It featured itinerant preachers, mass exhibitions
of religious fervor, and renewed religious commitments by the masses.
It also had a strong antiestablished church emphasis, since it was reacting
against the perceived formalism and dead orthodoxy of the existing,
usually established churches. This emphasis was strengthened when most
of the established churches and their clergy reacted negatively to the
Great Awakening, and sometimes used their influence with civil authorities to obtain the imposition of fines and imprisonment.

The second partner in the "strange coalition" consisted of the Enlightenment liberal rationalists. Led by figures such as Thomas Jefferson
and James Madison these people were religious—even Christian—in a
broad, generic sense, but largely rejected or saw as irrelevant to govern-

ment the traditional doctrines of historic Christianity. These people were well read, cosmopolitan, and revolted by the religious persecutions that had marked Europe in the recent past and that were also present in the colonies. They were rationalists who felt that human reason could discern the basic precepts of religion that were necessary for a stable, moral society and political order. Doctrines peculiar to the various religious traditions were unnecessary and even dangerous for the public order, and thus they could and should be separated from the public realm and relegated to the private sphere.

These two movements came together in the last quarter of the eighteenth century to provide the impetus for the disestablishment of the churches. The Enlightenment liberals, as an intellectual and political elite, provided most of the rationale in support of disestablishment; the popular Great Awakening provided mass support for disestablishment. The events surrounding the disestablishment of the Anglican church in Virginia proved to be especially crucial for the subsequent development of church-state concepts. Events began to unfold in 1776 when the Virginia legislature repealed most of the legal privileges that had been granted Anglicans and suspended the collection of taxes for the Anglican church.[15] Then in 1784 Patrick Henry introduced a General Assessment Bill that made clear there was to be no established church, but also provided for a tax whose proceeds were to be distributed in support of all Christian churches. It appeared to have majority support in the legislature, but Madison won a year's postponement of the vote on it. In the meanwhile Madison wrote his soon-to-be-famous "Memorial and Remonstrance against Religious Assessments." In it he condemned all public tax support for churches, arguing "that the same authority which can force a citizen to contribute three pence only of his property for the support of any one establishment, may force him to conform to any other establishment in all cases whatsoever."[16] With Madison supplying the intellectual firepower, the dissenting churches with roots in the Great Awakening—largely Baptist and Presbyterian—supplied the popular opposition to the Henry bill. They amassed over 11,000 signatures on petitions opposing the bill. In 1785 the Virginia legislature turned down the General Assessment Bill and enacted instead Jefferson's "Bill for Establishing Religious Freedom" that provided in part, "no man shall be compelled to frequent or support any religious worship, place or ministry whatsoever . . . but all men shall be free to profess, and by argument to maintain, their opinions in matters of religion, and that the same shall in no wise diminish, enlarge, or affect their civil capacities."[17] Subsequently other states that had had laws creating various forms of religious establishment repealed them. In 1833 Massachusetts, the last of the states to abandon church establishment, did so.

Soon after these events and the writing of the First Amendment, church-state relations entered a third stage, from roughly 1800 to 1950. By the beginning of the nineteenth century Christianity seemed to be losing its presence in society. The churches had lost their establishment status, and only about 10 percent of the population were members of any church.[18] In 1800 Jefferson, who was so unorthodox in his religious views that he was labeled an "infidel" by many of the orthodox church leaders, was elected president. Yet in 1888 James Bryce, the respected English commentator on U. S. government and society, wrote: "The National Government and the State governments do give to Christianity a species of recognition inconsistent with the view that civil government should be absolutely neutral in religious matters. . . . The matter may be summed up by saying that Christianity is in fact understood to be, though not the legally established religion, yet the national religion."[19] The nineteenth century, against all odds, saw an informal reestablishment of Protestant Christianity.

One cause of this reestablishment of religion was the Second Great Awakening in the early years of the nineteenth century.[20] Revival again swept through the land, especially on the rapidly growing frontier. Church membership swelled. Another cause for the reestablishment of religion was the fact that the eighteenth-century disestablishment movement was clearly committed to the formal, legal disestablishment of churches, but never directly addressed the question of whether or not to allow a host of public supports for religion more generally. Clearly, the heirs of the Great Awakening assumed that government support for such measures as Sunday observance, suppression of gambling , and other such marks of a "Christian society" would continue. Even Enlightenment liberals such as Madison and Jefferson were ambiguous on this issue. Madison as president, for example, issued proclamations calling for days of national prayer and approved chaplains to be paid from public funds for the Congress, although he later wrote that on reflection he felt such actions unconstitutional.[21]

Thus when Christianity experienced a surge in the early nineteenth century, a vigorous, populist Protestant Christianity overwhelmed any tendencies to maintain a more strict separation of church and state. Prayers and Bible readings were a regular part of state-supported common schools, Christian missions to Native Americans were subsidized by government, and laws enforced Sunday observance. In 1890 most state colleges and universities had chapel services and some even required Sunday church attendance.[22]

Then after World War II, at mid-twentieth century, the United States entered a fourth stage of church-state relations, one that can be termed the second disestablishment of religion. Enlightenment liberal thinking reemerged and came to dominate Supreme Court decisions and the thinking of society's leadership echelon, even if not of the broader public. The words of the Supreme Court decision quoted at the beginning of this chapter represent this decisive turn of events. Jefferson's wall of separation metaphor was resurrected and embraced by the courts and a majority of the American people. As will be seen in more detail later, the Supreme Court banned religious elements from the public schools, declared almost all aid to religiously based schools unconstitutional, and found other forms of church-state cooperation or recognition unconstitutional. The liberal view of society clearly triumphed in the United States. In the other democracies considered in this book Enlightenment liberalism was forced into compromises with more conservative religious forces. But not in the United States. The paradox is that in what is clearly the most religious of the five countries considered, religion seems to have had the least impact in protecting a legitimate role for itself in the public life of the nation.

The historical explanation for this paradox resides in three key characteristics of nineteenth-century American Protestantism: its cultural dominance, its anti-Catholic fervor, and its intellectual shallowness. Throughout the nineteenth and into the twentieth century Protestantism was culturally dominate: it set the terms of public debate and determined much of the course of social history. Catholics were largely marginalized and Enlightenment liberalism as an independent force was weak. The Protestant elite had no need to make common cause with Catholics to oppose a secularized liberalism, as happened in the Netherlands and elsewhere, since it was culturally dominant by itself. Nineteenth-century Protestantism also had strong anti-Catholic leanings.[23] Roman Catholics tended to be seen as subservient to a foreign pope and thereby their allegiance to the Untied States was drawn into question. The recent-immigrant status of most Catholics and their tendency to send their children to parochial schools reinforced the image of them as a foreign, somehow un-American element that posed special problems of assimilation into American life and values.

Various commentators have also noted the intellectual shallowness of nineteenth-century Protestantism. It was a religion of the people—populist and entrepreneurial. Historian Nathan Hatch has described this aspect of nineteenth-century Protestantism: "Increasingly, assertive common people wanted their leaders unpretentious, their doctrines self-evident and down-to-earth, their music lively and singable, their churches in local hands."[24] Historian Sidney Mead has argued that as a result nineteenth-century populist Christianity "effectively scuttled much of the intellectual structure of Protestantism."[25] In addition to these three characteristics of nineteenth-century Protestantism, it is helpful to note that American liberalism did not have the strong, obvious anticlerical tendencies that often marked European liberalism. It was willing to make allowance for and pay respect to a generic sense of religion and even biblical morality.

In the nineteenth century Protestant and liberal leaders often cooperated. This unlikely cooperation was encouraged by their common fear and distrust of Catholicism and by liberalism's lack of a strident anticlericalism and a willingness to accommodate a generalized Christianity. In addition, the intellectual shallowness of nineteenth-century Protestantism meant its leaders never developed a well thought-out rationale for religion playing the public role that they supported. Then in the early twentieth century American Protestantism was undercut and weakened by modern theological trends that it did not have the intellectual vigor to resist. In less than a generation theologically conservative, biblically oriented Protestants lost their dominance in the mainline Protestant denominations, the universities, and among other cultural leaders, and were replaced by an intellectual and social elite largely attuned to the thinking of Enlightenment liberalism. In the post-World War II era—with there being no well thought-out rationale for religion's playing a public role and Enlightenment liberal thinking now dominant among the social and cultural elite—the Supreme Court read into its church-state interpretations of the First Amendment a liberal understanding of religion as a purely private matter with no legitimate role in the public realm.

All these tendencies can be seen in the common school movement as it developed in the nineteenth century, a story crucial for subsequent church-state developments. This movement has exerted a powerful force in American society. From the founding of the nation in 1789 Americans have worried about how to maintain national unity in the face of wide geographic distances, sharp class differences, and disparate, recurring waves of immigration. The answer Americans developed in the nineteenth century and have clung to since is the common school. In the early nineteenth century, European efforts at universal, state-run education caught the attention of Horace Mann and other New England elites. These reformers viewed the common school as the basic means by which the children of all classes—but especially the children of the lower, uneducated classes—would be taught social and political virtues. The common school advocates consistently saw the common school primarily in terms not of teaching skills in such areas as reading and mathematics, but in teaching the virtues thought necessary for national unity and free, democratic society. As Os Guinness has observed, "It [the public school] was to move beyond instruction in mere skills to education in character, ideals, and loyalties; and thus to be a moral force for character-forming and nation-building."[26]

When immigration surged in the middle decades of the nineteenth century, the concept of the common school was already well launched among the elites of the young American nation and readily available for application to this new turn of events. Surging immigration from Ireland, Italy, and other predominantly Catholic countries from whom the United States had previously had relatively few immigrants raised fears of American society being overwhelmed and undermined by millions of hard-to-assimilate immigrants unschooled in democratic values. These fears turned the common school ideal from an elite theory into a popular ideal broadly held in American society. Charles Glenn reports, "What in the 1830s was a cause appealing to a relatively limited elite, concerned to shape the American people in their own image, came in the next two decades to be perceived as an urgent necessity by virtually all Americans of social and political influence. . . ."[27] The common school came to be seen as an increasingly crucial means for achieving national unity, assimilation, and the inculcation of habits of good citizenship.

Religion of a particular type played an important role in the vision of the common school as the crucial inculcator of civic virtue and as the crucial instrument of cultural and national assimilation. Mann was a Unitarian—as were many of his fellow New England education reformers—and as such rejected both particularistic religion and nonreligious secularism. The schools were to be rational, Christian, and consensual. Glenn writes,

> Unitarians believed that they were preserving the essence of Christianity, purged of "sectarian" and divisive doctrines which—they argued—were no part of the message of Jesus. This essential Christianity could and should be taught in the common schools, since it represented a "religion of heaven" to which no right-minded parent could object, whatever additional doctrines he might hold privately and teach to his children at home.[28]

Thus the Christianity to be taught in the common schools was—in the eyes of the Unitarian backers of the common school—rational and consensual. One ended up with a nonsectarian, generalized Protestantism. Mann once wrote:

> Although it may not be easy theoretically, to draw the line between those views of religious truth and of christian faith which are common to all, and may, therefore, with propriety be inculcated in school, and those which, being peculiar to individual sects, are therefore by law excluded; still it is believed that no practical difficulty occurs in the conduct of our schools in this respect.[29]

Carl Kaestle has described the resulting common school ideology as being "centered on republicanism, Protestantism, and capitalism, three sources of social belief that were intertwined and mutually supporting."[30] The common school ideal thereby was definitely within the tradition of Jefferson, Madison, and other Enlightenment liberals.

There were some protests to this form of liberal religion both from a few evangelical conservative Protestants and from Roman Catholics, but Catholics in the nineteenth century were largely marginalized politically and socially, and conservative Protestants surprisingly came largely to accept the vision of the common school religion espoused by Mann and others. Especially in light of the perceived threat arising from large numbers of Catholic immigrants flooding into the United States, many conservative Protestants—by far the numerically dominant group within nineteenth-century Protestantism—felt common schools that included Bible readings and moral lessons represented a bulwark against the Catholic threat, even if it was not exactly biblical, orthodox Christianity that was being taught. Guinness has expressed it well: "In the nineteenth century, therefore, Protestant evangelicals were public-spirited in supporting state-run public schools. But it was also their way of 'establishing' a vague, nonsectarian, and moralistic Protestantism as the de facto civil religion."[31] The intellectual shallowness of Protestantism meant its leaders did not discern all that they were conceding to the Enlightenment liberals leading the common school movement. Instead, there was virtual unanimity among the culturally dominant Protestant elites that in the common school the ideals of democracy, America, and Christianity were joined together in a powerful device for uniting the nation. The elements of Christianity in the common schools meant even the then dominant conservative evangelical Protestants saw no need for their own separate schools, and enabled them to join fully in the common school enterprise. The common school movement was supported by the same "strange coalition" that had led the disestablishment movement of the late eighteenth century. When in the mid-twentieth century the Supreme Court largely embraced a liberal, strict separation interpretation of the First Amendment and applied it to the field of education, a weakened Protestantism had neither the intellectual nor political forces to resist this trend.

The Free Exercise of Religion

All five democracies included in this study support religious freedom for all. No person will be fined or imprisoned for whether, where, and how he or she worships God (or gods). Nevertheless, the United States—along with its fellow democracies—faces some tough, contentious issues over the exact meaning and application of religious freedom. Most difficult is the question of whether religiously motivated behavior that is thought to be contrary to societal welfare or norms should be protected. The United States has not followed a consistent path in its efforts to answer this question.

The First Amendment states: "Congress shall make no law . . . prohibiting the free exercise [of religion]." The Supreme Court has fashioned a wavering, uncertain path in interpreting these words—whether it is because of or despite their brevity. The waters were significantly muddied in the 1870s in the first case to come before the Court that called on it to interpret these words. It dealt with a federal law that prohibited polygamy, which was being challenged by Mormons who at that time practiced polygamy as a part of their religious beliefs. The Supreme Court ruled that the federal law did not violate the constitutional rights of Mormons since it was beliefs, and not actions, that the First Amendment protected: "Laws are made for the government of actions, and while they cannot interfere with mere religious beliefs and opinions, they may with practices."[32] The decision then went on to argue that to hold otherwise "would be to make the professed doctrines of religious belief superior to the law of the land, and in effect to permit every citizen to become a law unto himself."[33]

This belief-action distinction led to what has been termed the secular regulation rule: as long as the government has a valid secular purpose in mind and otherwise has the legal authority to engage in a certain form of regulation, the fact that it interferes with or hampers people's free exercise of their religion is not a basis for them to escape the regulation.[34] The secular regulation rule and the belief-action dichotomy on which it rests raise the question of what is left of free exercise protections. If the free exercise clause protects only beliefs (which presumably would be protected by other provisions of the Constitution anyway) and not religious practices, and if any law with legitimate secular purposes can be enforced on religious groups irrespective of sincerely and deeply held religious beliefs underlying their practices, is there any protection given by the free exercise clause that citizens would not enjoy anyway? There are two responses to this question. One is that the Supreme Court continues to hold that any act that intentionally singles out a religious group for disadvantages or limitations violates its free exercise rights. In 1993, for example, the Supreme Court struck down several ordinances of the city of Hialeah, Florida on the basis they were specifically aimed at outlawing animal sacrifices of the Santeria religion. "The ordinances had as their object the suppression of religion."[35] It reached this conclusion on the fact that the ordinances had been narrowly drawn to outlaw the religious sacrifice of animals, but not to outlaw such practices as hunting, slaughter of animals for food, and the kosher slaughter of animals. Since they were specifically aimed at the ritual sacrifice of animals as practiced by the Santeria religion, they were held to be in violation of the free exercise clause.

A second answer to the question of what is left of free exercise protections in light of the secular regulation rule is the compelling state interest test. This is an area of extreme legal uncertainty. The Supreme Court has wavered in its application of this test, recently seeming effectively to have abandoned it, and Congress has sought to reinstate it by legislation. The compelling state interest test holds that if an apparently neutral, secular law has the effect of significantly burdening or disadvantaging people's exercise of their sincerely held religious beliefs, that law can only be enforced on those persons if the state has a compelling reason for doing so. It thereby modifies the secular regulation rule. On this basis the Supreme Court held that the Amish did not have to send their children to school beyond the eighth grade, a Seventh-Day Adventist could not be excluded from receiving unemployment benefits because she refused Saturday work, and a pacifist could not be refused unemployment compensation when he lost his job because of refusing to work on manufacturing armaments.[36] In all three of these cases the Court ruled that the government had not demonstrated a compelling societal interest that would be endangered if exceptions to existing law were made in order to accommodate religious convictions.

The Supreme Court, however, has never consistently or fully followed the compelling state interest standard. In 1961 the Court failed to extend free exercise protections to Orthodox Jewish businesspeople who had been disadvantaged by Sunday closing regulations. In 1982 it did the same in the case of an Amish employer and his Amish employees who felt their religious scruples were violated by having to pay Social Security taxes, and in 1986 it did not uphold an Orthodox Jewish air force officer who had insisted on wearing a yarmulke as required by his faith.[37] In all three cases, the Supreme Court essentially followed the compelling state interest standard, but set a low threshold for meeting it, holding each time that the government had successfully demonstrated a compelling interest that overruled the claimed free exercise right.

In 1990 the Supreme Court considered a case dealing with adherents of a Native American religion who had used peyote as part of a traditional religious ceremony. As a result they had tested positive for drug use, were fired from their jobs, and were denied unemployment compensation since they were held to have been fired "for cause." The Court held that "an individual's religious beliefs [do not] excuse him from compliance with an otherwise valid law prohibiting conduct that the State is free to regulate."[38] The compelling state interest test was left in shreds: "To make an individual's obligation to obey . . . a law contingent upon the law's coincidence with his religious beliefs, except where the State's interest is 'compelling[,]' . . . contradicts both constitutional traditions and common sense."[39]

Widespread criticism greeted this decision of the Supreme Court. People and groups that traditionally have been divided on questions of religious establishment united in condemning it. A coalition of these groups came together and persuaded Congress to pass the Religious Freedom Restoration Act (RFRA) in 1993. This act reads in part: "Government may substantially burden a person's exercise of religion only if it demonstrates that application of the burden to the person is in furtherance of a compelling governmental interest; and is the least restrictive means of furthering that compelling governmental interest."[40] The act sought to write into law the compelling state interest standard the Supreme Court had first articulated, never fully applied, and then largely rejected. In the 1996 the Supreme Court accepted for review a case out of San Antonio, Texas concerning a church that sought to use the RFRA as a basis to escape the full consequences of certain local zoning laws. In 1997 the Supreme Court will hand down a crucial decision that will determine the constitutionality of the act and may either restrict or strengthen its impact. That decision will do much to determine whether the RFRA will restore the compelling state interest standard and make it a robust standard in free exercise cases. The RFRA, the wide coalition of groups that came together in support of it, and the wide margins by which it passed Congress all stand as testimonies to the normal commitment of the broader society and its political institutions to protect religious freedoms. When that normal commitment breaks down, however, unpopular religious minorities are vulnerable, and the free exercise clause, as interpreted by the Supreme Court, is an uncertain protection.

Also instructive is the fact that on several occasions the Supreme Court has rejected arguments that would use the free exercise clause to assert certain positive religious rights, as we will later see has sometimes been done in the Netherlands and Germany. The concept here is that if people are to enjoy full religious freedom, not only must they be free from direct legal restrictions on their right to act on their religious beliefs, they may sometimes need to be aided by government in doing so, especially if nonreligious people are being assisted by government to act on their secular beliefs. Two examples of the Supreme Court's rejection of such reasoning are instructive. The first comes from two basic decisions in which the Court ruled eight to one that neither a state-composed prayer nor the Lord's Prayer and a Bible reading could be a part of public school programming.[41] The lone dissenting justice in both these cases was Potter Stewart and in both cases he made a free exercise argument. He wrote, "There is involved in these cases a substantial free exercise claim on the part of those who affirmatively desire to have their children's school day open with the reading of passages from the Bible."[42] He then went on to explain more fully that

> a compulsory state educational system so structures a child's life that if religious exercises are held to be an impermissible activity in schools, religion is placed at an artificial and state-created disadvantage. Viewed in this light, permission of such exercises for those who want them is necessary if the schools are truly to be neutral in the matter of religion. And a refusal to permit religious exercises thus is seen, not as the realization of state neutrality, but rather as the establishment of a religion of secularism, or at the least, as government support of the beliefs of those who think that religious exercises should be conducted only in private.[43]

Stewart went on to argue that if public school religious exercises could be made voluntary in nature, the free exercise rights of those who desired them would be protected without violating the rights of those who did not desire them. As we will see later, this is the precise position the German Constitutional Court has taken. But the U. S. Supreme Court decisively rejected it.

Similarly, some justices have made a free exercise argument in cases dealing with public aid to religiously based schools. Justice Byron White, for example, in one such case dissented on free exercise grounds from the Court majority's conclusion that public aid to religious schools violates the First Amendment:

> The Establishment Clause, however, coexists in the First Amendment with the Free Exercise Clause and the latter is surely relevant in cases such as these. Where a state program seeks to ensure the proper education of its young, in private as well as public schools, free exercise considerations at least counsel against refusing support for students attending parochial schools simply because in that setting they are also being instructed in the tenets of the faith they are constitutionally free to practice.[44]

In another case dealing with public aid to religious schools he again made a free exercise argument when he argued that denying parents who send their children to such schools any financial relief "also make[s] it more difficult, if not impossible, for parents to follow the dictates of their conscience and seek a religious as well as a secular education for their children."[45]

But Justices Stewart and White have been lonely voices on the Supreme Court. The Court has consistently held that First Amendment restrictions on the establishment of religion trump a positive right to government support in freely exercising one's religion. It has not seen the free exercise clause as requiring government to take positive actions to assure room or space for religious people to practice their faith. In fact, it has, at best, been ambiguous in protecting religious people from laws that would hamper and disadvantage them in practicing what their religious consciences demand. As interpreted by the Supreme Court, the free exercise clause has remained limited, truncated in nature. It thereby has not been effective in affording wide protections to religious minorities when popular sentiment and the elected branches of government fail to do so.

The Establishment of Religion and Elementary and Secondary Education

As will become clear as this book develops, the U. S. approach to church–state issues differs sharply from the other democracies considered. The heart of these differences lies in the contrasting approaches taken to religion and education. Thus it is important to look carefully at the American approach to this crucial area of church–state relations. This section first considers religion in the public state-run elementary and secondary schools, and then the question of governmental aid to private religiously based schools.

In two decisions that continue, more than thirty-five years later, to be highly controversial, the Supreme Court in the early 1960s decided that prayer or Bible readings in the public schools violated the Constitution. In the first of these decisions the Court held that a brief, nondenominational prayer the New York authorities had composed for recitation at the start of the school day ("Almighty God, we acknowledge our dependence upon Thee, and we beg Thy blessings upon us, our parents, our teachers and our Country.") violated the establishment clause of the First Amendment ("Congress shall make no law respecting an establishment of religion . . ."). The Court argued that "in this country it is no part of the business of government to compose official prayers for any group of the American people to recite as a part of a religious program carried on by government."[46] A year later the Court ruled that programs of Bible reading and recitation of the Lord's Prayer at the start of the school day were also unconstitutional. Here the Court argued that what was at issue were "religious exercises, required by the States in violation of the command of the First Amendment that the Government maintain strict neutrality, neither aiding nor opposing religion."[47] The Court further ruled that to pass establishment clause scrutiny "there must be a secular legislative purpose and a primary effect that neither advances nor inhibits religion."[48] Prayers and Bible readings passed neither of these tests. The fact that the religious exercises were voluntary (children who objected could be excused) made no difference since a violation of the establishment clause does not require coercion to be present.

In subsequent cases the Supreme Court has consistently taken a strict separationist position on religious exercises in the public schools, as when it ruled against prayers at ceremonial occasions such as graduations and against moments of silence at the start of the school day for prayer or meditation.[49] In all these decisions the Court has primarily relied on the principle that government may not favor, encourage, or promote religion.

There have been continuing efforts to overturn some of these decisions of the Supreme Court by way of a constitutional amendment, legislation, or finding loopholes in the Court's decisions, spurred no doubt by the public's continuing support for certain religious elements in the public schools.[50] George Gallup reports: "Since the U.S. Supreme Court's 1962 and 1963 rulings that religious exercises and devotional

Bible reading in the public schools were unconstitutional, the courts have consistently struck down efforts to restore those practices. Surveys show that Americans have just as consistently favored some form of school prayer."[51] One survey, for example, showed 77 percent of the public favoring "a moment of silence each day for students to pray if they want to."[52]

The Supreme Court has also taken a strict separationist position in its rulings on integrating religion into the public school curriculum. It has ruled unconstitutional a released time program in which the schools and religious groups would cooperate by the schools releasing the students for an hour or so a week with various religious groups coming into the school to offer instruction to the adherents of their faiths. Students not desiring any religious instruction were given alternative activities. Justice Hugo Black spoke for the Court majority when he reasoned that such programs utilized "the tax-established and tax-supported public school system to aid religious groups to spread their faith."[53] A few years later the Court did allow a similar program, but one where the classes of religious instruction were held on sites away from the public schools.[54] The Court has also ruled against a Louisiana law requiring that whenever evolution is taught as a theory of human origins, equal time must also be given to a literal version of creationism.[55]

Sometimes individual schools or school districts, with the acquiescence of the lower courts, have gone beyond what even the Supreme Court would seem to require. A fifth-grade teacher was told she could not keep a Bible on her desk or silently read it during her class's silent reading period. A federal Court of Appeals upheld the school.[56] A ninth-grade teacher assigned her class a research paper and when one of her pupils wrote on the life of Jesus Christ she gave her an "F" on the paper, explaining that "the law says we are not to deal with religious issues in the classroom." The lower federal courts upheld the teacher.[57] In another instance a class valedictorian had been invited to give a talk at her graduation ceremonies and informed the principal of her school that she intended to devote a portion of the talk to the importance of Jesus Christ in her life. She was ordered to delete that portion of her talk and when she refused was removed from the graduation program. In this instance also, the lower federal courts upheld the principal.[58] Instances such as these may be due to overly zealous teachers, principals, or local school boards, but when the Supreme Court bans even silent prayer or meditation from public school classrooms on the basis of "wall of separation" and no-aid-to-religion reasoning, such efforts to ferret religion out of the schools are not too surprising.

On the other hand, the Supreme Court has insisted it is not hostile to religion. It has stated that public schools are permitted to teach about religion, to teach about the role religion has played in history, and to teach the Bible as literature. In one decision, for example, the Court stated that the "study of religions and of the bible from a literary and historic viewpoint, presented objectively and as part of a secular program of education, need not collide with the First Amendment's prohibition [against supporting religion]. . . ."[59] In 1984 Congress passed the Equal Access Act, which provided that if a school allowed extracurricular clubs to use school facilities outside normal instructional hours, it could not refuse a religiously based club to form and also use school facilities. The Supreme Court upheld this law and ruled that clubs formed under it do not violate the establishment clause, as long as "a religious club is merely one of many different student-initiated voluntary clubs. . . ."[60] In August 1995 President Bill Clinton released a report put together by the Department of Education that sought to define what religious practices could or could not be included in the public schools.[61] It stressed that private, voluntary prayer, students seeking to influence the religious beliefs of their fellow students, and the objective study of religion were permissible, but that teacher-led prayers or religious meetings and any advocacy of religion by the school were not.

On balance, however, the permissible role for religion in the public schools is extremely small. The line that has time and again been drawn excludes any official recognition or support for religion. At the same time, the public schools have been called increasingly to deal with morally sensitive issues such as teenage pregnancies, AIDS awareness, racial and ethnic respect, school violence, juvenile crime, and good citizenship. The very issues that religion has sought to address and that a majority of Americans turn to their communities of faith for answers must now be addressed in a thoroughly secular fashion by the schools. This results in a dilemma that the Supreme Court and most American societal elites have failed to recognize. On the one hand, for the public schools to integrate certain religious perspectives into the curriculum or to conduct certain religious exercises would violate the norm of governmental neutrality on matters of religion. Even generalized, consensual religion that has the support of a majority of the community—maybe even the overwhelming majority—are rejected by some parents in the community. Those parents and their children would be disadvantaged by such practices. And allowance for individual students to be excused from religious exercises or from lessons with religious dimensions may stigmatize those students in the eyes of their peers as "different." Thus the incorporation of consensual religious exercises and teachings into the public schools would be a violation of religious neutrality. Under the influence of Enlightenment liberalism this has been rightly recognized and given weight by the Supreme Court and societal elites.

On the other hand—and this is what the Supreme Court and American elites have failed to recognize—once religion is removed from the schools what is left is not a zone of neutrality between religion and secularism; what is left is secularism. As A. James Reichley has written, "Banishment of religion does not represent neutrality between religion and secularism; conduct of public institutions without any acknowledgment of religion *is* secularism."[62] The result is not the explicit promotion of secularism as an antireligious movement, but its implicit promotion as a latent ethos or force. If issues such as crime, AIDS, bigotry, and urban racial disturbances must all be discussed without reference to religion as an active moral force—not even in in-school released time programs—the implicit message is that religion is either irrelevant or unimportant. Thus removing religion from the public schools also violates the norm of governmental neutrality, since government is then indirectly and implicitly favoring secularism. Religious parents and their children are thereby disadvantaged.

There may not be a completely satisfactory answer to this dilemma, but in-school released time programs for religious instruction and moments for silent private prayer represent efforts to recognize or honor the faith communities of the students in a manner that makes allowances for the rich religious diversity of most public schools. They would lead to a greater measure of neutrality than would either incorporating certain consensual religious elements or banning all religion. Yet even in-school released time programs and moments of silence for prayer or meditation have been banned by the Supreme Court's interpretations of the First Amendment. Those decisions, as well as the reasoning the Court has used in reaching them and other decisions in regard to religion in the public schools, reveal that the Court does not recognize the dilemma outlined above. It sees only the first horn of the dilemma. As we will see in the following chapters, the other democracies studied here have taken a different approach to this issue.

This brings us to the question of governmental aid to private religiously based schools. Here also the Supreme Court has largely taken a strict separation, no-aid-to-religion approach. The initial decision in this area from which we quoted at the start of this chapter laid down the terms clearly: there was to be a "high and impregnable" wall between church and state and no taxes could go to support "any religious activities or institutions." It was twenty-four years later, in *Lemon v. Kurtzman* (1971), that the Court clearly and decisively ruled against public funds going to support private religious schools. In doing so it articulated a three-part test that—although highly controversial even today—has been used in many subsequent establishment clause decisions. To pass muster under the so-called *Lemon* test, a government program must meet all three of the following standards: "First, the statute must have a secular legislative purpose; second, its principal or primary effect must be one that neither advances nor inhibits religion; finally, the statute must not foster 'an excessive entanglement with religion.' "[63]

The Court has ruled in most cases involving state aid to nonpublic schools that there was a valid secular purpose: to help provide a general education for the children attending the nonpublic schools. But a number of state attempts to aid religious schools were held to fail the second part of the *Lemon* test: that they must not have the principal or primary effect of advancing or inhibiting religion. A well-known constitutional law scholar, Laurence Tribe, has pointed out that, in practice, the Supreme Court tends not to ask if the "principal or primary" effect is to aid religion, but if the aid has any effect at all of aiding religion. "The constitutional requirement of 'primary secular effect' has thus become a misnomer; while retaining the earlier label, the Court has transformed it into *a requirement that any non-secular effect be remote, indirect and incidental.*"[64] The accuracy of Tribe's observation can be seen in a case in which the Court found unconstitutional a program in which public school teachers were placed in private religious schools to teach nonreligious subjects. The Court acknowledged "that respondents adduced no evidence of specific incidents of religious indoctrination in this case."[65] Nevertheless, it went on to hold there was "a substantial risk, overtly or subtly, [that] the religious message . . . will infuse the supposedly secular class.[66] Also, it referred to the importance of appearances: "An important concern of the effects test is whether the symbolic union of church and state effected by the challenged governmental action is sufficiently likely to be perceived by adherents of the controlling denominations as an endorsement, and by the non-adherents as a disapproval, of their individual religious choices."[67] There need only be a risk of state action having a religious effect or of it giving the impression of religious support to reach a conclusion that the state action is a violation of the second facet of the *Lemon* test.

The third aspect of the *Lemon* test is that there must be no excessive government entanglement with religion. The Supreme Court used this test to invalidate a New York City program that supported remedial assistance for children from low-income families in nonpublic schools.[68] It ruled that the system New York had established to make certain that religious elements were not being introduced into the remedial program resulted in an excessive entanglement of church and state.

The Court has ruled that payment of bus transportation to and from school is permissible, as is the loan of certain secular textbooks, payment for certain diagnostic psychological tests, and a few other largely minor forms of aid. But for the most part the Supreme Court has ruled that public tax dollars may not go to support religiously based elementary and secondary schools. The few forms of aid that have been approved were approved on the basis that they were primarily benefiting the students, not the schools, and that any religious elements could easily and clearly be kept out of them.

There is more popular support for denying government aid to religious schools than there is for removing religious observances from the public schools. The common school ideal, as noted earlier in the historical section, has roots deep in the American culture, apparently resulting in societal leaders and a majority of the public rejecting public aid for religious schools. A 1988 nationwide public opinion survey, for example, found societal leaders in academia, the media, government, and business opposing financial aid to religiously based schools by 2–1 to 3–1 margins. Among academicians 74 percent opposed it, among leaders in the media 67 percent did so, and among both high-ranking federal executive branch officials and business leaders 62 percent did so.[69] The same survey found the public sharply divided on the question of whether government should provide financial help to religiously based schools, with 41 percent favoring such aid and 50 percent opposing it.[70]

In short, the Supreme Court—with the active support or acquiescence of most of society—has largely rejected the permissibility under the First Amendment of government providing aid and support for private religiously based elementary and secondary schools. It has seen such programs as aiding religion, and aiding religion is a violation of its own enunciated principles of a wall of separation between church and state and of no aid to religion. When one combines the decisions forbidding religious elements and in-school released time programs in public schools with the decisions forbidding any significant aid to private religious schools, one can readily see the difficult position into which deeply religious parents who desire a religious education for their children have been put. The religious elements they desire in the public schools have been eliminated; yet they can receive no financial help if they therefore decide to send their children to schools sponsored by their religious tradition. They have been disadvantaged by government policy in a way nonreligious parents who desire no religious education for their children have not been. None of the other democracies included in this study has taken this position—in fact, we know of no other democracy anywhere that has taken this position. The likely reason this position has won acceptance in the United States—at least among the intellectual and leadership elite—can be traced back to the common school ideal as *the* key agent of assimilation and moral education. Nevertheless, the common school ideal was predicated on the schools including religious elements of a generalized nature. To close out religious elements in the public schools and to close out state aid to religious schools raise questions of evenhandedness, or neutrality, toward religious and nonreligious parents alike. Later we will return to the question of why the United States has taken this route and other democracies have not.

The Establishment of Religion: Other Issues

Given the strict separation position taken by the Supreme Court in establishment questions related to elementary and secondary education and the strong language with which it has done so ("No tax in any amount, large or small, can be levied to support any religious activities or institutions, whatever they may be called . . ."), one would understandably assume that its constitutional interpretations have equally restricted governmental cooperation with and support of other types of religious activities and organizations. The surprising fact is that outside of elementary and secondary education the Supreme Court—with the support of the American public and other political institutions—has done almost a complete about-face, finding many forms of cooperation and support to be constitutional. The strict separation principle for which American church-state relations is famous has largely been limited to elementary and secondary education. Yet the principles and concepts established in the field of education have important consequences for the bases on which other forms of church-state cooperation have been approved.

The United States, for example, is marked by many private colleges and universities. Forty-nine percent of all colleges and universities are private nonprofit institutions, enrolling 20 percent of all higher education students.[71] Of these, 78 percent have a religious affiliation, and almost all receive large amounts of government funding.[72] Four cases challenging programs sending government funds to religiously based colleges and universities have come before the Supreme Court; in all four cases the Court held that the public funding programs did not violate the First Amendment establishment clause. The Supreme Court was able to maintain its strict separation, no-aid-to-religion line of reasoning, while approving aid programs to religiously based colleges and universities, largely because of its application of two legal principles.

One of these legal principles is the sacred–secular distinction. The aid programs under challenge were approved, first, because the Supreme Court was willing to accept the separability of the secular and sacred aspects of education at religiously based colleges, and therefore it could accept the theory that public funds were supporting the secular mission, but not the religious mission of the colleges. By making a clear-cut distinction between the religious and the secular elements in a college education and then funding only the secular elements, one can have government financial aid to a religious college without giving aid to religion (at least in legal theory). In one of the cases, the Court observed that the challenged program of aid "was carefully drafted to ensure that the federally subsidized facilities would be devoted to the secular and not the religious function of the recipient institutions."[73] Another decision noted that "the secular and sectarian activities of the colleges were easily separated."[74]

But this approach in itself does not distinguish the cases dealing with higher education from those dealing with elementary and secondary education, since the Supreme Court has largely rejected it in regard to elementary and secondary schools. The key distinction the Court has made is that in its view religiously based colleges and universities are not "pervasively sectarian," while religiously based elementary and secondary schools are. In a case dealing with a South Carolina program assisting in the construction of college and university buildings, a six to three majority of the Court made the point concerning the importance of a pervasively religious nature: "Aid normally may be thought to have a primary effect of advancing religion when it flows to an institution in which religion is so pervasive that a substantial portion of its functions are subsumed in the religious mission. . . ."[75] The decision then went on to make the point that the college whose receiving of government funds was under challenge was not marked by such a pervasively religious nature.

Less clear, however, are the exact characteristics that distinguish a pervasively sectarian from a nonpervasively sectarian institution. The plurality opinion by Justice Harry Blackmun in *Roemer v. Maryland Public Works Board* (1976) is the most complete and carefully crafted of the decisions reached by the Supreme Court in the aid-to-religious-colleges cases. Blackmun includes an extended discussion of the meaning of "pervasively sectarian." The first indication that the four Catholic colleges whose receipt of government aid was being challenged were not pervasively sectarian was the institutional autonomy of the colleges. The fact that they neither were controlled by the Catholic Church nor received funds from the church was important. Second, Blackmun noted that religious indoctrination was not "a substantial purpose or activity" of the four colleges. This in turn was demonstrated by the fact that participation in religious exercises was not required and "spiritual development" was not a primary objective of the colleges.[76]

Third, Blackmun noted the presence of academic freedom on the four campuses. Instructors were free to teach courses in an "atmosphere of intellectual freedom."[77] The existence of mandatory religion or theology courses did not indicate a pervasively sectarian situation, since such courses "only supplement a curriculum covering 'the spectrum of a liberal arts program.'"[78] Fourth, although prayers at the beginning of classes and religious symbols on campus were common, the courses were taught in such a manner as to meet normal academic standards. Given that fact, prayers and religious symbols were not enough to indicate a pervasively sectarian situation. Fifth, Blackmun noted that religion was not taken into account in the hiring of faculty members. "Hiring bias" or an effort "to stack its faculty with members of a particular religious group"[79] would point toward a pervasively sectarian situation, but that was not the case here. Sixth, the student bodies at the four colleges were "chosen without regard to religion."[80]

These six observations made by Blackmun in the *Roemer* case ought not to be taken as essential criteria, all of which, or even a preponderance of which, must be present if an institution is to avoid the "pervasively sectarian" tag. As Blackmun himself wrote, "To answer the question whether an institution is so 'pervasively sectarian' that it may receive no direct state aid of any kind, it is necessary to paint a general picture of the institution, composed of many elements."[81] Blackmun saw the six points as important characteristics of the four colleges that to him painted a general picture of nonpervasive sectarianism. Which ones and how many could be missing (or substituted by others) and a college still not be "pervasively sectarian" is unknown. It is hard to disagree with the conclusion Blackmun himself reached ten years later when he acknowledged that the "pervasively sectarian" standard is "a vaguely defined work of art."[82]

In addition to the sacred-secular distinction and the pervasively sectarian standard that the Supreme Court has largely relied on to approve public funds for religious colleges and universities, it has sometimes made reference to the indirect nature of the funding. The most recent case dealing with public money going to a religiously based college was a 1986 case that concerned a blind student attending a Protestant college to study to be a pastor or other church leader. A unanimous Supreme Court overturned the Washington state supreme court, insisting that this program of aid to the student and, indirectly, to the college he was attending did not violate the establishment clause. Key to this decision was the indirect nature of the aid. The public money that ended up in the coffers of a religious institution was due to the individual student's decision. "Any aid provided under Washington's program that ultimately flows to religious institutions does so only as a result of the genuinely independent and private choices of aid recipients."[83] The fact that the public funds were supporting a student studying for a religious career at a religious college—and the unanimity of the decision—bears striking testimony to the Court's much greater willingness to approve public money flowing to colleges and universities than to elementary and secondary schools.

In addition to providing government support of private religiously based colleges and universities, the United States provides massive amounts of public funds to private nonprofit service organizations, many of which are religiously based.[84] In a recent year, for example, 65 percent of the Catholic Charities' revenue came from government sources, as did 75 percent of the Jewish Board of Family and Children's Services' revenues and 55 percent of the Lutheran Social Ministries' revenues.[85] One study found that a majority of religiously based child and family service agencies receive over 40 percent of their budgets from government sources.[86]

Despite large amounts of public tax dollars going to religiously based service organizations, only two cases have come before the Supreme Court challenging this practice, and in both instances the Court found the practice constitutional. One case, from the end of the nineteenth century, dealt with aid to a District of Columbia Catholic hospital. The Supreme Court based its approval of the program of aid on the sacred-secular distinction. The Court saw the hospital as "simply the case of a secular corporation being managed by people who hold to the doctrines of the Roman Catholic Church."[87] Further, the secular nature of the hospital's function assured the constitutionality of the aid: "The act of Congress, however, shows there is nothing sectarian in the corporation, and 'the specific and limited object of its creation' is the opening and keeping a hospital in the city of Washington for the care of such sick and invalid persons as may place themselves under the treatment and care of the corporation."[88]

The constitutional issues at stake were raised more clearly in the 1988 case of *Bowen v. Kendrick.* The Adolescent Family Life Act (AFLA) had authorized federal grants for both public and private nonprofit organizations for the purpose of providing services relating to teenage sexuality and pregnancies. By a close five to four vote, the Supreme Court ruled that on its face the act did not violate the First Amendment establishment clause and remanded the case to the lower courts to determine whether it did so as actually administered. The key issue with which the Court struggled concerned the second part of the *Lemon* test, namely, whether the act advanced religion. The Supreme Court majority ruled that "the programs established under the authority of the AFLA can be monitored to determine whether the funds are, in effect, being used by the grantees in such a way as to advance religion."[89] The money could only go to support the secular aspects of the agencies' programs. Further, the Court majority ruled that the agencies receiving government funds were not pervasively sectarian, but seemed to be more like colleges and universities for whom public funds had previously been approved than like elementary and secondary schools for whom public funds had largely been rejected: "In this case, nothing on the face of the AFLA indicates that a significant proportion of the federal funds will be disbursed to 'pervasively sectarian' institutions."[90]

In summary, under the no-aid-to-religion strain in Supreme Court reasoning, public money may flow to religiously based nonprofit organizations as long as the money goes to support secular services and programs and the nonprofit organizations to which the money goes are not "pervasively sectarian." The chances of public funding programs being found constitutional is also enhanced when money is funneled to religious nonprofits indirectly through recipients of their services.

It is important to note that the Supreme Court has occasionally decided church-state establishment issues on a basis other than the ones thus far discussed. This is the equal treatment, or neutrality, principle. A decision that illustrates the use of this principle is the 1995 decision in *Rosenberger v. Rector.* The University of Virginia had refused to fund a Christian student publication, even though it had funded fifteen other student opinion publications, since it was convinced that doing so would violate church-state separation. In a five to four vote the Court held that the university's refusal to fund the publication violated the students' free speech rights, and that funding it would not violate the establishment clause. The majority opinion is clearly rooted in the equal treatment, or neutrality, principle. It states:

> A central lesson of our decisions is that a significant factor in uphold-ing governmental programs in the face of Establishment Clause attack is their neutrality towards religion. . . . We have held that the guaran-tee of neutrality is respected, not offended, when the government, following neutral criteria and evenhanded policies, extends benefits to recipients whose ideologies and viewpoints, including religious ones, are broad and diverse.[91]

A program funding a clearly—some would say pervasively—religious publication was saved from establishment clause violation because reli-gion was not singled out for favored treatment and the funding was extended to "the whole spectrum of speech, whether it manifests a reli-gious view, an antireligious view, or neither."[92]

The neutrality line of reasoning illustrated in this decision is clearly distinguishable from the no-aid-to-religion line of reasoning. It would allow limited forms of governmental accommodation and assistance—even financial assistance—to religious groups and their activities as long as that assistance was offered equally to all religious groups and to reli-gious and nonreligious groups on the same basis. This line of reasoning has thus far not been used to challenge directly the no-aid-to-religion line of reasoning, yet it has the potential for doing so. When religious groups may not be excluded from participating in public programs or activities in which all other nonreligious groups are participating—even without giving up or segregating the deeply religious aspects of their programs—clearly the no-aid-to-religion principle and the sacred-secu-lar and pervasively sectarian distinctions are being ignored, if not chal-lenged. The four dissenting justices in the *Rosenberger* case clearly saw that the decision undermined the no-aid-to-religion principle and the sacred-secular distinction under which religious groups have sometimes been permitted to receive public funds. They wrote: "Even when the Court [in the past] has upheld aid to an institution performing both secular and sectarian functions, it has always made a searching enquiry to ensure that the institution kept the secular activities separate from its sectarian ones, with any direct aid flowing only to the former and never the latter."[93] They went on to advocate the continued reliance on "the no-direct-funding principle" over "the principle of evenhandedness."[94] As will be seen later, the other democracies considered in this study have tended to use variations of this equal treatment line of reasoning rather than the approach more typically taken by the U. S. Supreme Court.

There are examples of the Supreme Court approving various other forms of church-state cooperation: tax exemptions for churches were found constitutional, the opening of legislative sessions with prayer by a paid chaplain was approved, and a crèche and a menorah as parts of holiday displays won approval.[95] These were approved while still upholding the no-aid-to-religion, wall of separation theory, since the religious elements in these cases were held to have been overshadowed or neutralized by long practice or secular goals or aspects. Other common forms of government acknowledgment of and cooperation with religion have never even been challenged before the Supreme Court. Examples include chaplains in the armed forces paid by the government, the acknowledgment of God in the Pledge of Allegiance to the flag and on coins, prayers at various ceremonial occasions such as inaugurations of presidents, and church services held in national parks.

In short, outside the area of elementary and secondary education, the Supreme Court has frequently found various forms of church-state cooperation or recognition constitutional, but it has usually done so on bases that still preserve the strict separation, no-aid-to-religion principles it had developed in its education decisions.

In so doing the Supreme Court has had the implicit, even if often not the explicit, support of the other branches of government and the American people. The strongest evidence in support of this conclusion is the frequent passage of such programs by the political branches of government on the national and state levels with little or no controversy over including religious organizations within their funding provisions. The Basic Education Opportunity Grants and work-study grants regularly are given to private colleges and universities—religiously based and secularly based alike—without the great stirring of controversy that typically accompanies programs that would grant aid to religiously based elementary and secondary schools. The same can be said of the earlier GI Bill that provided tuition grants to post-World War II veterans and could be used in either public or private (including religiously based) institutions. Similarly, in 1993 two *Newsday* reporters wrote a series of articles documenting the hundreds of millions of public dollars going to a variety of New York Catholic archdiocesan social agencies. No great stir—nor even a small stir—followed their disclosures. One of the reporters stated he was "amazed at the nonreactions."[96] Similarly, the various examples of government cooperation with and acknowledgment of religion mentioned earlier are routinely practiced with only rare protests.

One final example occurred in 1996 when Congress passed a welfare reform bill. It incorporated an amendment introduced by Senator

John Ashcroft of Missouri that sought to make more use of private service organizations to deliver welfare services than had been done previously. It provided that states could contract with private organizations or create voucher systems to deliver welfare services, and that any state that did so would have to consider religious organizations on an equal basis with secular organizations. Most significantly, it then went on to protect the religious freedom rights of religious agencies that receive government funds, by providing that agencies receiving such funds shall maintain the right to develop and express their religious orientation, may keep religious pictures and symbols in their facilities, and may favor members of their own religious faith in hiring decisions.[97] This amendment was adopted by wide margins in Congress, President Clinton did not raise objections to it in signing the bill into law, and it was not widely criticized in the media.[98] It helps illustrate the fact that basic support for church-state cooperation is usually present in the political system, as long as it is outside the field of elementary and secondary education.

As noted earlier, even when the Supreme Court has approved programs of aid to or cooperation with religious organizations, it has usually sought to maintain the principle of no–aid–to–religion. It has done so on the theory that the government is only aiding the secular aspects of the program, which have been carefully split off from the religious or sacred aspects of the program, and that the aided organizations are not "pervasively sectarian." But one crucial consequence of using this legal basis to approve public financial support for religiously based organizations is that questions arise over whether religious elements may be integrated into the presumably secular activities that are being subsidized. May religious pictures or symbols be displayed in a homeless shelter receiving public funds? May a religious college receiving public funds hire only faculty members of its own faith? May a home for abused children insist on standards of behavior for its staff in keeping with the religious beliefs of the sponsoring faith? The problem is that if in actual fact religious organizations such as these are truly providing secular services with no relevance to their religious beliefs, it is hard to think of logical reasons why they should have a right to insist that certain religious standards or elements be a part of them. In addition, the ambiguity present in the standard that says religious organizations receiving public funds may not be "pervasively sectarian" opens the way for officials administering a program or the lower courts to pressure religious agencies to give up certain religiously motivated practices. For example, a homeless shelter in Connecticut was forced to take down a picture of Jesus before it could receive federal funds, and a lower court ruled a Salvation Army spouse abuse program in Mississippi could not fire a counselor who was a believer in the pagan religion of Wicca.[99] What more systematic evidence is available, however, suggests that usually religious organizations receiving public funds are able to integrate religious elements into the services they provide, but that periodically and unpredictably they can run into restrictions on their religious freedom.[100] Especially given the absolutistic-sounding wall of separation, no-aid-to-religion rhetoric of some Supreme Court decisions and the bases on which it has found funding programs for religiously based organizations constitutional, it is not surprising that problems have arisen periodically. As will be seen in the following chapters, most other democracies have avoided such issues by not embracing a strict no-aid-to-religion standard and basing their granting of public funds to religious organizations on equal treatment or evenhandedness grounds rather than a sharp sacred-secular distinction.

Concluding Observations

As seen in this chapter the United States has embraced in theory even if not always in practice the strict church-state separation model; as will be seen in the following chapters it is the only country in this study that has done so. In this concluding section we both return to the question of why the United States has taken this position and seek a tentative evaluation of it. The most persuasive explanation of the U. S. position is that in the nineteenth century Enlightenment liberals and the dominant Protestants came together to oppose Catholic influence in the United States and to impose their own generalized Protestant establishment on all of society. Throughout the nineteenth and into the twentieth century Protestants were the dominant force in this liberal-Protestant coalition. But by the mid-twentieth century, conservative Protestantism had been routed in internal church battles and replaced by a liberal Protestantism that accepted many of the basic tenets of Enlightenment liberalism. Neither evangelical Protestantism nor Catholicism was numerically or socially powerful enough to command the political and media influence to make their positions felt in the courts and among the influential elites. As a result the Enlightenment liberal view of church and state was left in a commanding position, and came largely to be incorporated into Supreme Court interpretations of the First Amendment, especially in relation to the public schools that traditionally had been seen as playing a crucial leveling, assimilating role in an otherwise divided society.

The prevailing church-state situation as we have described it in the United States carries with it three distinct disadvantages or problems. One is the confusion, uncertainty, and even anger that the current state of church-state law and practice engenders. Scholars have used terms such as "incoherent," a "tangled body of law," and "eccentric" to describe current church-state law.[101] No one seems to be happy with the status quo. Steven Smith made a telling point when he wrote that "in a rare and remarkable way, the Supreme Court's establishment clause jurisprudence has unified critical opinion: people who disagree about nearly everything else in the law agree that establishment clause doctrine is seriously, perhaps distinctively, defective."[102] The Supreme Court justices themselves issue closely divided rulings on church-state questions, with even the majority and dissenting justices often unable to reach agreement on why they have reached their conclusions. As a result respect for the law suffers, uncertainty abounds, and government authorities—as noted earlier in the case of some positions taken by public schools officials—have sometimes taken stances that appear clearly violative of personal religious rights. The other countries studied in this book seem to have handled church-state issues with less controversy and less uncertainty. Perhaps there is something to be learned from them.

A second problem posed by the current state of church-state relations and the concept of strict separation on which they are largely based is that implicitly, by default, a secular cultural ethos is favored over an ethos in which religion is respected as a significant force in society. The norm of governmental neutrality on matters of religion we put forth in chapter 1 is thereby violated. We took note of this situation earlier in our consideration of the U. S. insistence that all elements supportive of religion be removed from the public schools. When that is done, government does not occupy a neutral zone between religion and secularism, for the removal of all things religious results in an implicit secularism. If all subjects and a host of contemporary problems and issues must be presented and discussed without reference to religion, the implicit message is one of religion's irrelevancy. Similarly, when the public schools—whose teachings are more compatible with the worldviews of secular parents—are fully funded with public funds, but religious schools—which some parents believe essential in order to have their children taught the religious perspectives they treasure—may receive almost no public funds, is not religion being disadvantaged by government action?

This problem relates directly to a third problem in current church-state theory and practice, namely the vulnerable position that the basic right to the free exercise of religion has been put. Religious minorities or adherents of non-traditional faiths face this danger. Such faith groups as the Amish, Orthodox Jews, and Native Americans have usually not found much protection for their free exercise of religion in the First Amendment of the Constitution. But the problem extends beyond such nonmainstream religious groups to include more traditional and much larger groups because of the almost total absence of a concept of positive religious freedom in the American setting. Religious freedom is typically seen as the freedom to be free from government restraints on one's religious beliefs and practice. Since government is seen as properly occupying a neutral zone between the various religious groups and between religion and nonreligion, it is assumed there is no need for government to take certain positive steps to support or encourage religion. After all, government is to be neutral. To give certain religious groups or religion as a whole special support would be to violate neutrality. But a case can be made that a government that recognizes, favors, and aids all sorts of secular enterprises and perspectives is not neutral if it systematically excludes religious enterprises and perspectives. Secular perspectives and belief structures represent a point of view, a worldview as much as various religious perspectives and beliefs do. Thus to support secular groups and programs over religious ones is anything but neutral.

Rooting its approach to church-state relations on the liberal Enlightenment assumption that strictly separating government and religion assures governmental neutrality on matters of religion may violate the very neutrality that liberals are rightly eager to attain. As we view the contrasting approaches to church and state of the other countries considered in this study we will ask whether the assumptions and ideals of Enlightenment liberalism are adequate to assure a genuine religious neutrality on the part of government in today's world.

Notes

1. *Everson v. Board of Education,* 330 U.S. at 16 (1947).
2. *Everson v. Board of Education,* at 18.
3. From the dissent of Justice Robert Jackson, *Everson v. Board of Education,* at 19.
4. See Ted G. Jelen and Clyde Wilcox, *Public Attitudes Toward Church and State* (Armonk, N.Y.: Sharpe, 1995), 57–97.
5. Phillip E. Johnson, "Concepts and Compromise in First Amendment Religious Doctrine," *California Law Review* 72 (1984), 817.
6. These figures are from a 1996 poll by the Pew Research Center for the

People and the Press. See Gustav Niebuhr, "Public Supports Political Voice for Churches," *New York Times* (June 25, 1996), A1 and C18.

7. Barry A. Kosmin and Seymour P. Lachman, *One Nation Under God: Religion in Contemporary American Society* (New York: Crown, 1993), 256.

8. Robert Booth Fowler and Allen D. Hertzke, *Religion and Politics in America* (Boulder, Colo.: Westview, 1995), 35, and George Gallup Jr. and Jim Castelli, *The People's Religion: American Faith in the 90's* (New York: Macmillan, 1989), 114. Some figures put the American Muslim population as high as 2 percent of the population. See "Campaign Highlights Muslims' Quandary," *Los Angeles Times* (August 10, 1995), B4.

9. See James Davison Hunter, *Culture Wars: The Struggle to Define America* (New York: Basic Books, 1991), 76, and Niebuhr, "Public Supports Political Voice for Churches," C18.

10. "Spiritual America," *U.S. News & World Report* 116 (April 4, 1994), 48.

11. *The Public Perspective* (April/May, 1995), 25.

12. Everett Carll Ladd, "Secular and Religious America," in Richard John Neuhaus, ed., *Unsecular America* (Grand Rapids, Mich.: Eerdmans, 1986), 16.

13. Sidney E. Mead, *The Lively Experiment* (New York: Harper & Row, 1963), 17.

14. The term "strange coalition" is Mead's. See Mead, *The Lively Experiment,* 35. For more on the role played by these two disparate movements in the disestablishment of the churches in the eighteenth century see Stephen V. Monsma, *Positive Neutrality* (Westport, Conn.: Greenwood, 1993), 83–113.

15. For an account of these events see Leonard W. Levy, *The Establishment Clause: Religion and the First Amendment,* 2nd ed. (Chapel Hill: University of North Carolina Press, 1994), 58–75.

16. James Madison, "Memorial and Remonstrance Against Religious Assessments," in Robert S. Alley, ed., *The Supreme Court on Church and State* (New York: Oxford University Press, 1988), 19–20.

17. Thomas Jefferson, "Bill for Establishing Religious Freedom," in Alley, *The Supreme Court on Church and State,* 26.

18. See Robert Handy, *A Christian American: Protestant Hopes and Historical Realities* (New York: Oxford University Press, 1984), 24–25.

19. James Bryce, *The American Commonwealth,* rev. ed., vol. 2 (New York: Macmillan, 1911), 769–70.

20. On the Second Great Awakening and its consequences for American Christianity see Nathan Hatch, *The Democratization of American Christianity* (New Haven: Yale University Press, 1989).

21. See Daniel L. Dreisbach, *Real Threat and Mere Shadow: Religious Liberty and the First Amendment* (Westchester, Ill.: Crossway, 1987), 151–55.

22. See George M. Marsden, "The Soul of the American University: A Historical Overview," in George M. Marsden and Bradley J. Longfield, eds., *The Secularization of the Academy* (New York: Oxford University Press, 1992), 11.

23. See John Higham, *Strangers in the Land: Patterns of American Nativism* (New Brunswick: Rutgers University Press, 1955), Stephen V. Monsma, *When Sacred and Secular Mix* (Lanham, Md.: Rowman & Littlefield, 1996), 136–142, and Barbara Welter, "From Maria Monk to Paul Blanshard: A Century of Protestant Anti-Catholicism," in Robert Bellah and Frederick E. Greenspahn, eds., *Uncivil Religion: Interreligious Hostility in America,* (New York: Crossroad, 1987), 43–71.

24. Hatch, *The Democratization of American Christianity,* 95.

25. Mead, *The Lively Experiment,* 54.

26. Os Guinness, *The American Hour* (New York: Free Press, 1993), 228. Also very helpful on this point is Carl F. Kaestle, *Pillars of the Republic: Common Schools and American Society, 1780–1860* (New York: Hill and Wang, 1983), especially chap. 5.

27. Charles Leslie Glenn Jr., *The Myth of the Common School* (Amherst: University of Massachusetts Press, 1987), 84.

28. Glenn, *The Myth of the Common School,* 154. Also noting the Unitarian nature of the Christianity of the common schools is George M. Marsden, *The Soul of the American University* (New York: Oxford University Press, 1994), 89.

29. Quoted in Glenn, *The Myth of the Common School,* 164.

30. Kaestle, *Pillars of the Republic,* 76.

31. Guinness, *The American Hour,* 229.

32. *Reynolds v. United States,* 98 U.S. at 166 (1879).

33. *Reynolds v. United States,* at 167.

34. See C. Herman Pritchett, *The American Constitution,* 3rd ed. (New York: McGraw-Hill, 1977), 392–94.

35. *Church of the Lukumi Babalu Aye v. Hialeah,* 508 U.S. at 542 (1993).

36. The cases were *Wisconsin v. Yoder,* 406 U.S. 205 (1972), *Sherbert v. Verner,* 374 U.S. 398 (1963), and *Thomas v. Review Board,* 450 U.S. 707 (1981).

37. The cases are *Braunfeld v. Brown,* 366 U.S. 599 (1961), *United States v. Lee,* 285 U.S. 252 (1982), and *Goldman v. Weinberger,* 475 U.S. 503 (1986).

38. *Employment Division v. Smith,* 58 LW at 4435 (1990).

39. *Employment Division v. Smith,* at 4435.

40. Public Law 103–141, 103d Congress, Section 3 (b).

41. The cases are *Engel v. Vitale,* 370 U.S. 421 (1962) and *Abington v. Schempp,* 374 U.S. 203 (1963).

42. *Abington v. Schempp* at 313.

43. *Abington v. Schempp* at 313.

44. *Lemon v. Kurtzman,* 403 U.S. at 665 (1971).

45. *Committee for Public Education v. Nyquist,* 413 U.S. U.S. at 814 (1973).

46. *Engel v. Vitale,* 421 U.S. at 425 (1962).

47. *Abington School District v. Schempp,* 203 U.S. at 225 (1963).

48. *Abington School District v. Schempp,* at 222.

49. See *Lee v. Weisman,* 60 LW 4723 (1992) and *Wallace v. Jaffree,* 472 U.S. 38 (1985).

50. See Kenneth D. Wald, *Religion and Politics in the United States,* 2nd ed. (Washington, D.C.: Congressional Quarterly, 1992), 158–61.

51. Gallup and Castelli, *The People's Religion,* 20.

52. *The Williamsburg Charter Survey on Religion and Public Life,* (Washington, D.C.: Williamsburg Charter Foundation, 1988), Table 34.

53. *McCollum v. Board of Education,* 333 U.S. at 210 (1948).

54. See *Zorach v. Clauson,* 343 U.S. 306 (1952).

55. See *Edwards v. Aguillard,* 107 S.Ct. 2578 (1987).

56. See *Roberts v. Madigan,* 921 F.2d 1047 (10th Cir. 1990).

57. See *Settle v. Dickson County School Board,* 53 F.3rd 152 (1995).

58. See *Guidry v. Broussard,* 897 F.2d 181 (5th Cir. 1990).

59. *Epperson v. Arkansas*, 393 U.S. at 106 (1968). Also see a similar statement in *Abington School District v. Schempp*, at 225.

60. *Westside Community Schools v. Mergens*, 58 LW at 4727 (1990).

61. See Steven Holmes, "Clinton Defines Religion's Role in U.S. Schools," *New York Times* (August 26, 1995), A1 and A8.

62. A. James Reichley, *Religion in American Public Life* (Washington, D.C.: Brookings Institution, 1985), 165. Reichley's emphasis.

63. *Lemon v. Kurtzman*, 403 U.S. at 612–613 (1971). The quoted material is from *Walz v. Tax Commission*, 397 U.S. at 674 (1970).

64. Laurence H. Tribe, *American Constitutional Law*, 2nd ed. (Mineola, N.Y.: Foundation Press, 1988), 1215–16. Tribe's emphasis.

65. *Grand Rapids School District v. Ball*, 473 U.S. at 388 (1985).

66. *Grand Rapids School District v. Ball*, at 387.

67. *Grand Rapids School District v. Ball*, at 390.

68. See *Aguilar v. Felton*, 473 U.S. 402 (1985).

69. *The Williamsburg Charter Survey*. More specifically the academics were a random sample of 155 university faculty members of Ph.D.-granting departments of political science, sociology, history, and English; the media leaders were a random sample of 100 radio and television news directors who were members of the Radio and Television News Directors Association and newspaper editors in cities of over 100,000 population; the government leaders were a random sample of 106 high-level federal executive branch political appointees; and the business leaders were a random sample of 202 executives listed in *Who's Who in Industry and Finance*.

70. *The Williamsburg Charter Survey*, Appendix, Table 37.

71. Lester M. Salamon, *America's Nonprofit Sector* (New York: Foundation Center, 1992), 73.

72. "Institutional Identifying Characteristics," HEPS Profile of Independent Higher Education 1 (April 1991), 8, and Monsma, *When Sacred and Secular Mix*, 64–80.

73. *Tilton v. Richardson*, 403 U.S. at 679 (1971).

74. *Roemer v. Maryland Public Works Board*, 426 U.S. at 764 (1976).

75. *Hunt v. McNair*, 413 U.S. at 743 (1973).

76. *Roemer v. Maryland Public Works Board*, at 755.

77. *Roemer v. Maryland Public Works Board*, at 756.

78. *Roemer v. Maryland Public Works Board*, *at* 756. The quotation is from the district court decision.

79. *Roemer v. Maryland Public Works Board*, at 757, quoting from the district court opinion.

80. *Roemer v. Maryland Public Works Board*, at 758.

81. *Roemer v. Maryland Public Works Board*, at 758.

82. See *Bowen v. Kendrick*, 487 U.S. at 631 (1988).

83. *Witters v. Washington Department of Services for the Blind*, 474 U.S. at 487 (1986).

84. For a thorough consideration of this field see Monsma, *When Sacred and Secular Mix*, 4–10 and 64–80.

85. On the first two of these organizations see Sean Mehegan, "The Federal Connection: Nonprofits Are Looking More and More to Washington," *The*

Nonprofit Times 8 (November 1994): 43. On the third of these organizations see 1996 Annual Report (Chicago: Division of Church and Society of the Evangelical Lutheran Church in America, 1996).

86. Monsma, *When Sacred and Secular Mix,* 68.

87. *Bradfield v. Roberts,* 175 U.S. at 298–299 (1899).

88. *Bradfield v. Roberts,* at 299–300. No source is given in the Court's opinion for the quoted phrase, but from the context it appears to be from the act of Congress that incorporated the hospital.

89. *Bowen v. Kendrick,* at 615.

90. *Bowen v. Kendrick,* at 610.

91. *Rosenberger v. Rector,* 1995 WL 382046 (U.S.), at 10–11.

92. *Rosenberger v. Rector,* at 11.

93. *Rosenberger v. Rector,* at 24.

94. *Rosenberger v. Rector,* at 27.

95. See *Walz v. Tax Commission, Marsh v. Chambers,* 463 U.S. 783 (1983), *Lynch v. Donnelly,* 465 U.S. 668 (1984), and *Allegheny v. ACLU,* 109 S.Ct. 3086 (1989).

96. Telephone interview with Thomas Maier (April 7, 1994).

97. See Public Law 104–193, section 104. For an excellent description and explication of this section of the law see *A Guide to Charitable Choice: The Rules of Section 104 of the 1996 Federal Welfare Law Governing State Cooperation with Faith-based Social-service Providers* (Washington, D.C.: Center for Public Justice, and Annandale, VA: Center for Law and Religious Freedom of the Christian Legal Society, 1997).

98. There were a few exceptions. See, for example, J. Brent Walker, "Separating Church and State," *New York Times* (September 14, 1995), A17.

99. See "Picture of Jesus Blocks Public Funds for Salvation Army," *Church and State,* 42 (October 1989), 207, and *Dodge v. Salvation Army,* 1989 WL 53857 (S. D. Miss.).

100. See Monsma, *When Sacred and Secular Mix,* 80–99.

101. See Michael A. Paulsen, "Religion, Equality, and the Constitution: An Equal Protection Approach to Establishment Clause Adjudication," *Notre Dame Law Review* 61 (1986), 317, Reichley, *Religion in American Public Life,* 117, and Johnson, "Concepts and Compromise," 817.

102. Steven D. Smith, "Separation and the 'Secular': Reconstructing the Disestablishment Decision," *Texas Law Review* 67 (1989), 955–56.

Chapter 3

THE NETHERLANDS: PRINCIPLED PLURALISM

$\mathcal{T}$he Netherlands has a justified reputation as a stable, prosperous de-mocracy with a long tradition of religious liberty. It is also a tolerant—some today would even say a permissive—society. Prostitution and the use of marijuana are tolerated in some quarters and euthanasia is not uncommon. The Dutch social welfare system is often linked with Swe-den's as being the two most generous in the world. In cross-national studies it ranks near the top in educational achievement—certainly higher than the United States.[1] The death penalty was abandoned in 1876. Since the seventeenth century the Netherlands has often served as a refuge for persecuted religious groups and, along with Denmark, is often cited as doing the most to protect its Jewish citizens during the Nazi occupation. Moreover, it has one of the most theoretically rooted, thought-out approaches to church-state relations of any of the western democracies. Its study, therefore, should prove particularly enlightening.

This chapter opens with a brief description of the Netherlands and its system of government. It then considers the historical background for the Netherlands' approach to church-state issues, next it considers the Dutch approach to free exercise issues and questions, and then it does the same for establishment issues as they relate, first, to education and then to nonprofit social service agencies. The last section makes some concluding observations.

The Nation

The Netherlands, with fifteen million people crowded onto 16,000 square miles of land, is one of the most densely populated countries in the world. It is often said that Dutch history and geography have molded people that are, paradoxically, both fiercely independent and strongly committed to cooperation. The independence of the Dutch has resulted in a surprisingly large degree of societal pluralism for so small a country. It was historically fostered by the low-lying, marshy ground of the deltas of the Rhine, Meuse, and Scheldt Rivers that resulted in areas developing in relative isolation from each other.[2] This geography kept even the Romans from ever uniting under their rule the area that is today the Netherlands. During the Middle Ages this area consisted of several autonomous duchies. It was only in the late sixteenth century that a loose confederation of provinces came together to form a single republic. Even today the Netherlands has two official languages, Dutch and Frisian, the latter spoken by 400,000 Frisians living in the northern part of the country.

The Protestant Reformation resulted in the Dutch being further divided between a Catholic south and a Protestant north. The Protestants, in turn, were divided among the dominant Reformed, or Calvinist, group and other Protestant groups such as Lutherans and Mennonites. Meanwhile, the "golden age" of Dutch commercial prosperity developed in the seventeenth century, when truly the business of the Dutch was business. The commercial elites of Amsterdam and elsewhere concentrated more on making money than pursuing theological truth, with the result that the Dutch tolerated a variety of religious traditions when much of Europe was still at war over religious issues. The result is that even today the Dutch are a mosaic of religious, ethnic, and regional groupings, each jealous of its distinct identity and independence.

But this pluralism and independence of the Dutch is only one part of the picture. The other is a strong commitment to cooperation. Many observers of the Dutch scene trace this characteristic to the relentless battle against the sea. Sixty percent of the population inhabits the 25 percent of the Netherlands that is below sea level. This is made possible only by a complex, integrated series of canals, pumps, and seawalls. Dutch survival down through the centuries has necessitated cooperation. As recently as 1953 spring runoff and a series of heavy storms resulted in over 1,800 people drowning. As the population of the Netherlands has swelled in the twentieth century from 5 million to 15 million, cooperation has also been necessitated by the need for urban planning, housing development, and public transportation.

The famous Dutch toleration for differing religious, ethnic, and lifestyle groups is often said to arise out of the combination of these qualities of independence and cooperation. Cooperation in fighting the sea and building a prosperous economy could only be achieved by accepting the differences that were there and working together despite them.

Religiously, Catholics and Reformed Protestants (that is, Calvinists) are the two largest religious communities. In rough terms, of the 15 million population about 4.7 million are Catholic, 4.5 million are Protestant, and 6 million have no religious affiliation. Of the 4.5 million Protestants, 3.3 million belong to the two largest Reformed churches. There are also 25,000 Jews, 600,000 Muslims, most of whom are immigrants from Turkey and Morocco, and 80,000 Hindus and Buddhists, most of whom are also overseas immigrants.[3]

Since the 1960s there has been a strong secularization trend in the Netherlands. From 1959 to 1986 the percentages of the population reporting membership in the Roman Catholic Church dropped from 37 to 31 percent, and in the two largest Reformed churches from 38 to 21 percent, while those professing no religious preference rose from 21 to 44 percent over the same time span.[4] Even more telling is the drop in church involvement. Among Catholics, weekly church attendance dropped from 87 percent in 1959 to only 26 percent in 1986; among the Reformed denominations it also dropped over the same time period, but by a much smaller amount: from 36 to 33 percent in the larger of the two main Reformed churches and from 88 to 65 percent in the smaller of the two.[5]

Despite this secularization trend, strong religious belief also remains. Michael Fogarty once described the Netherlands as having "not only the highest percentage in western Europe of 'unchurched' adults, topping even Britain, but also the highest percentage of 'core' Christians, not only practicing but actively involved in their church: 23 per cent in 1990."[6] A 1981 survey bears out Fogarty's conclusion. Among the continental western European nations only Italy and Spain had higher rates of church attendance of at least once a month, and only Denmark and France had higher rates for never attending church.[7] The Netherlands, with a 40 percent level for at least monthly church attendance and a 41 percent level for no church attendance, ranked high in both attendance and nonattendance! Religiously, the Netherlands is a polarized nation with many strong believers and many nonbelievers.

Politically, the Netherlands is a constitutional monarchy, with Queen Beatrix serving as the head of state.[8] It has a parliamentary form of government with a bicameral legislature called the States-General. The upper house has seventy-five members elected indirectly by the members of provincial councils and the lower house has one hundred fifty members elected directly by the populace by a strict system of proportional representation. Most legislation originates with the cabinet and must be passed by both houses of the States-General, but only the lower house may amend or introduce bills. There are four major political parties: The Christian Democratic Appeal (CDA), the Labor Party (PvdA), the People's Party for Freedom and Democracy (VVD)—a liberal (in the traditional sense) business-oriented party—and Democrats '66 (D66), a change-oriented, political reform party. The current government, formed after the 1994 elections, is a coalition of the PvdA, the VVD, and D66. The CDA lost twenty seats between the 1989 and 1994 elections (a huge loss by Dutch standards) and is not a part of the government for the first time since 1918.

The Dutch political system has been described as corporatist and consociational.[9] The former term emphasizes the tendency for institutionalized representatives of key societal organizations to make public policy through a process of negotiation and compromise among themselves and with governmental officials. Consociational democracy emphasizes the tendency in segmented, or sharply divided, societies for the elites of the various segments to replace the incompatible demands of their constituent groups with pragmatic compromises that maintain the unity of society. Although the Dutch political system has been undergoing significant change in the past ten to twenty years, the corporatist concept of the Dutch political system is still accurate. Rudy Andeweg and Galen Irwin have written that "obituaries of neo-corporatism seem premature. . . . [T]he incorporation of interest groups into the decision-making process . . . is still characteristic of Dutch policy-making in many fields."[10] Although the number of advisory bodies has recently been reduced, the Department of Welfare, Health, and Sports, for example, still has thirty-three advisory councils and the Department of Agriculture has eleven.[11] Questions have been raised concerning whether the consociational concept is still applicable to the current Dutch scene.[12] But whatever one's position on that issue, it is clear that the Dutch political system continues to be marked more by negotiation, discussion, and compromise than by adversarial confrontations with outright winners and losers.

All these are themes to which we will return later in the chapter as we seek to understand Dutch church-state principles and practices. But first it is important to gain insight into the historical forces that have shaped the distinctive Dutch church-state practices and the assumptions and perspectives that underlie them.

The Historical Background

In the nineteenth century, liberal Enlightenment thinking then ascendant in the western world confronted both the United States and the Netherlands with a similar challenge. The United States took one road; the Netherlands another. As a result the two countries' approaches to church-states issues have sharply diverged down to today. The story of this challenge, how the Dutch responded to it, and the consequences for church-state relations largely revolve around the issue of education. The Dutch liberals in the nineteenth century reacted against the old conservative order that had featured a semiestablished Reformed Church (Nederlands Hervormde Kerk) and a host of privileges for the aristocratic classes. In contrast, the liberals worked for more popular participation in government, a more limited role for the state, and no state favoritism toward religious groups.

Underlying the reforms advocated by the Enlightenment liberals was a particular view of the ideal society, which explains why they believed there could be more popular participation in the political system without societal divisions and greed destroying societal stability as the conservatives feared. Dutch scholar Siep Stuurman has described this basic liberal view of that time: "Through education and propagation of (Liberal) 'culture' among all classes the circle of citizens could be broadened and the basis of the state as well. On this course a homogeneous Dutch nation would come into being, and would naturally take on a liberal coloration."[13] The liberal goal was a society marked by a consensus of values that were common and nonsectarian. Such a society would make possible broad democratic participation and a removal of the old prerogatives of the aristocratic classes without creating the social and political chaos the conservatives were predicting. The public schools were to play an especially important role in the teaching of a common, liberal culture of national unity, tolerance, and virtue.

Therefore, at the beginning of the nineteenth century a strong movement developed in the Netherlands to create publicly funded common schools that all children would be required to attend. Stuurman also wrote that the homogenization of the nation was "the political core of the liberal school policies. The school as nation-forming institution must not be divided among competing 'sectarian schools' or left in the hands of an exclusive political or church party."[14] Johannes van der Palm (1763–1840) was a Protestant clergyman, university professor, and leader in the liberal movement. He once described in strong terms the problem with leaving schooling in the hands of churches when he wrote that national regulation of education was needed in order to assure that "opinionated and fanatical idiots [not be appointed] in the position of teacher, lest rural youth in particular remain submerged in the wallow of prejudices whose destructive results have become all too apparent in these days of civic dissension."[15] But in his view religion and morals were not to be ignored; instead, he wrote, children ought to be taught a "Christianity above doctrinal differences."[16] This was the core of the liberal view of education and was very similar to the view of education advocated in the United States by Horace Mann and his supporters, as we saw in chapter 2. Education ought to be universal and carefully regulated by the government to make sure that divisive, parochial Christian doctrines were eliminated in favor of broad moral themes that would produce national unity and good, responsible citizens.

But where did that leave the diverse religious communities of the Netherlands? The answer is that in the liberal scheme of things particularistic, divisive religious beliefs were to be relegated to the purely private sphere. As a result schools outside the common school scheme of things were at best viewed with suspicion, and simply banned at worst. It was not until the 1848 constitution and, later, the 1857 school law that the freedom of parents to establish their own schools for their children was made clear.

As the nineteenth century wore on, increasing opposition to this concept of education grew among Catholics and especially among a number of orthodox Reformed groups (the largest of which was the Gereformeerde Kerk) that had split off from the large, semiestablished Reformed Church (the Hervormde Kerk), believing it was deserting traditional, orthodox Calvinist theology and practice.[17] From out of this opposition both the orthodox Reformed and the Catholics started to develop their own political movements in the 1860s.

Meanwhile liberalism was also changing, leading to a hardening of the lines. It was becoming more anticlerical and more committed to a secular philosophy. Political scientist Stanley Carlson-Thies summarizes the changes in Dutch liberalism in the 1870s: "Progress, advance through science, . . . liberation from outmoded dogmas—these were the watchwords of the younger generation. Simple dismissal of the benighted, who clung tenaciously to outmoded Christian beliefs, was no longer enough; those beliefs, and the schools and political initiatives embodying them, had to be confronted and defeated."[18]

The tensions that had been building for some time between the Enlightenment liberals, who were dominant in parliament, and the more orthodox Reformed groups that had split off from the large Hervormde Kerk and the Catholic forces came to a head in reaction to the passage of a new school law in 1878. Led by Kappeyne van de Coppello, the liberals pushed through parliament a new education law. It mandated new and higher standards for all schools—public schools run by municipalities, as well as alternative schools being run by Catholic and orthodox Reformed groups. It then provided generous financial subsidies from the central government to pay for these mandated improvements for the public schools, but not for the religious alternative schools. The alternative schools would have to come up with the additional funds, and if they could not, they could be closed by the education authorities. In the context of the times, the Catholics and orthodox Reformed viewed it as an all-out attack on the religiously based schools and as reneging on the freedom of education liberals had earlier supported in the 1848 constitution and the 1857 school law.

The law ignited a firestorm out in the country. It led to a mass political movement and drove the orthodox Reformed and Catholics— two groups with long histories of antagonism and distrust—into a formidable, politically active alliance. In only five days—between the time parliament passed the new law and the king gave his assent to it—the orthodox Reformed groups collected over 300,000 signatures in opposition to it and the Catholics over 160,000. As Carlson-Thies has written, "Compared to the total population of only some four million and an electorate of 122,000, this was a outpouring of popular sentiment of startling size."[19] Within a year the Reformed groups had established the Anti-Revolutionary Party (ARP), which, Hans Daalder has reported, "pioneered modern mass-party organization techniques in the Netherlands."[20] By 1883 a program for a Catholic party had been written and was receiving wide circulation among Catholics, although it was several decades before the formal establishment of a Catholic party.

The 1878 school law led to a "monstrous alliance," as one Dutch observer termed it,[21] between the orthodox Reformed groups and the Catholics. The ARP-Catholic alliance quickly became a major political force, winning an absolute majority of the lower house in 1888. Over a period of forty years and in a series of stages it won total approval of its vision of education: religiously based schools of various types and public schools espousing a "neutral," consensual philosophy all sharing fully and equally in public funding. This concept was enshrined in the Dutch Constitution in 1917 where it remains today. This constitutional victory was made possible by a pragmatic coalition among the ARP-Catholic forces, which wanted equal funding for their schools; the social democrats, who wanted universal male suffrage; and the by now small Liberal Party, which wanted a proportional representational electoral system. All three received what they wanted in what has been termed "the pacification of 1917."

The powerful Catholic-Reformed alliance has continued to play a prominent role in Dutch politics. The Catholic People's Party, the ARP, and the Christian Historical Union (a second Reformed party formed in 1908) in 1980 merged to form the Christian Democratic Appeal (CDA). This party continues to be a major force in Dutch politics, with it or its forebears being a part of every government from 1918 to 1994.

Equally important, however, is the fact that this alliance prevailed over the liberals on the intellectual front. Led by several Reformed thinkers, but also supported by the Catholic leadership, explicit, well worked-out theories based on a pluralistic view of society were developed to uphold its position on government support for all education, public and private alike. Those theories were also applied to areas of society other than the schools, and gained broad acceptance in Dutch society. In conducting interviews in 1996 with many Dutch government, church, education, and social service leaders, we were often struck by the extent to which these concepts have become part of the Dutch mindset on issues of church and state. It is important to understand them well. They form the heart of the *principled* pluralism we have noted in the title of this chapter.

One might suppose that Dutch Protestants would have reacted in one of two ways to the liberal vision of common schools imbued with a generalized moralistic, religious culture that in the nineteenth century would have been rooted in a genial Christian Protestantism. They might have accepted this as good and appropriate. After all, it was a general Protestant spirit that would infuse the classrooms. Catholics and nonbelievers would thereby receive some introduction to a nonsectarian Christianity that was much more congenial to Protestantism than to either Catholicism or a militant secularism. As seen in the previous chapter, nineteenth-century Protestants in the United States essentially reacted in this way when faced with a similar situation. And the large, more liberal Hervormde Kerk mostly reacted in this same way. It was the more "extreme," splinter groups that were Calvinist in a more orthodox, traditional sense—led by the Gereformeerde Kerk—that rejected the liberal-inspired common schools.

A second way the orthodox Reformed critics of the common schools could have reacted was by demanding that the common schools become thoroughly Reformed, reflecting—from their point of view—

the true faith. Similarly, Catholics could have demanded that the schools become thoroughly Catholic. Historically, there have been times and places where both of these religious traditions have sought to establish theocracies, where the power of government was used to help or favor their religious views or even to impose them onto all of society.

But in the Netherlands both the orthodox Reformed groups and the Catholics chose a different route, one of a pluralism that respects and gives room for a variety of religious-intellectual movements. The pragmatic situation both groups found themselves in may have encouraged this response, since both were minority groups that were unlikely to be able to impose their beliefs on the nation as a whole. Nevertheless, they developed a principled rationale for the positions they took and this rationale has had a lasting impact in Dutch society. Three persons—two Calvinists and one Catholic—are especially important in understanding how this came about.

Guillaume Groen van Prinsterer (1801–76), a historian and member of parliament, was an early leader of the more orthodox groups that were leaving the large Hervormde Kerk to form their own churches. He was a transitional figure, with his conservative tendencies leading him to hold certain theocratic views, but he clearly leaned toward more pluralistic thinking. This can be seen when in 1840 he argued that the public schools ought to be divided into separate Reformed, Catholic, and Jewish schools, with each school giving religious instruction in keeping with its religious tradition. He argued that common schools were inherently unable to serve all elements of a religiously diverse society, since education was necessarily based on one point of view or another and those points of view left out would be discriminated against.

The central figure in the path taken by the orthodox Dutch Calvinists was Abraham Kuyper (1837–1920), theologian, educator, and prime minister from 1901 to 1905. Fogarty has written that Kuyper was "the greatest leader whom Dutch Protestantism in modern times has produced."[22] Even today "Dr. Kuyperstraat" in The Hague is the street on which one finds the headquarters of the CDA. In it there is an Abraham Kuyper room containing various historical memorabilia from his long career. The influence of Kuyper and the orthodox Reformed party he founded, the ARP, is hard to overestimate.

Kuyper decisively, explicitly rejected the creation of a theocracy where the state would promote Christian beliefs and values. Time and again he spoke in favor of, and when in political power worked for, a political order that recognized and accommodated the religious pluralism of society. His goal "was not a theocratic recasting of the public order as a substitute for the liberals' project of privatizing religion. As cabinet head and leader of the confessional bloc, Kuyper forcefully reiterated as the confessional goal a system in which all views would be accorded equal rights in state and society."[23] When in 1898 Kuyper was invited to give the Stone Foundation lectures at Princeton University, one of his lectures was on "Calvinism and Politics." In it he stated that government should allow "to each and every citizen liberty of conscience, as the primordial and inalienable right of all men."[24] He also praised the concept of "a free Church, in a free State" and criticized czarist Russia and the Lutheran concept of secular rulers determining the religion of their kingdoms as violating this ideal. But—and this is highly significant—he also criticized "the irreligious neutral standpoint of the French revolution" as violating the ideal of a free church in a free state.[25] Kuyper often spoke in support of "parallelism," that is, the right and freedom of differing religious and philosophical perspectives and movements to develop freely on separate, parallel tracks, neither hindered nor helped by the government.

The Canadian political scientist Herman Bakvis has concluded: "It was the example of the Calvinists under the leadership of Groen van Prinsterer and Abraham Kuyper that gave the Catholics impetus towards developing some sort of party organization."[26] The person who emerged to lead this drive was a Catholic priest, journalist, and member of parliament, Herman Schaepman (1844–1903). In 1883 he called for a Catholic political party and outlined in a journal he coedited the program such a party would pursue. Much in Schaepman's thinking paralleled Kuyper's. The Catholic party he desired, according to Carlson-Thies, "would seek only equality for the Catholic church, not predominance, and would promote freedom of religion, independence of the churches from the state, and equal rights for all citizens and all religious bodies. . . . No special rights were needed, but there must be acceptance of the special character of Catholic desires and demands."[27] He also argued there was "a common cause to be made between Catholics and Anti-Revolutionaries on the schools issue; both groups wanted control of their own educational system."[28]

It was these pluralistic principles—tolerant, yet insisting that a variety of religious views and perspectives had as much right to sit at the public policy table as their secularly based counterparts—that triumphed over liberal thinking in the early twentieth century. When this victory was ensconced in the Constitution in 1917 by the guarantee of full funding of schools for all faiths on par with the public schools, the principles of pluralism came to dominate public thinking and to be copied in many other areas of public life. From the 1920s to the 1970s—and some would say down to today—a system referred to as pillarization (*verzuiling*) came to mark Dutch society.

Under pillarization most areas of group human activity—from political parties to labor unions to education to television broadcasting to retirement homes to social service agencies to recreation clubs—were marked by separate organizations representing the different religious and secular points of view.[29] There were four main pillars: Reformed, Catholic, socialist, and neutral (that is, liberal). This meant, for example, that there was a Catholic political party, a Catholic labor union, Catholic schools from primary to university, a Catholic television network, a Catholic newspaper, various Catholic recreation clubs, and more. These organizations would constitute the Catholic pillar. A person growing up in a Catholic household would largely live his or her life in the context of Catholic organizations (the Catholic pillar). A person growing up in a Reformed home or in a home without particular religious commitments but of a socialist (for the working class) or liberal (for the business and small entrepreneur) bent would face a similar situation. This social structure fit well with the principles articulated by Groen van Prinsterer and Kuyper and adopted by Catholics. If all of life is touched by religion, one's religious beliefs (or their secular counterparts) would be relevant to what one reads, how one votes, how one seeks an education, and even how one recreates. As foreign as such a system seems to the American observer, it worked well in the Netherlands in the 1920–60 period. In contrast to nearby continental European nations such as Germany, France, Spain, and Italy, a diverse people lived and prospered in social and political stability.

In the 1960s things began to change. The strong secularization trend noted earlier undercut much of the meaning that the religious pillars had had. Voting by religion, especially among the Catholics, fell precipitously. Although 70 percent of Dutch children still attend private schools today, parents now seem to select schools largely in terms other than their religious character. Many Protestants attend Catholic schools, Catholics attend Protestant schools, and nonbelievers attend both. Support for other forms of pillarized organizations has dissipated. As a result, many of the formerly pillarized organizations are combining: Protestant with Catholic, and both with secular. The Dutch no longer live most of their lives within a single pillar, but pick and choose. A family may be members of the Gereformeerde Kerk, yet send their children to a Catholic school. Meanwhile, the wife may work at a secular drug treatment center, the husband may belong to the CNV (a Christian—Catholic and

Protestant—labor union), they may largely listen to the new commercial television channels, and in the last election they may have voted for the nonreligious, reform-oriented D66 Party. In fact, pillarization in the Netherlands today has a negative connotation—something that is in the past and referring to an era of religious exclusiveness and division.

Is then pillarization dead? Some would say yes. But others say pillarization is not dead, but radically changed from thirty or forty years ago. An official with the CNV insisted in a 1996 interview that if by pillarization one means distinguishing between "neutral" and Christian or otherwise principled organizations, it is still very much alive. In many fields, organizations rooted in religious or secular principles still exist and are recognized and allowed for by official government policy as organizations reflecting a particular religious or secular point of view. And in corporatist fashion the leaders of these groups are often called upon to advise the government on issues of concern to them. The head of a Muslim organization serving the elderly told us with some pride that he had recently been asked to meet with a government group in order to relate the special perspectives and problems of elderly Muslims (previously, he related, only representatives of Protestant, Catholic, and humanist organizations had been invited to make presentations). It is instructive to see him—and the government—thinking in terms of the religious-philosophical bases of the organizations. It is not assumed that a neutral, secular organization of the elderly can speak for all the elderly. The religious-belief-ethnic pluralism of society is still being recognized and accommodated.

Pillarization has changed since the 1950s, but it is still a part of the Dutch way of governing and thinking about societal organizations. The term itself is no longer very descriptive. What is still in existence are societal-political organizations segmented by religious-philosophical orientations, and a society and a government that accept the legitimacy of and seeks to accommodate such organizations in a wide variety of fields. They are seen as reflecting points of view of significance in the populace and as serving segments of the taxpaying populace, and for both reasons deserving recognition and support. In the following sections the significance of this pluralistic view of society for church-state relations is developed.

The Free Exercise of Religion

The basic right to the free exercise of one's religion is laid down in Articles 1 and 6 of the Dutch Constitution, newly revised in 1983. Article 1 states:

All persons in the Netherlands shall be treated equally in equal circumstances. Discrimination on the grounds of religion, belief, political opinion, race or sex or on any other grounds whatsoever shall not be permitted.[30]

And Article 6 reads:

1. Everyone shall have the right to manifest freely his religion or belief, either individually or in community with others, without prejudice to his responsibility under the law.
2. Rules concerning the exercise of this right other than in buildings and enclosed places may be laid down by Act of Parliament for the protection of health, in the interest of traffic and to combat or prevent disorders.

In seeking to understand these constitutional provisions it is important to realize that the Dutch judiciary does not have the power of judicial review over acts passed by parliament. Article 120 clearly states that "The constitutionality of Acts of Parliament and treaties shall not be reviewed by the courts." The courts, however, can find, and sometimes have found, acts of municipal and provincial councils and executive branch agencies to be unconstitutional. In addition, Article 94 provides that acts of parliament and other statutes that conflict with treaties or with resolutions by international institutions—such as those of the European Union—are not applicable. The Dutch courts have historically been hesitant to hold acts of local councils and executive agencies unconstitutional or to enforce Article 94 against acts of parliament, although they have become somewhat more activist in doing so in recent years. Also relevant is the fact that Dutch citizens and groups, when compared to Americans, are slower to assert their perceived constitutional rights in the courts. The Dutch culture is more committed to negotiation and working situations out through discussions than to legal confrontations. Therefore, judicial interpretations have not been a dominant influence on the development of free exercise rights, as they have in the United States. Nevertheless, the constitutional provisions are important, both as a reflection of Dutch thinking and as legally enforceable provisions.

There are four aspects of the religious freedom language contained in Articles 1 and 6 that are important to note. One is that Article 6 provides for the free exercise of both religion and "belief." Protection of "belief" as well as religion was a change made in the 1983 revisions to the Constitution in order to make clear that secularly based beliefs were to have the same legal protection as religiously based beliefs. This is fully in keeping with the Dutch concept of pluralism discussed earlier—that all religions, as well as their secular equivalents, deserve respect and protection. The Dutch word translated as "belief" is *levensovertuiging* and more literally could be translated as "life conviction." It is not just any belief that has constitutional protection, but firm convictions that guide one's life, even though they are not rooted in religion in the traditional sense.

Second, Article 6 makes clear that one's freedom to manifest religion or belief is protected whether one exercises it as an individual or "in community with others." Individual rights are protected, but so are the rights of people to act as part of a larger community or group. This communitarian emphasis can probably again be traced back to Dutch pluralism, with its emphasis on a plurality of religious and "life conviction" groups and associations and the important, legitimate role they play in society. It contrasts with the approach of Enlightenment liberalism that currently dominates American thinking. Liberalism tends to assume that the protection of individual, private religious belief is sufficient and downplays the importance of the fact that religion is almost always lived out in faith communities.

Third, the second section of Article 6 contains an exception similar to the American "compelling state interest" test. The exercise of the right to religious freedom may be regulated in the interest of public health, the free flow of traffic, or the prevention of civil disorder.

A fourth point to note is especially important. Article 1, by stating that all people are to be "treated equally in equal circumstances," lays the groundwork for the free exercise right of religious organizations to receive the same sort of governmental assistance that their secular counterparts receive. Legal scholar Sophie van Bijsterveld, probably the foremost authority on church-state relations in the Netherlands today, has written:

> It [Article 1] guarantees equal treatment in equal circumstances to all persons. . . . It is clear that under the Constitution public-authorities in the Netherlands shall be neutral with respect to the various religious and non-religious denominations. . . . [I]t is clear that once authorities subsidize or support certain activities, religious counterparts cannot be excluded for that reason. Article 1 forbids this.[31]

Later she goes on to note that "equal treatment requires that financial support be available to organizations whether they operate under a religious or a non-religious banner."[32] In an interview Van Bijsterveld gave an example of what she had in mind when she explained that government should enable the free exercise of religion, not make it impossible. So [it means] the positive protection of religion, so to say. In the case of ancient church monuments, we say the government supports old castles and other old buildings, so it should also protect ancient church monuments. They should not be excluded. That is what equal treatment means.[33]

In the Dutch mindset, nondiscrimination and equal treatment in equal circumstances means that general programs of aid or support may not exclude religiously based belief structures and organizations. One sees the application of the basic concept of pluralism discussed in the previous section. A variety of religious and secular beliefs and their organizations and programs are to be treated equally by government. This principle is as basic to the Dutch approach to church-state issues as is the contrasting American no-aid-to-religion principle.

In addition to the relevant constitutional provisions, it is helpful to note how in practice the Netherlands has dealt with minority religions whose practices may conflict with otherwise valid regulatory laws. In doing so the already noted Dutch toleration and tendency to solve problems by discussion, as well as the limits of that toleration and willingness to work things out, can be observed. One area of concern has been the observance of religious holidays, especially how their observation affects working hours and school attendance. Since 1919 legislation regulating working hours has provided that Jews and Seventh-Day Adventists may have Saturdays off instead of Sundays, and store closing laws have provided that those merchants whose day of rest is other than Sunday may choose either Sunday or that other day as the day on which they close.[34] The courts have also declared that in principle employees are entitled to a day off on festivals of their religion, if sufficient notification is given. Similarly, the Compulsory Education Act frees children from school attendance on their religion's holidays, if advance notice is given. Special legislation has been passed to allow Hindus to scatter the ashes of their dead and Muslims to bury their dead without the use of coffins, as long as proper health concerns are met. Recently the Commission for Equal Treatment—a special body that was created to deal with the treatment of minority religions and that has the status of a court—ruled that school principals could not forbid the wearing of a head covering by Muslim girls.[35] A leader in the Jewish community, when asked if the Jews are fully included in the pluralism of Dutch policies, answered with an unambiguous yes.[36]

Nevertheless, the Netherlands continues to struggle with the increasing pluralism resulting from the rise of non-Christian religions.

Complete freedom for minority religions is not always achieved. One issue that has arisen is that of the ringing of church bells or other public forms of calling people to worship and prayer. In 1988 a Public Manifestations Act was passed that explicitly allowed church bell ringing and other calls to worship, but allowed local municipal councils to regulate the length and volume level. Van Bijsterveld, however, has noted:

> Church bell ringing is still a generally accepted form of expression and local communities concerned have used their powers of regulation mainly for islamic convocations. Normally, these convocations are permitted once a week under a set of maximum of sound frequency. . . . A very small number of local communities allow islamic convocations daily or more than once a day.[37]

Van Bijsterveld has also pointed out that the Dutch courts have held that the religious holidays of non-Christian religions need not be treated in the exact same manner as the Christian Sunday, since "Sundays and christian holidays not only have a religious function but a general social function, as well."[38] She also reports on another problem area—the use of buildings for religious purposes that conflict with local planning ordinances:

> [R]eligious communities, often islamic communities, but also small evangelical communities, use buildings contrary to their legally designated purpose. Local councils tend to tolerate or ratify these situations. Sometimes they do not. Courts have taken the view that despite the strict wordings of the Constitution on freedom of religion and belief, local community regulations in this area can be enforced.[39]

We interviewed the leader of a Muslim organization who stated that some employers do not allow their Muslim workers to take time off on Friday for prayers or give them the flexibility they need on days they are required to fast until sundown.[40] He also told us that Muslim children sometimes experience problems in the schools, as when the girls have to go to gym or sport activities with boys in clothes the traditional Muslim would consider immodest. He reported that some school principals make allowance for such concerns, but others do not. When that happens most Muslims feel there is nothing they can do. Some have been told, "You are now in the Netherlands, you have chosen to come here, so now you have to follow our rules." He reported that in a few instances such as this the courts have protected the Muslim students, but that most Muslims are hesitant to go to the courts. Nevertheless, he concluded by saying that there is greater freedom and less discrimination and problems in the Netherlands than in most western European countries—so much so that a certain pacifism has developed in the Dutch Muslim community that makes building strong Muslim organizations difficult.

In dealing with minority religions and their practices, accommodation is the norm, but there are exceptions. As the Netherlands has become home to increasing numbers of non-Christian minorities—and especially to Muslims—there have been areas of tensions where the Dutch proclivity for toleration and flexibility has not been fully extended. But it cannot be denied that the Dutch have a broad, expansive understanding of the free exercise of religion. It is interpreted to include the equal treatment of religious and nonreligious organizations and programs, and usually includes the practices of minority religious groups.

Church, State, and Education

The Dutch concept of pluralism translates, when applied to education, to a deep and lasting commitment to freedom of choice. There is strong support for the proposition that parents should be able to choose the sort of education their children receive, whether that be Catholic, Reformed in a genial, broad sense, Reformed in a strict, orthodox sense, Muslim, Hindu, secular, or secular with certain special teaching techniques or philosophies such as Montessori. A recent study by the Organization for Economic Cooperation and Development (OECD) concluded that " 'the central value of freedom of choice' was an aspect of Dutch education beyond debate at the present time."[41] One official with a national organization representing the boards of Protestant schools told us: "We are so much for freedom of education. . . . This is a part of the Dutch way of thinking." He went on to state that the potential problem of separate schools dividing Dutch society rarely comes up, but that "if it is discussed the desire for freedom always prevails."[42]

This freedom of choice is enshrined in Article 23 of the Constitution, which provides: "All persons shall be free to provide education . . ." and "Private primary schools . . . shall be financed from public funds according to the same standards as public-authority schools." It also states that private secondary schools shall receive public funding, as determined by the States-General. L. S. J. M. Henkens, the director of secondary schooling in the Ministry of Education and Science, has stated that Article 23 protects three distinct freedoms: the freedom to found schools, the freedom to determine the principles on which schools are to be based, and the freedom to organize the instruction. The second of these freedoms "entitles the competent authority of a school to choose the ideological or philosophical principles on which teaching at the school is to be based. The third . . . [entitles] the competent authority to decide on the content of teaching and the teaching methods to be used in the school."[43] Later he writes that "these freedoms remain untouched eighty years after they were first enshrined in our Constitution."[44]

Wilfred Vollbehr, the head of a Reformed research center, related a recent incident where a cabinet minister had suggested that Article 23 be changed or even done away with:

> Well, that took a lot of discussion and everyone was agreed we should leave the article as it is and not change it because it is a very fundamental article in our Constitution: that all groups can have their own education. It was still very important, a very important article in our Constitution. . . . Even the liberals say it is important to have pluralistic education, to have freedom for education.[45]

In this section we consider how this freedom of educational choice—enshrined in Article 23 of the Constitution and rooted in the Dutch concept of pluralism—works out in practice and how it affects church-state relations.

Under Article 23 of the Constitution the central government provides virtually full funding for all schools, including public schools run by local governments, privately run religious schools, and privately-run nonreligious schools. In order to assure maximum freedom of choice, whenever there are sufficient numbers of parents who want a new school that incorporates a certain distinctive religious or secular philosophy (*richting*, or direction), the government is committed to fund it as fully as it does the public schools. This includes the construction of facilities. And this is the case even if there are underutilized schools already in existence in the area where the new school is being proposed.

In the Netherlands today 69 percent of the primary students and 73 percent of the secondary students attend nonpublic schools, by far the highest level of the five countries considered in this study.[46] As of 1993, on the primary level there were 2,900 public schools, 2,400 Catholic schools, 2,200 Protestant (liberal) schools, 260 Protestant (orthodox) schools, 320 private secular schools, 76 Rudolph Steiner schools, 30 Islamic schools, 3 Hindu schools, and 2 Jewish schools.[47] A similar situation prevails on the secondary level, although there are presently no

Islamic or Hindu secondary schools. The Dutch policy of full funding for private schools clearly has resulted in a wide choice of schools.

In practice the Netherlands' basic policy of fully funding all schools still leaves many unresolved issues. One issue is how many parents and pupils asking for a new school are sufficient for the government to accede to their request. The numbers of students needed to found a new, publicly funded school are set by national standards and they vary based on pupil density in the area. In rural areas as few as eighty pupils may be enough, while two hundred to three hundred are generally required in urban areas. Whether a school of the same or similar orientation is nearby is also considered, as well, of course, as what constitutes "nearby." If there already is a school of the same religious or secular orientation in the area, the authorities may require three hundred fifty or more pupils before they approve a new school, even though attending the existing school may require a lengthy trip. The Netherlands' compact size, excellent public transit system, and ever-present system of bicycle paths make lengthy trips to reach school less onerous than might be supposed. Government officials also need to determine exactly what constitutes a new or distinctive religious or secular direction. If there already is a Protestant school in a community, but some parents believe it is too modern or contemporary in its theology, is that a sufficient basis for the government to fund a new school? Some Muslims have thought that the government has been insensitive to the differing groups within Islam. Another issue is when a school must close as the number of its students declines. If the number of pupils falls to less than thirty in a rural area or less than one hundred fifty in an urban area, the school faces the possible loss of government funding. Or there may be pressure for such a school to merge with a school of a similar nature. Again, there are no hard and set rules; public authorities must make many judgment calls. In recent years the government has been seeking economies of scale by avoiding very small schools. It has been slower to fund new schools and quicker to encourage small schools to combine or merge with others.

Two factors seem to make a system with as much potential for conflict and abuse in fact work with a manageable number of tensions and conflict. One is that Dutch society as a whole—including the public authorities—is genuinely committed to a pluralistic education system. Thus groups of parents wishing to maintain or start a school—while not automatically granted their request—are received with respect and given serious consideration. Second, the famous Dutch system of governing by discussion, negotiation, and consensus-building comes into play. There are umbrella organizations representing the various religious and

secular groups active in education, and thus active discussions and nego-
tiations ensue when an issue arises over the founding or closing of a
school of a particular group. Although our interviewees occasionally
expressed unhappiness over the decisions of the government authorities,
we received the distinct impression that public authorities are basically
committed to funding schools of a wide variety of religious and secular
perspectives, and will do so if there is a demonstrated demand for them
and the parents wishing the schools are organized and persistent.

The exact form the funding of private schools takes is both complex
and in a state of flux. Traditionally, the central government pays all salaries directly. This means that all teachers, no matter in what type of
school they teach—public or private—are on the same pay scale. Normally, the local authorities pay for obtaining the necessary building and
then are reimbursed by the central government. Every school receives a
certain amount annually from the central government for expenses such
as building maintenance, utilities, supplies, and equipment.[48] Recently
there has been a move to give schools greater financial autonomy by
way of making lump-sum grants. These payments are determined by a
formula, based on the number of pupils in a school, the type of building
it has, and other relevant factors. All secondary schools were scheduled
to go under this system in 1996 and all primary schools in 1998. This
change is being instituted because government officials thought the education budget was too open-ended and desired a more predictable—and
more manageable—budget.

Schools are not allowed to charge additional fees, although they
may request parents to make voluntary contributions. Most private and
some public schools request such contributions, but they average only
about 100 guilders ($63) a year.

Relevant to the issue of church-state relations is the fact that the
vast majority of the private schools receiving full public funding are
religious in nature—Catholic, Protestant, Jewish, Muslim, and Hindu.
One of the Jewish schools receiving funding is Orthodox in nature.
When pressed as to the nature of the Catholic schools, Dominique Majoor of a Catholic umbrella education organization acknowledged that
some Catholic schools are Catholic only in name, but then went on to
state: "But I think still a lot of schools are Catholic not only in name but
also by what they are doing and how they are doing it. The ideal within
my organization is that we should work on it and improve it. . . . But I
look at my own schools—the schools I've seen—and you can really
recognize them as being Catholic."[49]

Even more telling is a school sponsored by one of the small, strictly

Reformed denominations that we visited, the Greijdanus College in Zwolle. Its principal, Kars Veling, reported that his school receives 100 percent funding from the government and stressed that the teachers are properly qualified and that they teach all the required subjects. But he also made clear that they have classes in religion and bring religious perspectives into all subject fields, when appropriate. "The way we teach the content of our lessons is our own, is our choice."[50] All their teachers must be members of their own denomination and 90 percent of their students are also members of it. In the term used by the American Supreme Court, it is "pervasively sectarian." In short, although many of the religious schools receiving full public funding are religious in a very general sense, many are also very specifically, distinctively religious in nature.

The Dutch typically characterize their system as one of church-state separation. "The system of church and state relationships is characterized throughout as one of separation of church and state."[51] When we asked the author of these words how church-state separation can be squared with financial support for religious organizations, including schools, she replied that the Netherlands has no established church and that the state does not directly finance the churches, but if the state subsidizes education and social work, it must not discriminate against religion. If it funds neutral organizations, funding religious ones does not violate church-state separation.

> There have also been court decisions [ruling] that government doesn't have to subsidize social work, charitable work, or youth work, but when it subsidizes this type of work it should make no discrimination on the basis of religion or belief. So if a "neutral" organization applies for this work it may receive it, but if a church or religious organization wants to carry out this work, it should not be excluded because that would not be equal treatment.[52]

It is on the basis of equal treatment—of making funds available neutrally for all types of religious schools and for religious and secular schools alike—that funding of religious schools and church-state separation are seen as being compatible.

This leads to the question of how much freedom or autonomy is granted religious schools. Are they fully free to be as religious as they wish? Or are there overt or subtle pressures to conform, to water down their religious message? First, it is clear that all schools—public and private, religious and secular—are under numerous limitations and constraints. The Netherlands is a highly regulated society, with government regulations affecting almost all areas of life. Education is no exception. Much of the curriculum is set on the national level, as are the certification standards and the working conditions for teachers. All students from all schools take the same comprehensive exams. Schools clearly are not free to have whomever they want, teaching whatever they want them to teach.

Nevertheless, schools are, in a formal sense, completely free to be as religious as they wish to be. Article 23 of the Constitution seeks to protect this religious freedom when it states that government standards shall give "due regard, in the case of private schools, to the freedom to provide education according to religious or other belief." It later goes on to state that the funding "provisions shall respect in particular the freedom of private schools to choose their teaching aids and to appoint teachers as they see fit." In this context "teaching aids" refer to such learning supports as textbooks, maps, and films. The director of an umbrella Catholic school association has written that "educational institutions at all levels are permitted to teach in the manner they please. They can choose their own texts and their own teachers, including the possibility of using religion and lifestyle as a criterion for hiring."[53] Veling, the principal of Greijdanus College, insisted to us that "we are totally free in what we teach in our classes."

This is not, however, the entire story. There are three sources of pressures or constraints on the religious character of the schools. First, several people associated with religious schools have reported feeling the pressure created by the national curriculum and comprehensive national exams. The curriculum even specifies how much time must be devoted to the various required courses, and comprehensive exams mean that the schools, no matter what their orientation, must prepare their students to do well on them. Thus whenever the national curriculum is expanded or additional topics are covered in the exams, less time is left for the schools to interject their own distinctive courses and perspectives. The continuing tendency is for the national government to impose more requirements and to specify more attainment targets. Recently, for example, a dispute broke out over whether the national exams were to include questions on evolution that would assume its validity. After much controversy, in which the Royal Academy of Sciences strongly opposed allowing the schools freedom of choice in teaching evolution, it was decided to accede to the wishes of the religiously based schools and not include questions on evolution. But this controversy stands as an example of the sorts of pressures government regulations can put on the religious freedom of religiously based schools.

A second way in which government pressures can be brought to bear on religious schools relates to their hiring practices. When there is a vacancy, schools are legally free to hire any qualified applicant, but there are certain financial advantages in hiring a currently unemployed teacher, whether or not he or she agrees with the religious character of the school. As the principal of one Protestant school has written: "At the moment we are forced to give precedence to teachers from other schools who have, for some reason or other, lost their jobs, unless there are very clear and relevant reasons for not doing so."[54] These pressures can be resisted, but they are there.

Third, as school enrollments drop and the government seeks greater economies of scale by discouraging very small schools, pressures can be brought to bear on schools with falling enrollments to merge with other schools, even if they are of a different religious orientation.

In short, the Netherlands is a highly regulated society, and this also extends to the schools. The schools face significant pressures on their religious character and they need to have a clear and distinct understanding of their own religious character, if they are to resist them. Without that understanding, the danger is great that they will not successfully resist the pressures on them and the formal freedom they are promised in the Constitution will not be realized in practice.

This leaves the question of the role of religion in the public schools. Article 23 stipulates: "Education provided by public authorities shall . . . [pay] due respect to everyone's religion or belief." This has been "interpreted as a neutrality clause which requires a positive attitude towards religion. . . . Provision is made for [voluntary] religious education in public-authority schools. . . . A whole series of court rulings established that instruction in non-religious (humanist) belief should be offered and subsidized on the same basis as religious instruction."[55] Exactly how these requirements are met varies from one locality to another. Usually they are met by some form of objective teaching about religions and the role they play in society. Sometimes released time programs have been adopted, where students are taught by representatives of the various faiths after normal school hours. Prayer and other devotional activities are very rare in public schools, but have never been explicitly outlawed by either court decision or parliament. There is no attempt to encourage or promote consensual religious beliefs and traditions in the public schools. Such efforts would run counter to the principle of religious pluralism embraced by the Dutch.

There is, however, little educational choice on the university level. In fact, there is only one Reformed university and two Catholic universities. Over 80 percent of the university students are in public universities, while only 7 percent are in the Reformed university, and 12 percent in Catholic universities.[56] But this is only a part of the story. The Protestant and Catholic universities are almost indistinguishable from their public counterparts. In fact, the universities are so similar that students are centrally assigned to the various universities, with a lottery system used in cases of excess demand. All universities, including those with a religious tie, are funded by the central government. Theological schools are also funded by the government, and here distinctive religious differences, of course, still exist. Since 1962 the education of humanist counselors has also been included in the system of government support.

Educational choice, as we said at the beginning of this consideration of education, is the cornerstone of the Dutch approach to education. Religious schools are fully funded, and this is seen not as a violation of church-state separation and religious neutrality, but as a necessity if government is to be truly neutral among competing religious and nonreligious belief systems. To do otherwise would be to pick sides and thereby violate the free exercise rights of those left out.

Church, State, and Nonprofit Service Organizations

The struggle over the financing of private religious schools and the settlement reached on that issue have done much to shape the Dutch approach to the role nonprofit service organizations play in society and their funding by the government. The field of education established the pattern of relying upon private nonprofit organizations to provide a vital public service, with the government providing the funding. That pattern is the one that has been followed in the health care, social service, broadcasting, and other public service areas. Private—often religiously based—agencies provide the services and government provides most of the funding. Herman Aquina has pointed out that "about 70 percent of GNP is allocated by government in some way, but only 10 percent of GNP is directly controlled by core government: the other 60 percent is accounted for by PGOs [Para-Government Organizations]."[57]

The situation that exists in the field of treatment for drug addiction is typical: "About 3,000 people, spread over 70 institutions at 200 addresses are working in specialized addiction care in the Netherlands. On an annual basis there are some 80,000 clients. Apart from a few municipal methadone programmes, the entire service is of a private character."[58] Television and radio broadcasting has also traditionally been in the hands of nonprofit organizations representing the various "directions," or religious-philosophical perspectives, present in the population. There is no government-run broadcasting system similar to the BBC in Britain. "By law, any non-profit organization is entitled to broadcasting time if it can mount a 'full programme' (i.e. a mixture of light and serious programmes, plus magazine-like items), if it represents a cultural or religious group, and if it has sufficient support measured by the number of subscriptions to the radio and TV guide that every broadcasting organization publishes."[59] Presently, 450,000 subscriptions are needed to qualify for support.

There is no article in the Constitution similar to Article 23 that guarantees government funding for nonprofit service organizations, and in fact the actual amount and form of funding they receive vary greatly from one organization to another. The head of an agency that works with mentally and physically handicapped people reported that of a total budget of 1.5 million guilders, they receive only 60,000 guilders from the government.[60] But his agency does have a related foundation that has several residential facilities and they are funded totally by governmental social insurance. The director of a Muslim agency working with the elderly told us that it receives no general government funding, but that it has received government funding for certain special projects. The head of a drug rehabilitation agency told us it took them nine years to qualify for government funds, but that now they receive almost full funding. Despite these diverse experiences two facts need to be kept in mind. One is, as the figures cited earlier by Aquina make clear, most social services are provided by private nonprofit organizations with extensive public funding. Another is that even those agencies that do not receive general public funding are able to apply for special project funds and are eligible to receive social insurance funds for their clients who qualify for such funds. Public funding of nonprofit social service organizations is extensive and pervasive.

Originally, most of these nonprofit service organizations were "organized mainly along denominational lines."[61] The same pillarization system that we noted in the case of schools and other voluntary organizations existed in the area of social services.

> During the last part of the nineteenth century and the first half of the twentieth century, . . . the diversity of religious motives and political ideologies led to the formation of Roman Catholic, Protestant (Calvinistic), socialistic, and nonsectarian humanistic organizations like separate pillars in an edifice. Thus, the whole society was structured by these religious and ideological organizations. This "pillarization"

was for the most part as true in politics as in the sphere of delivering nonprofit services.[62]

Although the nonprofit service sector was deeply affected by the more general "depillarization" and secularization trends that swept through the Netherlands, many religiously based nonprofit service organizations still exist and take part in government funding programs just as their secular counterparts do. Many of these are clearly religious in more than name. There are, for example, four international aid and relief agencies—one Catholic, one Protestant, and two secular agencies. Dutch aid and relief funds are given to all four organizations, with the two religious agencies receiving about 60 percent of the funds.[63] The head of special programs for the Catholic organization, Cebemo, told us: "Our roots are in the missionary movement and we cannot deny them, and we also do not have the need to deny them. We say we are Christians, and we have a Catholic philosophy. We believe a world with justice for all means that we . . . give support to the people in the South who do not have the same amount of justice we have in our own society."[64] Cebemo hires non-Catholics as well as Catholics to work for it, but requires that about ten key positions be filled by Catholics.

A Jewish rabbi reported to us that there are three Jewish homes for the elderly, a Jewish social welfare organization, and a Jewish child welfare agency, as well as many other Jewish organizations. When pressed on whether Jewish organizations receive public funds just as Christian organizations do, or if there is some subtle discrimination against them, he responded unambiguously that Jewish organizations receive public funding just as their Christian and secular counterparts do.[65] The lobby of the building of the NCRV (the broadly Protestant broadcasting organization) has the words of Psalm 8, "O Lord, how great is your name in all the earth," emblazoned on one wall, and its head of research told us that their broadcasts are biblically oriented and distinctively Christian, even though often more implicitly than explicitly so.[66] Two-thirds of its revenue comes from a radio and television tax.

De Hoop (The Hope) is a drug treatment residential program in Dordrecht. It is officially recognized as a psychiatric hospital and thereby qualifies for full public funding. It also sometimes receives public funding for certain special projects for which it applies. It is Christian in an evangelical Protestant sense, and a few minutes talking to staff during our visit revealed that it is clearly and distinctively Christian. All their workers are required to be Christian believers and there are prayers before meals, devotions and prayers every evening, and twice a week Bible studies. All these religious activities are voluntary in nature, but clients are invited to take part in them. Similarly, an agency that is Reformed in a strict, orthodox sense and that works with mentally and physically handicapped people receives, as noted earlier, 60,000 guilders a year from the government and the residential programs of its related foundation receive full funding by way of the government's social insurance program. It is clearly and explicitly religious in nature—from its name, Dit Koningskind (The Child of the King), to its goal of serving only members of its own denomination.

In brief, the Dutch make extensive use of nonprofit organizations to deliver a wide variety of public services and many of these organizations possess—to greater and lesser degrees—religious orientations.

To many Americans such practices would seem to be a denial of religious freedom. After all, tax money from nonbelievers is going to fund Jewish homes for the elderly, money collected from Jews is going to support deeply Christian drug rehabilitation programs, and taxes paid by Catholics are going to fund Protestant television broadcasts. But the Dutch response is to insist that not to fund such religious organizations would be a denial of religious freedom. This came out in our interviews time and again. Frans Koopmans, of De Hoop drug treatment center, made a point that is fundamental to the Dutch approach to state funding of religious service organizations when he stated, "Every hospital, every helping facility has its principles, its priorities, its fundamentals. Even though they are perhaps not Christian. Everyone is working out of a philosophy. We are working out of a Christian philosophy because we are wholeheartedly convinced it is the truth."[67] As a result of this perspective, neutrality or evenhandedness demands that religious and nonreligious organizations be funded in the same manner. As Koopmans also said, "We have Christians in the Netherlands and we should have facilities to help that specific part of our population. If people are humanistic, you should have a humanistic hospital. We even have a anthroposophic psychiatric hospital."[68] This reasoning is firmly rooted in the Dutch concept of pluralism noted throughout this chapter.

Similarly, when asked concerning possible negative reactions of nonbelievers, Jews, or Muslims over their taxes going to fund his explicitly Christian organization, Martin de Jong of The Child of the King responded:

> We almost never have that kind of discussion, because they can get money for the same kind of activities in their interpretation of life. It's a right for everyone to get money for such kind of activities. . . . They

have a right to get money for such kind of activities; we have the right
to get money for such kind of activities. So when they say that to me
I can say that is a common right, it is not only my right. . . . It's not a
right especially for Christians, or for the Jewish; it's a common right.[69]

Maria Martens of VKMO (an umbrella organization of Catholic
social service organizations) defended her agencies' receiving public
funds with these words: "When the government gives money for housing for the elderly, why not to Catholics? . . . When we are all paying
our taxes, for these kinds of initiatives, and we have our [initiatives],
why should we be left out?"[70]

Koopmans, De Jong, and Martens were appealing to a basic sense
of governmental neutrality or evenhandedness based on the concept of
a pluralistic society, whose various elements have distinctive philosophies
or approaches and are deserving of the same support. This is the same
concept to which Van Bijsterveld made reference in the words quoted
earlier when she said that "government doesn't have to subsidize social
work, charitable work, or youth work, but when it subsidizes this type
of work it should make no discrimination on the basis of religion or
belief. . . . [I]f a church or religious organization wants to carry out
this work, it should not be excluded because that would not be equal
treatment."[71] In the dominant Dutch mindset public funding of social
service organizations does not violate church-state separation or governmental religious neutrality, as long as such funding goes to the organizations of all religious traditions and to those of nonreligious secular groups
as well. In fact, to do otherwise is seen as discriminating against religion.
Undergirding this mindset is the rejection of an assumption often made
in the United States, namely, that religious organizations have a bias or
a distinctive ax to grind, while nonreligious secular organizations are
neutral. In the Netherlands secular and religious organizations alike are
seen as operating out of certain distinctive philosophies or beliefs.

This leads to the question of the amount of religious freedom pos-
sessed by religious nonprofit service organizations that receive public
funds. On the one hand, there are strong and convincing claims to the
effect that government funding has led to an enormous amount of government control over nonprofit organizations. Jaap Doek, a professor of
family law at the Free University of Amsterdam, has written:

> In conclusion: the government has strengthened its influence and
> control over the non-governmental organizations in the field of child
> protection. These organizations are in fact instruments of the govern-
> ment in carrying out her responsibility for children in need of care and
> protection. These organizations can only operate as child protection
> services if they are recognized by the government and this recognition
> is only possible if they meet the conditions set by the government.[72]

This same conclusion has been echoed by many others in other areas.[73] The control of the Dutch government over nonprofit service organizations that receive public funding is great. Since the 1980s the government has sought to achieve economies in the social service area by forcing mergers of smaller agencies and other changes, which have clear implications for the autonomy of the agencies. When this occurs, nonprofit service organizations do not even have the same protections that schools have by way of Article 23 of the Constitution.

On the other hand, there is persuasive evidence that the control exercised by government officials usually does not extend to the religious activities and identifications of nonprofit organizations. Koopmans of the evangelical drug rehabilitation program De Hoop gave this issue of government control following government funding the proper balance when he said: "What we do have, of course, are regulations for every psychiatric hospital—Christian or non-Christian, humanistic, anthroposophic—which we have to subscribe to. But they are not anti-Christian regulations or something like that. . . . The Netherlands always has been known as a very tolerant country in which everyone could believe whatever you wanted as long as you did not hurt anyone else. Well, it's still so."[74]

Paradoxically, several people reported to us that one of the most effective ways for religious agencies to resist increasing government control is to strengthen their distinctive religious nature. Van Bijsterveld stated that "it is easier for organizations to resist pressure to merge with other organizations if they are very distinctively Christian, and harder if they are more generally Christian. Then it is harder for them to document a distinct identification or direction—we say *richting*—that is lost if they would merge with another."[75] Similarly, Daan Buddingh, head of the research bureau of the Protestant broadcasting company (NCRV), stated in response to the question if his company is free to be as religious in its programming as it wants to be: "Yes, the more the better I would say. . . . From the point of view of the government the answer is yes. From the point of view of the viewers it is limited—television is mainly used for entertainment. And that is our limitation. . . . But what the government expects us to do is to show a maximum religious profile. They want us to be recognized via what is on the screen."[76]

Dutch policies in regard to religiously based social service organizations is similar to that in regard to schools. In both cases the government—supported by attitudes prevalent in Dutch society—provides generous levels of funding to a wide variety of service organizations, religiously and secularly based alike. This public policy is rooted in a pluralistic concept of society that recognizes a variety of religious and secular belief systems present in society, all of which are held to be legitimate, contributing forces and therefore possessing an equal right to expect an appropriate share of public support. As is the case throughout Dutch society, there are many government regulations affecting the service organizations receiving public funds, a situation reinforced by recent government efforts to achieve economies in the delivery of social services. Nevertheless, the religious missions of religiously based agencies appear largely to be respected, especially when those religious missions are clearly in evidence and articulated.

Concluding Observations

The Netherlands is a clear example of the third model of church-state relations presented in chapter 1, the pluralist model. The Dutch seek to attain governmental neutrality on matters of religion, not by a strict church-state separation that sees all aid to religion as a violation of the norm of neutrality, but by a pluralism that welcomes and supports all religious and secular structures of belief on an evenhanded basis. This is a system of principled pluralism—as we put it in the title of this chapter—in that the Netherlands' pluralist approach to church and state is rooted in certain self-consciously held beliefs.

The principled nature of the Dutch church-state pluralist system can be seen in two basic beliefs or assumptions that undergird it. One is a pluralistic view of society that sees a variety of religious and philosophical movements—even when full participants in the public life of the nation—as normal and no threat to the unity and prosperity of society. Such movements do not have to be relegated to the private realm, with only consensual civil religious beliefs and values allowed into the public realm. A second underlying belief or assumption is that nonreligious, "neutral" organizations and movements are not truly neutral—as is often assumed within the liberal Enlightenment view of society—but are yet another *richting,* or direction, equally legitimate but no more legitimate than a host of other religious and nonreligious philosophies or directions.

Public policies that respect, accommodate, and support public roles for a plurality of religious and secular belief structures emerge out of these beliefs. The comments of Bob Goudzwaard, a professor of economics at the Free University of Amsterdam, emphasized to us the importance of a certain mindset in order to understand Dutch policies in regard to church-state issues: "Nondiscrimination when it comes to religion always also means in the Dutch mindset that if you have an organization that thinks it good to have a Christian approach, that cannot be a reason in itself to withhold subsidies because that would be discrimination. That is still very often present in the mindset."[77] This is a basic point that has emerged at various points throughout this chapter. What is often viewed in the United States as discriminating in favor of religion, and thereby a form of establishing religion, is viewed in the Netherlands as necessary in order to avoid discriminating against religion. On this basis the government funds a wide variety of private religiously based schools, universities, theological schools, and social service and health agencies. To do otherwise would violate the free exercise rights of those not recognized or accommodated on a basis equal to other religious or secular movements. As Van Bijsterveld said, "Freedom of religion is not only a negative freedom in the sense that the government not infringe upon it, but also the structure of the law must create an atmosphere so that religion can really be exercised."[78] If religion is to be fully free, government must take certain positive steps to accommodate it so that religion, along with secular beliefs, can in practice be freely exercised.

By following this concept of pluralism the Netherlands has created an approach to church–state issues that appears to have achieved the traditional liberal goal of governmental neutrality on matters of religion. There is a paradox here. In the name of opposing the liberal vision of society based on privatizing particularistic religious beliefs and favoring a generic moral consensus, the Dutch have forged an approach to church and state that achieves the liberal goal of religious freedom for all. It does so by allowing the recognition and support for the full range of particularistic religious beliefs, a practice that liberalism traditionally had assumed inevitably would lead to divisiveness and religious repression of one group by another. Once one accepts the fact that consensual moral-religious beliefs that are accepted by most but not all of the population and that public institutions and programs purged of all religious elements are not truly neutral, but reflect certain philosophical or moral perspectives, it is hard to disagree with the basic Dutch contention that true governmental neutrality can only be attained by treating people and organizations of all religious and nonreligious perspective and beliefs equally—not by favoring one over the other.

In seeking to understand how the Netherlands successfully arrived at its commitment to a principled pluralism, the role played by Catholic-Protestant cooperation must be recalled. It was the "monster alliance," forged in the 1870s between Catholics and the more orthodox among the Reformed Protestants that was able to overcome the previously dominant liberal forces and carry the day politically. In the United States, as seen in the previous chapter, Protestants largely made common cause with liberals in opposition to the Catholic Church. Yet it is important to note that the theories of religious pluralism that were developed by this alliance were much more than a rationalization for the advancement of its members' own causes. It was an ideology to which they were in reality committed. Jews, socialists, and secular humanists were early included within it, and today Muslims and Hindus are as well. It was a genuine, not a sham commitment to pluralism.

Finally, it is helpful to note that in part this system may work as well as it does in the Netherlands because of certain unique Dutch conditions. Even the small, compact size of the country enters in, served as it is by excellent public transportation and an amazing system of bicycle paths. This means schoolchildren can safely ride to schools some distance from their homes, thereby making it easier to sort out the children by religious or philosophical conviction. The public transportation system makes it possible for citizens to reach the social or health service agency they wish to use. The sense of cooperation and national unity forged by a common history and language (except for a small minority of Frisian speakers) may also play a role. Countries without the same long tradition of working together may have a harder time maintaining a sense of national unity and purpose than has the Netherlands. Nevertheless, the Netherlands stands as a testimony to the possibility of combining genuine governmental religious neutrality, a broad system of recognition and support for religious and secular private schools and social service organizations, and national purpose and unity. There is much to learn from the Dutch experience.

Notes

1. See, for example, Roy W. Phillips, "Cross National Research in Mathematics Education," in T. Neville Postlethwaite, ed., *International Educational Research* (New York: Pergamon, 1986), 67–110.

2. For a brief, readable account of the historical background of Dutch pluralism see Robert C. Tash, *Dutch Pluralism* (New York: Lang, 1991), chap. 2.

3. *Statistical Yearbook, 1996* (The Hague: Central Bureau of Statistics, 1996), 53.

4. G. A. Irwin and J. J. M. van Holsteyn, "Decline of the Structured Model of Electoral Competition," in Hans Daalder and Galen Irwin, eds., *Politics in the Netherlands: How Much Change?* (Totowa, N.J.: Cass, 1989), 34. Some of these figures differ from those reported in the prior paragraph since these are based on survey research studies and the ones in the previous paragraph on actual mem-

bership figures reported by the various religious communities. On the recent secularization trend also see James Carleton Kennedy, *Building the New Babylon: Cultural Change in the Netherlands During the 1960s* (Ph.D. dissertation, University of Iowa, 1995).

5. Irwin and van Holsteyn, "Decline of the Structured Model," 36.

6. Michael Fogarty, "How Dutch Christian Democracy Made a New Start," *Political Quarterly* (1995), 142. Sophie van Bijsterveld has also noted: "Although the degree of secularization in the Netherlands is high compared to other Western European countries, the degree of active participation of church members in their church is also comparatively high." Sophie C. van Bijsterveld, "State and Church in the Netherlands," in Gerhard Robbers, ed., *State and Church in the European Union* (Baden-Baden: Nomos Verlagsgesellschaft, 1996), 210.

7. See Richard John Neuhaus, ed. *Unsecular America* (Grand Rapids, Mich.: Eerdmans, 1986), 116.

8. For an excellent introduction to Dutch government see Rudy B. Andeweg and Galen A. Irwin, *Dutch Government and Politics* (New York: St. Martin's Press, 1993).

9. See Andeweg and Irwin, *Dutch Government and Politics,* chaps. 2 and 7. On consociational theory see Arend Lijphart, "Consociational Democracy," *Comparative Political Studies* 1 (1968), 3–44.

10. Andeweg and Irwin, *Dutch Government and Politics,* 175.

11. Letter from Sophie C. van Bijsterveld, Catholic University of Brabant (May 31, 1996).

12. See the discussion in Andeweg and Irwin, *Dutch Government and Politics,* 33–44. Also see Arend Lijphart, "From the Politics of Accommodation to Adversarial Politics in the Netherlands: A Reassessment," in Daalder and Irwin, eds., *Politics in the Netherlands,* 140–53.

13. Quoted by Charles L. Glenn, Jr., *The Myth of the Common School* (Amherst: University of Massachusetts Press, 1987), 46.

14. Quoted by Glenn, *The Myth of the Common School,* 46. Emphasis removed.

15. Quoted by Glenn, *The Myth of the Common School,* 47.

16. Quoted by Glenn, *The Myth of the Common School,* 47.

17. Especially able accounts in English of this struggle are found in Glenn, *The Myth of the Common School,* 244–49, and Stanley Carlson-Thies, *Democracy in the Netherlands: Consociational or Pluriform?* (Ph.D. dissertation, University of Toronto, 1993), 44–231. Much of what follows is based on these accounts.

18. Carlson-Thies, *Democracy in the Netherlands,* 138.

19. Carlson-Thies, *Democracy in the Netherlands,* 144.

20. Hans Daalder, "The Netherlands: Opposition in a Segmented Society," in Robert A. Dahl, ed., *Political Opposition* (New Haven: Yale University Press, 1966), 201. The revolution the party was against was the French Revolution, and more particularly the liberal principles in which the Reformed groups saw it being grounded.

21. The term is from G. J. Rooymans—used in a publication put out by the KVP in 1948. See Carlson-Thies, *Democracy in the Netherlands,* 175.

22. Michael P. Fogarty, *Christian Democracy in Western Europe, 1820–1953* (London: Routledge & Kegan Paul, 1957), 172.

23. Carlson-Thies, *Democracy in the Netherlands,* 229.

24. Abraham Kuyper, *Calvinism: Six Stone Foundation Lectures* (Grand Rapids, Mich.: Eerdmans, 1943), 108.

25. Kuyper, *Calvinism,* 106.

26. Herman Bakvis, *Catholic Power in the Netherlands* (Kingston, Ontario: Mc-Gill-Queen's University Press, 1981), 61.

27. Carlson-Thies, *Democracy in the Netherlands,* 168–69.

28. Bakvis, *Catholic Power in the Netherlands,* 62.

29. On pillarization see Erik H. Bax, *Modernization and Cleavage in Dutch Society* (Aldershot, Netherlands: Avebury, 1990), chaps. 5 and 6, and Harry Post, *Pillarization: An Analysis of Dutch and Belgian Society* (Aldershot, Netherlands: Avebury, 1989).

30. This and the following quotations from the Netherlands Constitution are taken from the English translation of the Constitution published by the Constitutional Affairs and Legislative Division of the Ministry of Home Affairs (October 1989).

31. Sophie C. van Bijsterveld, "The Constitutional Status of Religion in the Kingdom of the Netherlands," *The Constitutional Status of Churches in the European Union Countries* (European Consortium for Church-State Research, proceedings of the 1994 meeting, University of Paris), 207 and 211.

32. Van Bijsterveld, "The Constitutional Status of Religion," 211.

33. Interview with Sophie C. van Bijsterveld (February 9, 1996).

34. On this and other legal provisions mentioned in the paragraph see Sophie C. van Bijsterveld, "Religious Minorities and Minority Churches in the Netherlands," *The Legal Status of Religious Minorities in the Countries of the European Union* (European Consortium for Church-State Research, proceedings of the 1993 meeting, Thessaloniki), 293–94.

35. Letter from C. J. Klop of the Institute for Policy-Research and Planning for the Christian Democratic Appeal (May 30, 1996).

36. Interview with Rabbi R. Evers (February 29, 1996).

37. Van Bijsterveld, "Religious Minorities and Minority Churches," 90.

38. Van Bijsterveld, "Religious Minorities and Minority Churches," 294.

39. Van Bijsterveld, "Religious Minorities and Minority Churches," 290–91.

40. Interview with Süleyman T. K. Damra (February 1, 1996).

41. Organization for Economic Cooperation and Development, *School: A Matter of Choice* (Paris: OECD, 1994), 68. The quotation is from an earlier OECD study.

42. Interview with W. Bos (January 26, 1996).

43. L. S. J. M. Henkens, "The Development of the Dutch Education System," in Tymen J. van der Ploeg and John W. Sap, eds., *Rethinking the Balance: Government and Non-Governmental Organizations in the Netherlands* (Amsterdam: VU University Press, 1995), 52.

44. Henkens, "The Development of the Dutch Education System," 55.

45. Interview with Wilfred Vollbehr of the Center for Reformational Philosophy (January 25, 1996).

46. OECD, "The Netherlands: Equal Treatment for Public and Private Schools," in OECD, *School: A Matter of Choice,* 68. These figures are as of 1990.

47. Bartho M. Janssen, "The Position of Umbrella Organizations, Advocacy

and Commitment to the Central Policy," in Van der Ploeg and Sap, eds., *Rethinking the Balance,* 65 and 66. Rabbi R. Evers reports that as of 1996 there were three Jewish schools, one of which was Orthodox. On the total number of pupils in private schools over time see Estelle James, "Public Subsidies for Private and Public Education: The Dutch Case," in Daniel C. Levy, ed., *Private Education: Studies in Choice and Public Policy* (New York: Oxford University Press, 1986), 118.

48. See James, "Public Subsidies," 119–21 and M. L. Kreuzen, "Freedom Within Bounds—Or the Regulated Autonomy," in Van der Ploeg and Sap, eds., *Rethinking the Balance,* 73–74.

49. Interview with Dominique Majoor of the General Bureau for Dutch Catholic Education (January 26, 1996).

50. Interview with Kars Veling (February 1, 1996). Incidentally, in 1991 this school was named by *Newsweek* magazine as one of the ten best schools in the world. See "The Best Schools in the World," *Newsweek* (December 2, 1991), 38–50.

51. Van Bijsterveld, "Church and State in the Netherlands," 215.

52. Interview with Sophie C. van Bijsterveld (February 9, 1996).

53. Janssen, "The Position of Umbrella Organizations," 68.

54. Kreuzen, "Freedom Within Bounds—Or the Regulated Autonomy," 73.

55. Van Bijsterveld, "State and Church in the Netherlands," 219.

56. Janssen, "The Position of Umbrella Organizations," 64.

57. Herman Aquina, "PGOs in the Netherlands," in Christopher Hood and Gunnar F. Schuppert, eds., *Delivering Public Services in Western Europe* (London: Sage, 1988), 94.

58. Marten J. Hoekstra, "The Division of Roles Between Government and Non-Governmental Organizations in Making Youth Drug Policy," in Van der Ploeg and Sap, eds., *Rethinking the Balance,* 98.

59. Aquina, "PGOs in the Netherlands," 99.

60. Interview with Martin J. de Jong of The Child of the King (January 30, 1996).

61. Ralph M. Kramer, "Governmental-Voluntary Agency Relationships in the Netherlands," *Netherlands' Journal of Sociology,* 25 (1979), 155.

62. Tymen J. van der Ploeg, "Changing Relationships between Private Organizations and Government in the Netherlands," in Kathleen D. McCarthy, Virginia A. Hodgkinson, and Russy D. Sumariwalla, eds., *The Nonprofit Sector in the Global Community* (San Francisco: Jossey-Bass, 1992), 194.

63. Interview with Ellen van Moorsel of Cebemo (January 31, 1996). Also see Bram van Leeuwen, "The Netherlands' Co-Financing Programme," in Van der Ploeg and Sap, eds., *Rethinking the Balance,* 115–19.

64. Interview with Ellen van Moorsel (January 31, 1996).

65. Interview with Rabbi R. Evers (February 29, 1996).

66. Interview with Daan Buddingh of NCRV (February 7, 1996).

67. Interview with Frans Koopmans of The Hope (February 5, 1996).

68. Interview with Frans Koopmans (February 5, 1996).

69. Interview with Martin J. de Jong (January 30, 1996).

70. Interview with Maria Martens of VKMO (February 5, 1996).

71. Interview with Sophie C. van Bijsterveld (February 9, 1996).

72. Jaap E. Doek, "Relations in Child Protection: An Overview," in Van der Ploeg and Sap, eds., *Rethinking the Balance,* 86.

73. This control over the nonprofit service organizations by the government appears to be of recent origins. As recently as 1981 Ralph Kramer wrote: "Despite the belief that he who pays the piper usually calls the tune, CRM [the Ministry of Culture, Recreation, and Social Welfare] evidently exerts relatively little central control over the PIs [voluntary agencies]." Ralph M. Kramer, *Voluntary Agencies in the Welfare State* (Berkeley: University of California Press, 1981), 32.

74. Interview with Frans Koopmans (February 5, 1996).

75. Interview with Sophie C. van Bijsterveld (February 9, 1996).

76. Interview with Daan Buddingh (February 7, 1996).

77. Interview with Bob Goudzwaard of the Free University (February 7, 1996).

78. Interview with Sophie C. van Bijsterveld (February 9, 1996).

Chapter 4

AUSTRALIA: PRAGMATIC PLURALISM

𝒯he most important principles in church-state relations in Australia are pragmatism and tolerance. Pragmatic considerations have structured the state's resolution of church-state issues at every point in Australian history, and because the "practical" solution to church-state problems has changed over time, Australia has vacillated among four different church-state models in its two-hundred-year history: establishment, plural establishment, liberal separationism, and pragmatic pluralism. As with the Netherlands, Australian policy is consistent with governmental neutrality and religious pluralism, but it is rooted in pragmatic concerns, not in basic, theoretical principles as in the Netherlands. At the same time, there has been very little support in Australia for an American separationist model that would challenge public finance of religious schools and religious service organizations. Underlying this policy pragmatism is a socially tolerant political culture—a live and let live attitude—that has led to a respect for and protection of the rights of religious minorities.

This chapter opens with a brief description of Australia's religious composition and the nation's political structures. It then considers the history of church-state relations in the Australian colonies, and after the colonies federated in 1901 to form the Commonwealth of Australia. The chapter follows with a consideration of the Australian approach to religious free exercise and establishment issues. The final section reviews the implications of Australia's pragmatic pluralism for public policy related to church-state issues.

The Nation

Australia has a population of seventeen million people spread over a continent roughly the size of the United States. Because of harsh envi-

87

ronmental conditions—much of Australia is virtually uninhabitable—
nearly 80 percent of the population lives along a thousand-mile stretch
of the southeastern seaboard between the cities of Adelaide and Brisbane.
Roman Catholics and Anglicans are the two largest religious communities in Australia; according to the 1991 census, there are 4.6 million
Catholics and 4 million Anglicans in the country. The other largest
Christian groups are the Uniting Church, 1.3 million, and the Presbyterians, 700,000. There are also 150,000 Muslims, 150,000 Buddhists, and
75,000 Jews.[1]

Over the past several decades, Australia has become more religiously diverse and more secular. Between 1971 and 1991 the percentage of the population reporting membership in a non-Christian religion
rose from 0.78 percent to 2.64 percent. Buddhists and Muslims have
grown the fastest in the past decade, mostly because of a rise in immigration from Asian and Middle Eastern countries. There has also been a
secularization trend in Australia. Between 1971 and 1991 those stating
no religion in the census rose from 6.7 to 12.9 percent and those not
stating a religion climbed from 6.1 to 10.1 percent of the population.
Monthly church attendance has also dropped, falling from 36 to 24 percent of the population between 1950 and 1989, and more than half of
Australians reported that they did not attend any church service in 1983.
The decline in church attendance has been particularly strong in the
historically powerful Anglican, Presbyterian, and Uniting churches, and
less pronounced in independent evangelical Christian churches and
among non-Christian groups. In comparative terms, the rate of monthly
church attendance in Australia is roughly twice that of Britain and half
the rate in the United States.[2]

In terms of its political structures, Australia combines England's parliamentary form of government with America's institutional federalism.[3]
The titular head of state of Australia is the British monarch, represented
by a governor-general, who has very little real power. The prime minister, who is responsible to the House of Representatives, has effective
executive power. The 148-member House of Representatives parallels
the British House of Commons and is the Australian Parliament's more
important chamber. There is also a 76-member Senate that has far less
political power than either the prime minister or the House of Representatives. There are two major and several minor political parties in
Australia. The largest parties are the Australian Labor Party (ALP), which
represents Australia's political left, and the pro-business Liberal Party.
The National Party, which represents rural interests, is a coalition partner
with the Liberal Party and, with sixteen seats in the House, is Australia's

most significant third party. John Howard leads the current Liberal Party government, formed after the 1996 elections. The ALP, which had governed since 1983, lost thirty-one seats between the 1993 and 1996 elections, which was its worst defeat since World War II.

As with most federal polities, Australia's federalism is a complex and dynamic relationship among the federal and six state governments and two self-governing territories. At the time of federation, the federal government's power was limited to its enumerated constitutional powers in interstate commerce, defense, foreign affairs, mass media, and immigration. States enjoyed "residual powers" which meant they could legislate in areas not specifically assigned to the federal government.[4] The balance of power, however, has shifted dramatically in the past fifty years toward the federal government. This is particularly clear in the commonwealth's financial authority. The national government has sole access to personal and corporate income taxes, sales tax, and excise duties. State and local governments, however, continue to have jurisdiction over important policy areas such as education, health, welfare, criminal law, urban affairs, and the administration of justice.[5] What this has meant is that the commonwealth government increasingly finances programs administered at the state and local levels. The commonwealth spends roughly one-third of its total budget on outlays to state and local governments.[6]

Australia's religious composition and political structures have had an important impact on the resolution of church-state practices. In order to appreciate how these factors have helped shape church-state policy, we turn now to an analysis of Australia's political history that has provided the framework for its model of pragmatic pluralism.

The Historical Background

Religion did not give birth to the Australian colonies as it did in America, and church-state issues assumed a very different form in the emerging Australian state. The original purpose of the British settlement in New South Wales in 1788 was to imprison criminals from English cities. The British needed to find an alternative location for their prisoners after the American Revolution stopped them from being shipped to Georgia; convicted criminals made up half of the fifteen hundred people in the first fleet of ships to settle Australia. This secular state intent shaped the relationship between religious and political institutions at least until England sent its last fleet of convicts to Australia in 1868. Colonial elites assumed there would be an established Church of England in the Australian colonies, as there was in England, and for the first several decades the Anglican Church alone received state aid for education, clergy, and church buildings. The primary goal for colonial authorities, however, was control of the convict population, not religious conversion or liberty.[7]

While the institutions were closely united, an activist and powerful state dominated the church and other institutions of civil society. The state took the lead in aiding religious institutions that were financially poor and had not experienced the religious revivals that generated so much energy in American churches and allowed them to flourish without state support.[8] The Australian Anglican Church was at the mercy of colonial authorities for financial aid and there were persistent disputes between chaplains and governors about the appropriate levels of state support. The state provided aid, but on utilitarian and pragmatic grounds. There was little or no religious motivation to the state's action; religion served the state's secular goal by providing moral order and social control among a penal population considered dangerous and morally corrupt. In return, colonial authorities expected the church to help foster political legitimacy in the new state.[9] Some Anglicans challenged the relationship on the grounds that it compromised the church's evangelistic message and independence, but Anglican clergy generally accepted their role as magistrates, moral policemen, and chaplains to the convict and settler population. Given the traditional dependence of the Church of England on the British crown, this is not surprising. The church had grown accustomed to looking to the state for support and providing political legitimacy in return.[10]

The degree of state regulation of religion varied among the Australian colonies. In the earliest days of colonial settlement in New South Wales, the state appointed Anglican clergymen and did not allow clergy from other faiths to minister to the convict population. Despite the fact that Irish Roman Catholics made up fully one-third of the convict population by the early 1800s, for example, prison authorities initially barred Catholic priests from celebrating the mass and required attendance at Anglican chapel services. Not surprisingly, the convict population largely rejected the established Church of England.[11] For the most part, however, the colonies did not regulate religious practices or place social and political disabilities on those who practiced other faiths. State officials were not all that committed to promoting the established Church of England, and what is more important they hoped to avoid the political disputes that pitted religionists against each other in England. As a result, a more liberal policy of religious free exercise rights developed in each of the colonies. The absence of a state-imposed religious monopoly allowed Australia to become a religiously diverse mix of Anglicans, Catholics, Presbyterians, and other nonconformists.

This diversity made it difficult for the colonies to maintain the English church-state model, however, as state support for the Anglican Church aroused hostility from the competing denominations. Because state elites did not feel obligated to an established church model for religious reasons, they could more easily contemplate a different political arrangement than their English counterparts, and they began to look for a more palatable church-state arrangement. The New South Wales Church Act of 1836 seemed to offer the ideal solution. The act revised the established church model by allocating colonial funds on a more equal basis to the three largest denominations (Anglicans, Catholics, Presbyterians) without discrimination. This plural or multiple establishment was a bold and innovative policy at the time, and the other Australian colonies followed with similar acts within a few decades.[12]

The Church Act was a secular response to religious diversity by a class of colonial governors who had little spiritual interest in religion. The state chose to be neutral among the largest denominations in order to depoliticize emerging religious disputes in the colonies and to enable churches more effectively to promote a Christian moral order and political legitimacy in the Australian state. Neutrality, in this view, did not mean the cessation of state aid or state finance to all existing religions; only the three largest and most politically powerful Christian denominations received money for churches and clergy. Contrary to the Dutch experience, Australian elites provided little philosophical or religious justification for this kind of state neutrality. It was not a principled commitment to pluralism that drove the policy; few people argued that the Church Act could be defended on the ground that the policy was a nondiscriminatory way to protect and promote Australia's religious diversity. The intent of the policy was to make life easier for colonial authorities who had grown weary of denominational conflict and to empower churches to provide moral guidance to their members.

At the same time, the Church Act established two important precedents that continue to shape public policy in contemporary Australia. First, as Michael Hogan notes, when the government provides funds to a religious denomination, they are generally available to all denominations on some basis of equality.[13] There was and is a basic commitment to a nondiscrimination principle among the churches when the state provides aid. This will become even more apparent when we look at the current policy on state aid to religious schools and nonprofit organizations. Second, pragmatism has been the norm when political leaders deal with church-state issues. Policy makers viewed religious issues as a problem to be solved in the most expedient manner possible, which in the mid-nineteenth century led them to support what was, for the time, a remarkable policy of plural establishment. The state initially limited aid to the three largest denominations, but these churches represented nearly all of Australia's religious population, and for its day the policy exhibited a respect for the rights of religious minorities, particularly Roman Catholics. In England, by comparison, the state barred Catholics from admission to universities and had only just granted them political emancipation when New South Wales passed the Church Act.

Despite the intent of the Church Act, it did not dissipate sectarian rivalry among the denominations. Most of the churches believed that the policy continued to advantage the Church of England because of its size, organization, and the lingering prejudice of the Anglican governing class against Roman Catholics and nonconformists. While the act reduced the disparity in state aid among the denominations, the Anglican Church continued to receive more than its fair share.[14] Roman Catholics pressed for a reformation of the act, nonconformists pushed for the voluntary principle of no state aid as a way to escape Anglican domination, and secularists—who were indifferent to Christianity—had gained a foothold in Australia by the end of the nineteenth century.[15] Finally, as the Australian state became more stable, it no longer looked to social institutions like the church for political legitimacy. In the absence of secular justifications for state aid, political leaders had fewer grounds on which to defend the policy. Because there had never been an overriding commitment by the state to promote religious pluralism, governing officials quickly abandoned the act when it proved costly, difficult to administer, and politically contentious. By the turn of the century each of the Australian states adopted a new policy of church-state separation rooted in the principles of Enlightenment liberalism. This meant an end to direct state funding for clergy and church buildings.

The major political challenge to the model of plural establishment occurred in the field of education. Religious schools, particularly Anglican schools, had a virtual monopoly on education in the Australian colonies in the early nineteenth century. Colonial governments, under the Church Act, funded denominational schools on a largely equal basis. Religious schools could not keep up with the demand for public education in the mid-nineteenth century, however, and pressure grew in all the Australian colonies for a free, compulsory, and "secular" education system.[16] Until the 1860s, Anglicans and Catholics formed a powerful political coalition that preserved the denominational system from religious dissenters and secular liberals who wanted to make education a state function and believed that religious control of education threatened to undermine the assimilationist purposes of a universal system of education.

Anglican church leaders were not, however, as committed to the principle that education should be a religious function as were their Catholic counterparts, and their opposition to state control of education gradually dissipated. Many of the church's leaders joined forces with secular rationalists to end state aid to denominational schools. As in the United States, the Protestant objection to public finance of religious schools had much to do with Protestant hostility to Catholicism. Protestants became convinced that state funding of the denominational system advantaged Roman Catholics, and because they strongly opposed Catholicism they united to stop state aid for all religious schools.[17] In addition, Protestants did not generally believe that a secular educational system threatened their religious values because it allowed for instruction and worship of the general principles of Christianity. In contrast to the Netherlands, there was no Protestant movement in Australia that saw public schools as a threat to their religious values. The New South Wales Public Instruction Act of 1880 typified this "secular" approach to teaching religion: "In all schools under this Act the teaching shall be strictly non-sectarian, but the words 'secular instruction' shall be held to include general religious teaching as distinguished from dogmatical or polemical theology."[18] To make clear that a secular education did not preclude religious instruction, the author of the act, Sir Henry Parker, noted: "it was never the intention of the framers of this Bill to exclude such a knowledge of the Bible as all divisions of the Christian Church must possess, or a knowledge of the great truths of Revelation."[19]

Australia's secular educational system shared several of the liberal presuppositions of the American common school movement. First was the belief that a primary function of the public school was to assimilate persons of different religious, class, and ethnic backgrounds by introducing them to the key values of Australian society. In Australia, this primarily meant Roman Catholics, who had "alien" religious views and suspect political sympathies. It is not surprising, for example, that all schoolchildren were required to pledge their loyalty to God as well as to the king or queen and the British Empire. Patriotism was among the key political virtues that the public schools would inculcate children with, particularly Irish Catholics who had a history of opposition to the British crown and who needed to be socialized with "proper" social and political values.

Second, the Enlightenment liberals leading the public school movement believed that a nonsectarian, moralistic religion had a place in the schools. While reformers viewed the particularistic elements of the various churches as divisive and dangerous, they thought that the core consensual features of the Christian faith could provide the basis for a common morality. They shared Horace Mann's optimism that common religious beliefs were discoverable by human reason. What this ignored was the incommensurability of religious and moral viewpoints and the political power structures that lay behind the rationalization that the established Protestant viewpoint was rational or consensual. Protestant church leaders did not challenge this liberal vision because they saw it as consistent with their understanding of the social role of Christianity. Nor did they appreciate that the rationalistic assumptions of the liberal educational model undermined a distinctively religious point of view in the schools.

The education acts passed by the various states allowed independent religious schools to operate, but they rescinded public finance of them. State officials expected that Catholic schools would collapse without state funding and that the public schools would become a vehicle for Irish Catholic assimilation. This did not happen. The Catholic hierarchy rejected the public schools as dangerously liberal and antireligious, defended their educational principles, and committed additional resources to the preservation of a Catholic school system. Catholic parents similarly viewed the public schools as unsympathetic to their cultural and religious sensibilities. Fueled in part by Protestant antipathy, the Catholic school system incorporated most Catholic children and the religious rivalry between Protestants and Catholics intensified in Australia for the next half-century.

Religion played only a small role as Australia moved toward federation at the end of the century. The six colonies that united to form the Australian commonwealth in 1901 asked for the "blessings of Almighty God" in the preamble to the new national Constitution, and the drafters self-consciously modeled Section 116 on the First Amendment of the U. S. Constitution. Section 116 states:

> The Commonwealth shall not make any law for establishing any religion, or for imposing any religious observance, or for prohibiting the free exercise of any religion, and no religious test shall be required as a qualification for any office or public trust under the Constitution.

The purpose of Section 116 was to depoliticize religion as much as possible in order to keep the commonwealth out of the religious field. As we have seen, sectarian strife was a political reality in each of the Australian colonies and political leaders did not want religious rivalries spilling over into federation politics. Australia's religious diversity made it difficult to defend an established church. At the time of federation, Anglicans represented a plurality of the nation's population at 40 percent, but Catholics were 23 percent, and Methodists and Presbyterians each had 12 percent.[20]

In addition, there were no practical reasons for the drafters of the new constitution to press for an Established Anglican Church in the Australian commonwealth. The Anglican Church lacked the political power to force this model on recalcitrant policy makers and, just as significantly, the state's interest in religion had always been pragmatic. Political elites in Australia did not assume, as they likely would have in England at the same time, that the state had a positive obligation to defend an established church. Without this philosophical commitment to an establishment model, political leaders did all that they could to maximize support for the federation. This meant giving individual states effective power over religious matters. While the Constitution forbade the commonwealth from formally establishing a church or restricting religious free exercise rights, states could do both. The importance of state governments in the resolution of church-state issues became particularly apparent in subsequent rulings of the Australian High Court dealing with free exercise rights.

The Free Exercise of Religion

As with each of the countries in our study, Australia struggles with the question of how far to go to permit religious beliefs and practices that conflict with social welfare and societal norms. Those who drafted the Australian Constitution modeled Section 116 on the First Amendment to the American Constitution, and the Australian High Court has wrestled with the nearly identical language that bars the government from making any law that prohibits the free exercise of religion. Australia, however, lacks the theoretical commitment to the free exercise of religion that is so evident in the Netherlands. The High Court has not aggressively protected religious liberty. In two key free exercise clause cases, the Court has established the precedent that the Constitution provides very little protection for the religious beliefs and practices of Australian citizens. The Court has interpreted Section 116 narrowly, which has meant that religious liberty rights are at the mercy of the political process. As we shall see later in this section, Australia has made major strides toward the ideal of religious liberty, but that progress has not come by means of the Court's decisions.

The first major Australian case that tested free exercise rights was *Adelaide Company of Jehovah's Witnesses Inc. v. Commonwealth* (1943). This case involved opposition by the Jehovah's Witnesses to Australian involvement in World War II. A number of Australian churches opposed the war on religious grounds, including the Quakers, but they were able to convince the government that they did not pose a security risk to the state. The Jehovah's Witnesses were not so fortunate and the commonwealth government seized church property and declared the Adelaide branch of the church a proscribed organization. Since the proscription came from the Australian commonwealth, rather than a state government, the church appealed on the ground that the law violated their free exercise rights guaranteed in Section 116 of the federal constitution.

In his decision, Chief Justice John Latham recognized that the purpose of Section 116 was to "protect the religion (or absence of religion) of minorities, and, in particular, of unpopular minorities." Nevertheless, he ruled that the state may infringe upon religious liberty when it is necessary to protect civil government or the continued existence of the community: "Section 116 of the Constitution does not prevent the Commonwealth from making laws prohibiting the advocacy of doctrines which, though advocated in pursuance of religious convictions, are prejudicial to the prosecution of a war in which the Commonwealth is engaged."[21]

Latham emphasized an important point in his decision: it is appropriate for the state to restrict religious freedom when the exercise of that right has the effect of endangering the entire political community. Australia faced the very real danger of being invaded by Japan during World War II, which had earlier bombed the city of Darwin. The state had legitimate concerns about the prosecution of the war, and understandable reasons to worry about groups that actively opposed the Australian state. The problem with the decision, however, is that Latham did not examine in any detail the words and actions of the Witnesses to determine if they posed a genuine threat to the government or the community. Instead, he inferred that the church's teaching that the commonwealth was an organ of Satan was necessarily prejudicial to the defense of the commonwealth and that the government could legitimately proscribe the organization. The Court did not use the decision, therefore, to articulate a standard by which to judge when it was appropriate for the state to limit free exercise rights. In failing to do that, the Court effectively sent the message that it would not be a strong advocate for religious freedom. The contrast with the Netherlands is again instructive. Article 6 of the Dutch Constitution specifically articulates the conditions under which the state can limit religious liberty.

A second significant Australian free exercise case, *Grace Bible Church Inc. v. Reedman* (1984), demonstrated again the limited nature of free exercise protections under the Australian Constitution. The case involved the conviction of a Grace Bible Church for running an unregistered nongovernment school contrary to South Australia's Education Acts between 1972 and 1981. Under that act, the state could fine the governing authority of an unregistered school that enrolled students for instruction. The church claimed that registration would place the church school under the state's authority, which violated their religious belief that God controlled the school. South Australian authorities convicted Grace Bible Church and fined the school's governing authority $365.

The school appealed the conviction to the High Court and argued that South Australia's Education Act interfered with the freedom of religious worship and expression that is an inalienable right under the Australian Constitution. The Court rejected this argument with the terse statement that the rights guaranteed in Section 116 "cannot be of any relevance because it only imposes a prohibition upon the law-making powers of the Commonwealth Parliament."[22] The Court refused to interpret Section 116 as a restriction of a state's power in the field of religion. The issue of whether a state's action limits a person's free exercise right was moot, therefore, because the Court did not have the power to overturn such a state law. The Court further contended, following its decision in *Adelaide*, that there is no inalienable right of religious freedom under the Australian Constitution or common law, and that even if there were such a right, it could still be "invaded by an Act of the Parliament of this State."[23]

The Court sympathized with the plight of the school and recognized that the registration of a nongovernment school is dependent upon the satisfaction of the education board, which gives state officials wide discretion to determine the appropriate place for religious instruction. The Court concluded, however, that the political process is the only avenue for groups dissatisfied with a state's law: "the remedy for this state of affairs, if a remedy is required, is a political one and not a legal one."[24] Interestingly, the Court did not discuss if South Australia's law placed a burden on religion and, if it did, whether the state's interest in the law could justify such a restriction. The High Court simply asserted that it was bound by the rule of law and the Constitution, which, when narrowly read, does not give it the power to overturn acts of state parliaments in the field of religious free exercise.

The Australian High Court has had fewer means than the U. S. Supreme Court to extend the religious rights of Section 116 because it has not incorporated those portions of the Constitution dealing with the provisions of the Australian commonwealth government and made them applicable to the states. There is no Australian equivalent to the due process clause of the U. S. Constitution's Fourteenth Amendment and its provision that "no state shall make or enforce any law which shall abridge the privileges or immunities of the citizens of the United States." A proposal to amend Section 116 to include coverage to the states failed in a referendum in 1944, as have more recent attempts to adopt a Bill of Rights or extend Section 116 to the states.[25]

A recent landmark decision of the High Court in *Australian Capital Television Pty Ltd and Others v. The Commonwealth of Australia* (1992) opened up, in principle, the possibility for the court to affirm a fundamental right of religious free exercise in the future.[26] In this case, the Court overturned a law that established a regulatory body to govern the broadcasting on television and radio of political advertisements. The act required broadcasting stations to provide free time for political advertising for each political party, but prohibited them from broadcasting other political advertisements or information. The stated purpose of the legislation was to safeguard the integrity of the political process by reducing the pressure on parties and candidates to raise substantial amounts of money for political campaigning on television and radio.[27]

Writing for the Court, Chief Justice Anthony Mason acknowledged that the Constitution does not guarantee a protection of fundamental rights and freedoms: "The framers of the Constitution accepted, in accordance with prevailing English thinking, that the citizen's rights were best left to the protection of the common law in association with the doctrine of parliamentary sovereignty."[28] Nevertheless, Mason asserted that the freedom of communication, though not stated in the Constitution, is "so indispensable to the efficacy of the system of representative government for which the Constitution makes provision that it is necessarily implied in the making of that provision."[29]

The implication of the decision is that the Constitution gives the commonwealth—and the High Court—an implied power to safeguard the rights and freedoms associated with a liberal polity. Although the Court has yet to test the idea of implied rights in the area of religious freedom, it could theoretically use this authority to read into Section 116 a fundamental guarantee of religious liberty, but only if it chooses to exercise its power aggressively in the area of religious rights.[30]

The High Court's decision in *Grace Bible Church* established the precedent that there are no constitutional grounds for the protection of religious liberties against the actions of state governments. In *Adelaide*, the Court failed to establish a clear standard by which to judge limits on religious rights and sent the message that it would not be an institutional advocate for religious freedom. The Court's approach to free exercise issues reflects the policy pragmatism that has marked the resolution of church-state issues throughout Australian history. The state has sought workable solutions to religious disputes, which in most cases has meant giving to colonies, or now individual states, the power to determine for themselves what is the best church-state policy.

The defense of religious rights in Australia comes less from the High Court than from each of the state constitutions and commonwealth and state legislation. In terms of state constitutions, Tasmania is the only state where there is a free exercise provision, but this provides little protection because it can be overridden by an act of Tasmania's parliament. Commonwealth legislation includes religion as a protected right, but it is not particularly strong and fails to deal with individual cases of religious discrimination. Religious discrimination exists in Australia and there are some cases where the political process protects the major churches but disadvantages minority faiths.[31]

As we noted earlier, however, Australia has made progress in the area of religious rights. Public opinion and cultural values have been the most significant determinants of this change, although the law is beginning to catch up. As Gary Bouma notes, Australia has developed "a notion of fair play, (the) equal worth of human dignity and live and let live."[32] In addition, Australia is a politically tolerant culture that has historically been open to a diversity of religious practices. These social values have contributed to an atmosphere that supports religious free exercise rights and has generally allowed immigrant religious groups to negotiate their way into Australian society. The best example of this is Australia's current school policy that, as we shall detail below, provides public finance for virtually every major and minor religious group in Australian society. This sense of fair play, evenhandedness, and social tolerance has also led to more laws specifically designed to protect religious freedom.

Equally important is the fact that many of the state governments have passed antidiscrimination laws that include religion as a protected freedom. In order to give meat to this legislation, states have established anti-discrimination boards to deal with individual cases of religious discrimination. The most populous Australian state, New South Wales, does not include religion in its Anti-Discrimination Act, although its anti-discrimination board has made a strong recommendation that religion should be included.[33]

Public opinion and cultural values are a nebulous way to protect religious freedom, but it is significant that Australia has not had the kinds of conflict around the rights of Muslims that is evident in England, another country in our study without constitutional or legal protections for the rights of religious groups. Australians seem committed to a process of negotiation and compromise with religious minorities, while Britain is more defensive of an established church-state model that limits religious rights and invites religious group conflict.

A primary cause for this shift has been the liberalization of immigration policy in the past two decades that has produced a much higher level of ethnic and religious heterogeneity into Australia. An open preference for white western immigrants characterized Australia's immigration policy for much of this century. From 1900 until 1945, the so-called White Australia immigration policy used racial characteristics to exclude nonwhites and most non-Christians from entering Australia. From 1947 to 1972, the state used public moneys to induce immigration among preferred migrant groups, which were the British and northern and southern Europeans. In 1957, for example, the state launched a "Bring out a Briton" campaign and worked closely with churches to implement the policy.[34] The purpose of the policy was to facilitate the migration of Protestants and Roman Catholics, groups that fit comfortably into the established cultural and religious molds, and could easily assimilate themselves into the dominant values of Australian society. As late as 1947, the three largest denominations, Anglican, Roman Catholic, and Uniting Church represented over 90 percent of Australia's religious population.

The big three still represent over 80 percent of the nation's religious population, but there has been a rapid increase in the numbers of new Christian groups (Pentecostal, Mormon, Jehovah's Witnesses, Orthodox Christians) and non-Christian religions (Buddhist, Hindu, Muslim). The immigration of new religious groups has helped to make Australia among the most ethnically diverse countries in the world, and increased the political power of non-Christian groups.[35] A growing number of organizations have begun to make provision for religious free exercise in such areas as dress codes, dietary restrictions, and recognition of religious holidays. It is also significant that Australia has not responded defensively to the immigration of non-Christian groups, as has occurred in other countries, but appears committed to a process of negotiation with them to minimize areas of religious conflict.

The current status of religious rights in Australia is not ideal; there is no enshrined, constitutional protection of religious liberty and no commonwealth law that specifically bars religious discrimination. The state has, nonetheless, made strides toward the pluralistic goal of equal treatment of all religious groups. A growing number of jurisdictions include religion among their grounds for complaints about discrimination, and the major religious groups work toward this ideal. As we will see in the next section, there is an equal commitment to this pluralistic model in religious establishment issues, particularly in public finance to religious schools and nonprofit organizations.

Church, State, and Education

As we saw in our historical overview, Catholics retained their independent school system at the end of the nineteenth century despite the fact that the state rescinded state aid to denominational schools. A smaller number of high-fee independent schools more loosely associated with a Protestant denomination also continued to exist. With limited financial resources and rising school costs, however, Catholic schools increasingly found it difficult to compete with government schools. By the late 1950s the disparity between state-run and Catholic schools became apparent and the church concluded that the Catholic school system would cease to exist without state support. The bishops committed themselves to preserving Catholic schools and they intensified their political pressure for state aid.

The federal election of 1963 brought the issue of state aid back onto the political agenda for the first time since the previous century. The push for state aid coincided with a growing split between the Catholic right and the secular left within the Labor Party. Working-class Catholics, who traditionally voted Labor, pressed the party to abandon its long-standing opposition to state aid for religious schools. Hoping to capitalize on Catholic disaffection with the Labor Party, Liberal Prime Minister Robert Menzies committed his party to a policy that would have provided commonwealth grants to public and private schools for the purpose of science education. Protestants had originally joined forces with secular liberals to oppose public finance of religious schools because of their hostility to Roman Catholics. By the early 1960s, however, Protestant opposition to Catholics had waned considerably, making it easier for the largely Protestant Liberal Party to support state aid to nongovernment schools. Support grew among Protestants for the right of parents to exercise a choice in schooling and for the government to fund students exercising that right. In response, Gough Whitlam, the Labor Party candidate for prime minister, successfully pressed his party to abandon its opposition to school funding.[36]

Menzies' initiative was the first formal entry of the commonwealth government into direct school funding, but it proved to be the tip of the iceberg. Both the Liberal and Labor Parties had a political imperative to press for state aid, and in the 1972 federal election both parties pledged major increases in grants to all nongovernment schools in need of support. The Labor Party, led by Whitlam, won the election and created the Schools Commission to formalize commonwealth educational policy. Under the policy instituted by the commission in 1974 the commonwealth provided direct grants to nongovernment schools.

Opponents of state aid challenged the policy on the grounds that the payment of government grants to denominational schools violated Section 116 of the Australian Constitution, which does not allow the commonwealth to make any law "for establishing any religion." Almost all nongovernment schools had some religious affiliation, and opponents contended that aid to religious schools constituted a de facto establishment of religion. In *Attorney General for the State of Victoria v. The Commonwealth of Australia* (1981), the High Court affirmed the validity of the legislative action. Relying upon what he called the "plain" or "usual" meaning of the words "for establishing any religion" in Section 116 Justice Garfield Barwick, writing for the majority, argued that establishing a religion involves "the identification of the religion with the civil authority so as to involve the citizens in a duty to maintain it and the obligation of, in this case, the Commonwealth to patronize, protect and promote the established religion."[37] According to this reading of Section 116, Barwick could not rationally see how "the law for providing the funds for the forwarding of the education of Australians by non-government schools is a law for establishing Christian religion."[38] In a concurring opinion, Justice Harry Gibbs put the point even more strongly: "I consider the words in Section 116 to mean that the Commonwealth Parliament shall not make any law for conferring on a particular religion or religious body the position of a state (or national) religion or church."[39]

The Court rejected the plaintiffs' attempts to use the U. S. Supreme Court's rendering of the First Amendment no establishment clause cases as a guide for this decision. Barwick contended that the American cases that barred aid to religious schools were irrelevant because of the "radically different language in our Constitution."[40] Barwick asserted that the wording of the Australian Constitution, "for establishing any religion" was narrower in meaning from the "respecting an establishment of religion" phrase of the American First Amendment. The Australian Constitution, Barwick argued, prohibits only those parliamentary laws that formally establish *a* religion (our emphasis), it does not involve "the prohibition of any law which may assist the practice of religion."[41] The decision removed the last serious obstacle to state aid for religious schools, but left unanswered the question of whether aid had to be non-preferential, i.e., available to any religious groups that wanted to form a school, or if public money could go only to existing church schools.

Nongovernment schools are eligible for commonwealth funding under the General Recurrent Grants Program, the Capital Grants Program, and the National Equity Program for Schools. General recurrent funding is provided on a per student basis. The government places each nongovernment school in one of twelve funding categories based on the amount of actual finance and income a school can raise on its own behalf.[42] The poorest schools receive the largest grants, but even the wealthiest nongovernment schools receive some state aid. Political efforts to stop funding the small number of very wealthy schools have failed, however, because of the power and unity of the nongovernment school lobby that has consistently opposed all such efforts. In 1993, the per student grants to nongovernment schools ranged from $423 to $1,701 for primary schools (315 to 1,275 US$) and from $671 to $2,486 for secondary schools (503 to 1,865 US$).[43] Recurrent grants from the commonwealth represent two-thirds of all commonwealth aid to private schools. The commonwealth also provides capital grants for maintaining school facilities, and funding under the National Equity Program for Schools, a policy that targets English as Second Language students and those with disabilities. Nongovernment schools also receive per student grants from state governments.

State aid to nongovernment schools has had a profound impact on education in Australia. Enrollment in nongovernment schools began to fall in the early 1960s from nearly 25 percent of all students to a low of 22 percent in 1971. With recurrent funding from the government, however, the percentage of students in private schools climbed to 29 percent in 1994. Proponents of state aid contend that this growth indicates that the natural market for nongovernment schools is between one-quarter and one-third of all students; state school supporters counter that private schools have increased their share because they are now more affordable.

State aid has lowered the cost of nongovernment schools and made them more attractive to middle-income parents. Nongovernment schools typically outperform state-run schools in test scores and graduation rates; as private schools have become more affordable it is natural that the demand for them would increase. As a proportion of total resources, state and commonwealth funding represents a significant source of revenue for most private schools, although it varies between Catholic and other nongovernment schools. Commonwealth and state funding provides 75 percent of the cost of educating students in Catholic schools,[44] 60 percent in schools affiliated with the Australian Association of Christian Schools (AACS), the peak body for the evangelical sector,[45] but significantly less in other nongovernment schools, which, on average, charge three to four times as much tuition as Catholic schools. The average annual fee in a Catholic secondary school in 1994 was $1,214 (910 US$) and $3,639 (2,730 US$) for all other nongovernment secondary schools.[46] The most elite private schools charge as much as $7,000 annually.

At the same time, the popularity of independent schools reflects a growing parental preference for an education infused with a religious perspective. This is particularly true for immigrant groups and evangelical Christians. A recent survey conducted by the Immigration Bureau of the Jewish community in Australia noted that the more than 8,800 children currently attending Jewish day schools in Melbourne represent over 70 percent of the school-age population in the Jewish community. The report concluded: "There is a growing and widely shared belief that young people are more likely to develop a solid and lasting sense of Jewish ethnic identity if they spend at least some of their school years in a pedagogical and social environment that is strongly supportive of Jewish ideas and values."[47]

A similar Immigration Bureau survey of the Australian Muslim community by Gary Bouma noted that a majority of parents expressed a preference for Muslim schools. The report concluded that "immigrants are banding together to establish schools and programs more suited to their culture."[48] The number of students enrolled in Muslim schools has increased from 325 in 1986 to 2,500 in 1994.[49] Evangelical Christian schools have also grown rapidly in the past few decades, reflecting a growing preference for a religiously based education. The AACS notes in its 1994 annual report that "the need to teach children to understand the world from a Christ-centered perspective and to equip them to follow Christ in every area of life is as urgent now as at any time in history."[50]

The original purpose of state aid was to save the Catholic school system. An unintended consequence of the policy has been the proliferation of non-Catholic, but religiously based nongovernment schools. In 1971, Catholic schools enrolled over 80 percent of non-government school students; by 1994 this proportion had fallen to 68 percent. Catholic school enrollments have only increased by a total of 3.5 percent since 1986, whereas the combined non-Catholic groups have increased by more than 33 percent. In 1994, there were 6,428 primary and secondary government schools and 1,977 nongovernment schools. Government funds went to a plethora of religious schools, including Roman Catholic (1686 schools), Anglican (120), Lutheran (72), Seventh-Day Adventist (71), Baptist (42), Pentecostal (21), Jewish (19), Assemblies of God (17), and Hare Krishna (2), to name some. In addition, the state provided aid to nonreligious private schools such as Montessori (19 schools) and Rudolph Steiner (34).[51]

The growth in the non-Catholic sector reflects the government's commitment to neutrality in funding private schools. When the High Court ruled that the commonwealth could fund religious schools, it left open the question of which religious schools would be eligible for aid. For the most part, state and federal administrators have consistently pursued a neutral policy in which aid is available equally to religious and nonreligious schools alike. This is a stark contrast with England where, as we will see in the following chapter, the system of public aid advantages the majority denominations, but disadvantages religious minorities, and with the United States which funds public schools but not independent religious ones. According to Aurora Andrushka, of the Department of Education, Employment, and Youth Affairs (DEEYA) "in terms of funding, we take a no favoritism approach; we look at a school regardless of its religious affiliation, its curriculum, or its philosophy."[52]

In our view, Australian policy is neutral in that it neither advantages nor disadvantages any particular religion, nor does it advantage or disadvantage religion or secularism generally. State aid to religious schools makes it possible for parents who want a religious education for their children to exercise that option, while parents who want a nonreligious secular education can opt for a state school or a nonreligious private school. The state has gradually come to recognize that educational choice is a value to be celebrated. A 1995 report by the Senate's Employment, Education, and Training Committee on commonwealth funding arrangements in education recognized this value in the current policy: "The committee considers that non-government schools clearly enrich the scope of educational choices available to the community at large."[53]

The government's guarantee of equal treatment in school funding is apparent in its policy of licensing new schools. A New Schools Committee, whose members come from the government, Catholic, and independent school sectors, assesses each application. The committee looks primarily at whether the new school can meet the minimum number of students to receive funding and if there is a need for a new school in the proposed location. The committee annually accepts a majority of new school applications. Because the demand for new religious schools has been high, and the government has been impartial in the kinds of schools it will fund, the number of religious schools has escalated.

The formation of dozens of independent school organizations, both denominational and peak bodies, has eased the application process for new schools and provided valuable political support for the sector as a whole. Organizations give advice to prospective new school applicants and represent their political interests before the various government agencies. Because state aid had foundered on the sectarian divide in the past, the major churches joined forces in the 1960s to present a united front for state aid and these school organizations advocate for government funding for all eligible independent schools. The executive officers of the National Catholic Education Commission (NCEC) and the Australian Association of Christian Schools indicated to us, for example, that they supported expanding government funding to Muslim schools.

The fastest growing religious schools are also the ones that have caused the most controversy in other countries: evangelical Christian and Muslim. There have been some questions raised in Parliament about the curriculum in these schools, but there has been no official challenge to nongovernment school autonomy and almost no public debate about the wisdom of the government's policy. Fergus Thomson, executive director of the National Council of Independent Schools Association (NCISA), the peak body for the nongovernment school sector, stated the view this way: "There is a general acceptance of the principle that Parliament should not tell schools what they should and should not teach."[54] Religious schools have also faced some questions about their hiring policy with the recent passage of the Sex Discrimination Act. In its 1994 annual report, the NCEC presented its case on hiring policy in this way: "The church must continue to have the right, as a matter of civil law, to discourage teachers who, either by teaching or by their lifestyles, explicitly or implicitly reject Catholic doctrine or Catholic morality."[55] Nongovernment schools are exempt from antidiscrimination legislation if they can demonstrate that the proposed policy violates a religious principle, and no Catholic school has lost a case brought against it on antidiscrimination grounds.[56]

In order to receive recurrent grants, private schools have to be licensed with DEEYA and by each state's Department of Education. Under Australia's federalism, states retain most of the regulatory power over nongovernment schools. In some states teachers have to be formally registered by the state, and schools must follow a satisfactory curriculum. In practice, state regulation is loose and nongovernment schools retain almost complete control over staffing, enrollments, and curriculum.[57] Most religious schools give a preference in hiring and admission to people who share the school's philosophy. They also have the right to develop their own curriculum. Member schools of the AACS "stand collectively for Christ-centered education,"[58] while the curriculum in Roman Catholic schools "must give a central place to education in faith and acknowledge the relevance to all areas of teaching of a Christian view of life as interpreted in the Catholic tradition."[59] DEEYA requires schools to account for grants received under commonwealth programs and to participate in various surveys to evaluate policy effectiveness, but the commonwealth does not strictly regulate nongovernment schools. According to Andrushka, it is "very difficult, particularly with General Recurrent grants, to get any clear picture of accountability."[60]

Commonwealth and state governments have tended to rely on an outcome-based strategy to regulate nongovernment schools. Private school graduates must take leaving exams to get a diploma, and they must take entry exams to secure a place at a university. As Dennis Doyle points out, "the standard to which the Australian private school is held is one of performance."[61] This means that nongovernment schools are often subject to internal pressures to provide a high-quality product. In order to attract students, schools presumably have to offer an education that will allow pupils to pass a leaving exam to get their diploma and score well on entry exams to get into a university. While the system uses market forces, it is best described as a system of managed choice and not a complete free market approach.[62] Nongovernment schools can lose their funding if they fail to attract a minimum number of students, and the government retains the power to license new schools and determine their funding levels. There are religious schools, for example, that teach creation science. The pressure such schools face is not generally from the government, but from school parents and Christian school educators who want students to do well on examinations at the end of secondary education. Peter Crimmins, executive officer of AACS, articulated precisely this view: "A Christian educational perspective is essential, but it is very important for our schools to get acceptability. If Christian schools are not aspiring to be as good as the best public schools in the country they are short-changing the kids and their parents."[63]

Ironically, it might be that nongovernment school advocates have more to fear from government finance than do government school supporters. There has been increased cooperation in the past decade among the various educational sectors, which has led independent school organizations voluntarily to agree to national goals for schooling and a move toward a framework for a national curriculum. The paradox, as many have noted, is that equalizing school funding and moving toward corporatist political arrangements among the various educational sectors often blurs the differences between private and public schools.[64] Crimmins pointed out to us that some of the schools in his organization had placed too much emphasis on academic performance and not enough on Christian witness. While state funding provides a potential threat to a religious organization's autonomy, we believe that the challenge has come less from overt government regulation than from changing norms of religious schools and agencies. The point is that religious schools and agencies, with a clear sense of their religious mission, have the capacity under the current system to retain their unique spiritual or philosophical perspective, and many have chosen to do just that.

There are numerous difficulties in comparing performances between private and public schools, but by virtually all measures nongovernment schools fare very well. Nongovernment school students, in both Catholic and other nongovernment schools, have higher retention rates than their state-run counterparts and a much higher percentage of private school graduates enter a university. Faculty to student ratios are actually higher in Catholic schools than in state-run schools, but much lower in other nongovernment schools. At the same time, the selectivity of the nongovernment sector and its ability to expel "problem" students likely gives it a competitive advantage over the state-run sector. While most religious schools are committed to educating church members regardless of socioeconomic circumstances, government schools are still much more likely to be assisted by the commonwealth under the National Equity Program, which aids disadvantaged schools and pupils, and have a much higher proportion of English as Second Language students than nongovernment schools.[65]

Finally, there is the question of the role of religion in the public schools.[66] Most states provide for nonsectarian secular instruction that includes general religious teaching (GRT). As we noted, liberal reformers opposed "sectarian" religious instruction in state-run schools, but they believed that secular instruction should include the consensual features of the Christian faith that would provide the basis for a common morality. The state justified religious observances as a method of reinforcing corporate identity and instilling essential social values. When states began to provide public education at the end of the nineteenth century, therefore, the legislation typically allowed for nondogmatic religious instruction. In practice, GRT focused almost exclusively on Christianity, even Protestant Christianity when antipathy to Roman Catholics remained high. GRT has become more generally Christian in recent decades, but questions have been raised about the appropriateness of religious instruction in the schools. The state supreme court of New South Wales ruled in 1976 that prayers, Bible readings, hymns, and grace before school meals were consistent with the provisions of GRT. The opinion of the court stated that religious instruction, even Christian instruction, was appropriate, so long as the state did not promote the teachings of a particular church: "It is natural that where a common form of teaching Christian beliefs had been adopted for use in State schools, and was acceptable to the various Christian churches, the State, in promoting secular education, should be at pains to prevent the beliefs of any one church from being advanced over others, and to ensure a lowest common denominator for general religious teaching."[67]

As Australia has become more religiously pluralistic, the problems with this approach have become apparent. The presence of Christian and non-Christian traditions that are uncomfortable with a lowest common denominator Christianity in the public schools challenges the optimistic assumption of the nineteenth-century legislation that it is possible to discern consensual religious beliefs, incorporate them into the public schools, and make them the basis for a common social morality. While there is a need for some common values and beliefs to bind society together, attempts to root them in religion run the risk of violating governmental religious neutrality. States have made some effort to include the study of other religions in their GRT, but in practice the lessons are drawn overwhelmingly from the Christian tradition. The state, in pushing these particular "consensual" religious values, implicitly gives mainstream Christian practices its imprimatur and violates the basic ideal of governmental neutrality that we believe should govern church-state relations. There is a concomitant danger that removing religious instruction from the school discriminates against deeply religious parents, but it is difficult to imagine how a curriculum of religious instruction could be genuinely neutral.

More in keeping with Australia's commitment to pluralism and neutrality are the Special Religious Instruction (SRI) programs instituted by each of the six states at the turn of the century and still in use today. Under SRI—what Americans term released time programs—visiting clergy can provide religious teaching at the school for those children whose parents want them to receive it. Parents have the right to withdraw their children from SRI. In 1980, the Minister of Education in New South Wales commissioned a report on religion in education in government schools that looked closely at the provisions for SRI. Two of the report's conclusions demonstrate the state's healthy commitment to neutrality in church-state matters. First, the report recommended that schools should broaden the criteria for determining religious groups' eligibility for access to schools to include "all groups which are widely recognized by the community as having essentially the character of a religion."[68] Second, the report concluded that children who opt out of SRI should be given "purposeful secular education."[69] These policies ensure that the government is neutral among religions and between religion generally and nonbelief generally.

Church, State, and Nonprofit Service Organizations

Public finance of religious schools is part of a broader pattern of state support to religious welfare organizations. Christian groups have dominated the nonprofit sector for much of Australia's history, but as with education the state has more recently adopted a "neutral" policy that has led to public finance for non-Christian welfare agencies. Churches took the lead in providing social welfare in colonial Australia. Evangelical Protestants, in particular, gave a religious impetus for the formation of charitable organizations that addressed the problems of poverty, child neglect, and homelessness.[70] There was little direct government provision of services in the early nineteenth century, so these organizations were the only means of aid for the unemployed and economically destitute. While much of the finance for these charities came from the churches and wealthy philanthropists, the state also gave substantial support to nongovernment organizations. Church agencies that worked toward the religious reformation of the "deserving" poor fit comfortably with the state's interest in the social control of a growing population of poor people.[71]

Reformist ideas that emerged at the turn of the century questioned the value of church-based charitable organizations by promoting the notion of a universal right to services and support based on need, and not the selective idea of moral worth. At the same time, church agencies could not meet the growing demand for services brought on by the economic depressions of the 1890s and 1930s. Gradually, the state began to take over more of the functions it previously had subsidized and adopted some reforming ideas with policies of basic income support, child care, and old age pensions. The Constitutional Amendment of 1946 overcame doubts about the commonwealth government's power with regard to social welfare by establishing its sovereignty to legislate in eleven key areas of social welfare, including maternity and family allowances, widow pensions, child endowment, and unemployment and sickness benefits.[72]

The federal government also emerged from World War II fiscally dominant over the states and a pattern emerged whereby the commonwealth collected most of the tax revenues and established national welfare priorities, but state governments or nongovernment agencies actually provided most of the human services.[73] The government expanded its welfare role in the 1960s and 1970s as public support grew for health insurance, income redistribution, and Aboriginal rights. Nongovernment welfare organizations (NGWOs) continued to be an important part of the social welfare network, but they became more dependent on state finance and they gradually adopted the norms of the emerging social welfare profession. A large number of secular NGWOs emerged in the postwar years that utilized a professional social work model in service provision. The Christian values base and the link between agencies and the local church of many existing religious agencies eroded during the next several decades as organizations hired more professional social workers and complied with the commonwealth's welfare priorities.[74]

The conservative critique of welfare systems in Britain and the United States in the 1970s and 1980s also affected Australian policy. Nongovernment organizations benefited, at least in the short run, from new right attacks on the welfare state because they were seen to be more flexible, efficient, and cost-effective than services provided directly by the government. Policy makers began to favor the devolution of services to NGWOs and in the decade between 1976–77 and 1986–87 direct support for nongovernment organizations by all levels of government in Australia more than doubled in real terms. According to one estimate, NGWOs currently provide more than half of all welfare services.[75] The combined total expenditure for the nongovernment welfare sector in 1992–93 was $4.4 billion; the government funded nearly 60 percent ($2.5 billion) of NGWO recurrent expenditures, though larger agencies tended to be less reliant on government finance than smaller ones.[76]

Australian welfare policy reflects an overiding pragmatism, which comes out most clearly in the government's commitment to economic efficiency and cost-effectiveness in service provision. The most common type of government payment to an NGWO is a fee for service. Organizations contract with the government to provide specified services, such as residential aged care, for a fixed fee. In terms of program monitoring, this conservative model focuses on the outputs delivered by an NGWO. Religious agencies, like their secular counterparts, have questioned the appropriateness of applying free market economic principles to social welfare provision. According to Community Services Australia, the peak body for Uniting Church welfare agencies, "quality of service is more about people's lives, well being and acceptance in the community than it is about economic efficiency."[77]

Debate is inevitable about what constitutes a positive client outcome in areas such as mental health or disability services. The government's focus on efficient and cost-effective services will not settle the difficult question of how to assess the quality of services an agency provides, but a virtue of policy pragmatism is that the government remains neutral in terms of how services are delivered and who provides them. David Pollard, executive director of the Industry Commission, an agency set up by the government to analyze and make recommendations about social services, describes funding arrangements in this way: "Funding is generally conceived as a contract for the supply of services to a target group from a range of suppliers some of which happen to be church auspiced."[78] Pollard's attitude is indicative of the government's pragmatic interest in the number of services an agency provides, and its relative indifference to who provides them and how they do it.

In addition to pragmatism, the principles of pluralism, tolerance, and governmental neutrality are well established in Australian social welfare policy. A large percentage of NGWOs retain a religious identification of some kind. According to a 1995 survey of the nonprofit sector conducted by the Industry Commission, twenty-one of the top fifty nongovernment agencies in terms of total income have a religious affiliation, including the Salvation Army, World Vision, Wesley Sydney Mission, Anglican Homes for the Elderly, and Baptist Community Services, to name a few. There are thousands of smaller Christian, Jewish, and Muslim agencies as well. The degree to which a religious ethos permeates the activities of these agencies varies a great deal. Many agencies have lost their original religious mission, but others have retained it. The Wesley Sydney Mission, Australia's fifth largest NGWO, describes itself as a church whose mission is "the proclamation of the Gospel of Jesus Christ and ministry of work and deed throughout Australia."[79] The government funds religious and nonreligious welfare agencies almost equally; the largest religious agencies received, on average, 48.4 percent of their total income from government funding, while the largest nonreligious agencies received 51.6 percent.[80]

In addition to providing funding to religious agencies, the government gives them considerable autonomy in how they deliver services. Religious agencies are generally exempt from equal opportunities legislation and are free to hire whomever they want for key positions within the agency. While not all agencies give preference to co-religionists in hiring, a majority of the ones we interviewed do, either explicitly or implicitly. Marilyn Webster of the Catholic Social Welfare Commission noted that "service agreements do not specify staff qualifications and the standard practice in most Catholic agencies is, whenever possible, to hire within the Catholic social welfare network."[81] World Vision, the Salvation Army, and the Wesley Sydney Mission also give a preference in hiring to co-religionists. Philip Hunt, executive director of World Vision Australia, justifies the agency's hiring policy in this way: "We believe that the only way for World Vision to maintain its religious mission is to select employees who are going to be consistent with our organization's values." World Vision also has religious services and Bible studies for employees, and while they are not mandatory Hunt said that most people choose to attend them.[82]

Agencies are generally allowed to offer religious services as a part of their program. Ed Dawkins, the community services secretary for the Salvation Army Eastern Command, noted that "we have drug and rehabilitation programs that have a strong spiritual dimension, including chapel services. We believe that the spiritual dimension is crucial to rehabilitation."[83] The Salvation Army makes clients aware of the religious elements of their various programs, but it does not discriminate against non-Christians who choose to sign up for one of them. Dawkins concluded that in his twenty-five years in social work the government had not once prevented him from "providing the spiritual ministry that I see as my mandate."[84] Overseas aid and development agencies are *not* allowed to use government money for religious purposes in their projects, but religious values and practices are still an important part of the work of many of these organizations. The initial point of contact for most

church-based development agencies is a local church, and a number
of these agencies, including the largest, World Vision, emphasize the
connection between development and evangelism in their literature.[85]

Some government programs require religious organizations to provide equal access and equity in the services they provide. There is often a
self-selection bias, however, on the part of clients who want a religiously
oriented social service. Paul Tyrell, executive director of Centacare, the
national body of Catholic welfare agencies, indicated to us that Centacare agencies do not discriminate among clients on the basis of religion,
but that the government understands that "as a Catholic agency a majority of our clients are going to be Catholic." According to Tyrell, half of
all Centacare clients are Roman Catholics, many of them having been
referred to the agency by a local priest. When we pointed this data out
to David Pollard, he simply stated that "the fact that religious agencies
may draw most of their customers from the ranks of their religious supporters is not of great concern."[86]

The devolution of services to nongovernment agencies in the 1970s
coincided with the immigration of new religious and ethnic groups into
Australia. This multiculturalism challenged the government's commitment to pluralism as immigrant groups often preferred services provided
by their own community organizations rather than the existing government and nongovernment agencies. According to a recent survey of the
Australian Jewish population, 53 percent of Jewish parents would prefer
Jewish child care services for their children and 82 percent of the elderly
would prefer accommodation in a specifically Jewish hostel or nursing
home.[87] The same is often true for Muslims and Buddhists, and the
government has responded by turning to religious and ethnic organizations as the primary service providers for those communities. A growing
number of NGWOs offer "ethno-specific services," a trend supported
by the Industry Commission in its recent report: "cultural differences
may necessitate a completely different approach to meeting community
need."[88] Government policy recognizes that ethnic and religious agencies are popular among immigrants and are likely to have the best access
to those targeted groups. As Pollard pointed out to us, "Islamic organizations have been funded because they have the best access to certain
target groups."[89] This comment reflects once again the pragmatism that
is the norm with aid to nonprofit organizations that has allowed for a
diversity of religious organizations to receive public aid.

Concluding Observations

In slightly more than two hundred years, Australia's church-state
policy has vacillated among four distinct models: religious establishment,

plural establishment, liberal separationism, and pragmatic pluralism. Because Australian policy makers have never committed themselves to a single church-state model, they have had the freedom to adopt the most politically favorable model at a given time. Political and pragmatic considerations, in other words, have been far more important in Australian church-state issues than theoretical considerations. This is in contrast to the Netherlands, where self-consciously held principles such as a positive right to governmental neutrality have always shaped church-state practices. Australia's church-state practices, though they are pragmatically based, come close to those of the Dutch. Both countries seek to accommodate and support a wide diversity of religious and secular systems of belief. Australian policy, therefore, fits most closely with the third of our church-state models: pluralism. The state recognizes that religious life is not limited to the private sphere, but has an important public component, and accommodates a wide variety of religious groups with funding for such diverse societal activities as education, mental health, and welfare services, to name a few. In addition, the government generally does not favor any one religious group over another, nor does it advantage religious over secular perspectives.

Australia's pragmatic pluralism has gradually increased the free exercise rights of religious groups. Australian practice in this area is not much different from that of the other countries in our study. Like these countries, Australia struggles with how far to extend religious rights, but there is a cultural commitment to the values of accommodation, tolerance, compromise, and neutrality that makes possible the free expression of religious ideas. A problem with the Australian approach, however, is that the state has not solidified its guarantee of religious liberty through judicial decisions or legislation. The Australian High Court has narrowly interpreted the free exercise right of Section 116 of the Constitution and there is no federal law that specifically bars religious discrimination. This is a significant deficiency, in our view, not because there is widespread religious discrimination in Australia, because there is not, but because there are no established guidelines as to how far groups can go to exercise their religious liberty.

Pragmatism has also driven the state's commitment to providing aid to religious schools and nonprofit organizations, and to the state's policy of religion in the public schools. The impetus for state aid to schools in the 1960's and 1970's was political and pragmatic; both major political parties hoped to secure Catholic support with schemes of direct aid to parochial schools. Similarly, a pragmatic concern about cost-effectiveness drove the government's decision to devolve service delivery to nongovernment organizations in the 1970s and 1980s. As the state became multicultural and the desire for religiously grounded education and services intensified, Australia successfully integrated new religious groups, such as Muslims, and allowed them to express their differences in publicly financed organizations. This demonstrates a practical commitment by the state both to encourage religious pluralism and to diversity. To its credit, Australia has adopted these policies without the level of political conflict that has occurred around identical issues in many of the other countries in our study. That is an impressive achievement.

Australian policy makers have rarely given much thought to the normative implications of Australia's church-state policy. There is little explicit reference to religious freedom as a positive right that the state has an obligation to accommodate. Nevertheless, Australia's pragmatic pluralism implicitly reaches the goal of governmental neutrality that we established as the basic ideal for church-state relations on this question. In practice, if not always in theory, Australian policy discriminates neither among religious groups nor between religious and nonreligious perspectives.

Notes

1. Peter Bentley, Tricia Blombery, and Philip J. Hughes, *A Yearbook for Australian Churches: 1994* (Melbourne: Christian Research Association, 1993).

2. Gary D. Bouma and Michael Mason, "Baby Boomers Downunder: The Case of Australia," in Wade Clark Roof, Jackson W. Carroll, and David A. Roozen, eds. *The Post-War Generation and Establishment Religion* (Boulder, Colo.: Westview, 1995): 27–58, and Peter Kaldor, *Who Goes Where, Who Doesn't Care?* (Canberra: Lancer Books, 1987).

3. David Solomon, *Australia's Government and Parliament* (Melbourne: Longman Cheshire, 1988).

4. Graham Maddox, *Australian Democracy: In Theory and Practice* (Melbourne: Longman Cheshire, 1985), chap. 5.

5. Campbell Sharman, "The Commonwealth, the States, and Federalism," in Dennis Woodward, Andrew Parkin, and John Summers, eds. *Government, Politics, and Power in Australia* (Melbourne: Longman Cheshire, 1985), 108–20.

6. Solomon, *Australia's Government and Parliament*, chap. 2.

7. Ian Breward, *A History of the Australian Churches* (Sydney: Allen and Unwin, 1993), chap. 2.

8. Hugh Jackson, "White Man Got No Dreaming: Religious Feeling in Australian History," *Journal of Religious History* 15 (1988), 1–11.

9. Bryan S. Turner, "Religion, State, and Civil Society: Nation-Building in Australia," in Thomas Robbins and Roland Robertson, eds. *Church-State Relations: Tensions and Transitions* (New Brunswick, N.J.: Transaction Books, 1987), 233–51.

10. Michael Hogan, *The Sectarian Strand* (New York: Penguin Books, 1987), chap. 1.

11. Roger C. Thompson, *Religion in Australia: A History* (Melbourne: Oxford University Press, 1994), chap. 1.

12. Gary D. Bouma, "The Emergence of Religious Plurality in Australia: A Multicultural Society," *Sociology of Religion* 56 (1995), 285–302, and Hans Mol, *The Faith of Australians* (Sydney: Allen and Unwin, 1985), chap. 9.

13. Hogan, *The Sectarian Strand*, chap. 2.

14. Breward, *A History of the Australian Churches*, chap. 4.

15. We are indebted to Gary Bouma for making this point clear to us.

16. Thompson, *Religion in Australia*, chap. 2.

17. Hogan, *The Sectarian Strand*, chap. 4.

18. Quoted in *Discrimination and Religious Conviction* (Sydney: New South Wales Anti-Discrmination Board, 1984), 319.

19. Quoted in *Discrimination and Religious Conviction*, 321.

20. Mol, *The Faith of Australians*, chap. 1.

21. Quoted in Hogan, *The Sectarian Strand*, 228.

22. *Grace Bible Church Inc. v. Reedman*, 54 ALR 571 (1984).

23. *Grace Bible Church Inc. v. Reedman*.

24. *Grace Bible Church Inc. v. Reedman*.

25. Pervaiz Ahmad Buttar and Lynette Joy Mattingley, *Religious Conviction and the "New Magna Charta"* (Brisbane: James Cook University, Centre for Southeast Asian Studies, 1986).

26. *Australian Capital Television Pty Ltd and Others v. The Commonwealth of Australia*, 108 ALR 577 (1992).

27. *Australian Capital Television Pty Ltd and Others v. The Commonwealth of Australia* at 587.

28. *Australian Capital Television Pty Ltd and Others v. The Commonwealth of Australia*, at 592.

29. *Australian Capital Television Pty Ltd and Others v. The Commonwealth of Australia*, at 596.

30. We are grateful to Michael Hogan for bringing this Court case to our attention.

31. For an outstanding review of religious free exercise issues in Australia, see *Discrimination and Religious Conviction*.

32. Gary D. Bouma, *Mosques and Muslim Settlements in Australia* (Canberra: Australian Government Publishing Service, 1994), 90.

33. This is the conclusion reached by the New South Wales Anti-Discrimination Board in its report, *Discrimination and Religious Conviction*.

34. Lois Foster and David Stockely, *Australian Multiculturalism: A Documentary History and Critique* (Philadelphia: Multilingual Matters, 1988).

35. Foster and Stockely, *Australian Multiculturalism*, 21.

36. Hogan, *The Sectarian Strand*, chap. 9.

37. *Attorney General for the State of Victoria (at the relation of Black) v. The Commonwealth of Australia*, 146 CLR 559 at 328 (1981).

38. *Attorney General for the State of Victoria (at the relation of Black) v. The Commonwealth of Australia*, at 330.

39. *Attorney General for the State of Victoria (at the relation of Black) v. The Commonwealth of Australia*, at 345.

40. *Attorney General for the State of Victoria (at the relation of Black) v. The Commonwealth of Australia,* at 326.

41. *Attorney General for the State of Victoria (at the relation of Black) v. The Commonwealth of Australia,* at 330.

42. Under a 1990 revision of the policy, new schools are only eligible for grants in categories one to six funding.

43. *National Report on Schooling in Australia: 1994* (Melbourne: Ministerial Council on Education, Employment, Training, and Youth Affairs, 1994).

44. *National Catholic Education Commission: School Funding Policy* (Canberra: National Catholic Education Commission, 1987).

45. *1994 Annual Report of the Australian Association of Christian Schools,* undated publication of the Australian Association of Christian Schools.

46. *Discussion Paper: Review of the New Schools Policy* (Canberra: Australian Government Publishing Service, 1995), 27.

47. John Goldlust, *The Melbourne Jewish Community: A Needs Assesment* (Canberra: Australian Government Publishing Service, 1993), 62.

48. Bouma, *Mosques and Muslim Settlements in Australia,* 52.

49. *Discussion Paper: Review of the New Schools Policy,* 15.

50. *1994 Annual Report of the Australian Association of Christian Schools,* 1.

51. *Discussion Paper: Review of the New Schools Policy.*

52. Interview with Aurora Andrushka, Department of Education, Employment, and Youth Affairs (July 26, 1995).

53. *Report of the Inquiry into Accountability in Commonwealth-State Funding Arrengments in Education* (Canberra: Australian Government Publishing Service, 1995), 76.

54. Interview with Fergus Thomson, executive director of the National Council of Independent Schools Association (July 27, 1995).

55. *1994 Annual Report of National Catholic Education Commission,* undated publication of National Catholic Education Commission, 12.

56. Interview with Kevin Vassarotti, executive officer, National Catholic Education Commission (July 28, 1995).

57. Helen Praetz, *Public Policy and Catholic Schools* (Hawthorn, Victoria: Australian Council for Educational Research, 1982), 63.

58. *1994 Annual Report of the Australian Association of Christian Schools,* 13.

59. *National Catholic Education Commission: School Funding Policy,* 3.

60. Interview with Aurora Andrushka, Department of Education, Employment, and Youth Affairs (July 26, 1995).

61. Dennis P. Doyle, "Family Choice in Education: The Case of Denmark, Holland, and Australia," in William Lowe Boyd and James G. Cibulka, eds., *Private Schools and Public Policy: International Perspectives* (London: Falmer Press, 1989), 53.

62. John Knight, Bob Lingard, and Paige Porter, "Restructuring Schools Toward the 1990's," in Bob Lingard, John Knight, and Paige Porter, eds., *Schooling Reform in Hard Times* (London: Falmer Press, 1993): 2–22.

63. Interview with Peter Crimmins, executive officer of The Australian Association of Christian Schools (July 27, 1995).

64. William Lowe Boyd, "Balancing Public and Private Schools: The Australian Experience and American Implications," in *Private Schools and Public Policy: International Perspectives,* 162.

65. *National Report on Schooling: Statistical Annex 1993* (Melbourne: Ministerial Council on Education, Employment, Training, and Youth Affairs, 1994).

66. For an excellent overview of religion in public schools, see *Discrimination and Religious Conviction*, chap. 6.

67. Quoted in *Discrimination and Religious Conviction*, 325.

68. Quoted in *Discrimination and Religious Conviction*, 339.

69. Quoted in *Discrimination and Religious Conviction*, 334.

70. Brian Dickey, *No Charity There* (Sydney: Allen and Unwin, 1989).

71. Elisabeth Windschuttle, "Women and the Origins of Colonial Philanthropy," in Richard Kennedy, ed. *Australian Welfare History: Critical Essays* (Melbourne: Macmillan, 1982): 10–31.

72. *Australia's Welfare 1993: Services and Assistance* (Canberra: Australian Government Publishing Service, 1993), chap. 1.

73. Adam Graycar and Adam Jamrozik, *How Australians Live: Social Policy in Theory and Practice* (Melbourne: Macmillan, 1989), 115.

74. Alan Nichols, "From Charity to Social Justice," in Dorothy Harris, Douglas Hynd, and David Millikan, eds. *The Shape of Belief: Christianity in Australia Today* (Canberra: Lancer Books, 1982), 140–62.

75. Mark Lyons, "Government and the Nonprofit Sector in Australia," in Kathleen D. McCarthy, Virginia A. Hodgkinson, and Russy D. Sumariwalla, eds. *The Nonprofit Sector in the Global Community* (San Francisco: Jossey-Bass, 1992): 254–77.

76. *Charitable Organizations in Australia* (Melbourne: Australian Government Publishing Service, 1995), chap. 12.

77. "Response to Draft Report: Charitable Organizations in Australia," undated publication of Community Services Australia.

78. Interview with David Pollard, Industry Commission (7/19/95).

79. *Wesley Sydney Mission Response to the Industry Commision's Draft Report on Charitable Organizations*, undated publication of the Wesley Sydney Mission.

80. *Charitable Organizations in Australia*, Appendix C.

81. Interview with Marilyn Webster, Catholic Social Welfare Commission (July 18, 1995).

82. Interview with Philip Hunt, executive director of World Vision Australia (July 21, 1995).

83. Interview with Ed Dawkins, community services secretary for the Salvation Army Eastern Command (July 31, 1995).

84. Interview with Ed Dawkins, community services secretary for the Salvation Army Eastern Command (July 31, 1995).

85. Laurie Zivetz and Anne Ryan, "World Vision of Australia," in Laurie Zivetz, ed. *Doing Good in Australia* (Sydney: Allen and Unwin, 1991), 267–80.

86. Interview with Paul Tyrell, executive director of Centacare (July 26, 1995).

87. Goldlust, *The Melbourne Jewish Community*, xv–xvii.

88. *Charitable Organizations in Australia*, 48.

89. Interview with David Pollard, Industry Commission (July 19, 1995).

Chapter 5

ENGLAND: PARTIAL ESTABLISHMENT

$\mathcal{E}$ngland is the only country in our study with a formally established church. The Church of England has been the established church in England since the middle of the sixteenth century. There has been a progressive dilution in the church's significant political powers and privileges since that time, but the fact that there is an established church is important. This church–state model, what we term a partial establishment, structures the resolution of church–state issues in England and, what is more significant, sustains a cultural assumption that religion has a public function to perform and it is therefore appropriate for the state and church to cooperate in achieving common goals.

This chapter begins with a very brief description of British political institutions and religious life. It then gives a historical survey of England's religious establishment, followed by a consideration of the formal and informal powers associated with the Church of England. The chapter then reviews how this church–state model structures the British approach to free exercise issues and questions, and establishment issues related to education and nonprofit organizations. Finally, the last section makes some concluding observations.

The Nation

Great Britain comprises the three countries of England, Scotland, and Wales. The United Kingdom includes these three countries plus Northern Ireland. This chapter focuses exclusively on England, by far the largest of the three countries with a population of forty-eight million.[1] Pragmatism characterizes English political culture, with a greater orientation toward what works than abstract theorizing. In this way,

England is much like Australia. As a result of this practical orientation, change in English history has been incremental, not revolutionary. Politically, England has gradually evolved from a limited representative democracy in the thirteenth century, with the signing of the Magna Charta, to a full and participatory democracy by the end of the nineteenth century. Today, England has a parliamentary form of government with a bicameral legislative branch. The 650 members in the House of Commons are popularly elected and politically powerful. The Commons selects the prime minister who serves as the head of the government. The nearly 1,100 members in House of Lords are not elected, but serve by virtue of birth, appointment by the Crown, or position. Although the prime minister and both houses of Parliament must formally pass legislation, by convention and law the Lords does not overturn a government bill and limits its role to discussion and debate.[2]

Unlike the other countries in our study, England does not have a codified constitution, which does have some effect on church-state issues. There is an uncodified British constitution that embodies the principle of a higher law, the most significant provisions of which are the rule of law, parliamentary government under a limited monarch, a unitary political system, and parliamentary sovereignty. Fundamental freedoms, including religious rights, however, do not lie in any constitutional mandate or bill of rights but in the capacity of the democratic society and Parliament to preserve shared values, which for the most part has been done.

The largest religious communities in England are Anglicans (37 percent), Roman Catholics (11 percent), and Methodists (4 percent). The importance of religion, however, has declined throughout the twentieth century. In terms of *active* church membership and attendance (once a week or more), England is the most secular country in our study. The rate of active church membership in England fell from 22 percent of the population in 1970 to 11 percent in 1990. It is slightly higher in Wales and significantly higher in Scotland and Northern Ireland. Anglican, Roman Catholic, Methodist and the Scottish Presbyterian churches have suffered nearly equal membership declines in the past two decades. Independent evangelical and Pentecostal churches are the only Christian bodies that have grown in the past few decades, but they are small by American standards with about 600,000 members among them. The Anglican Church is the largest Christian church in England with 1.5 million active members, followed by Roman Catholics, 1.3 million, and Methodists, 400,000.[3] The majority of the British population are "nominal" Christians, people who claim to believe in God, profess to be Anglicans, but are religiously inactive. According to a recent survey, 55 percent of the British consider themselves a religious person, 57 percent say that they believe in heaven, and about half the population is baptized into the Church of England.[4]

The largest non-Christian groups are Muslims, Sikhs, and Jews. Currently, there are a million Muslims in England, which is just over 2 percent of the country's total population. In terms of active religious members, however, Muslims are the third largest religious community, behind only Anglicans and Roman Catholics. In addition, there are an estimated 500,000 Sikhs and 300,000 Jews. Finally, a large number of people have no religious beliefs. While only 4 percent of those surveyed in a 1992 poll described themselves as a convinced atheist, 34 percent claimed to have no particular religion.[5]

The Church of England was once famously described as the Conservative Party at prayer, indicating the historically close political alliance between the two powerful institutions. According to a 1992 survey of Conservative Party members, there remains a strong link between party and church involvement, with 70 percent of party members claiming regular church worship.[6] On the other hand, political support for the Conservative Party among bishops, clergy, and active laity of the Anglican Church has declined. A survey of more than five hundred members of the General Synod of the Church of England indicated that only a quarter of the bishops or clergy voted Conservative in 1992, and Tory support among the laity dropped to 44 percent from 51 percent in 1983.[7] With the notable exception of Northern Ireland, the political salience of religion has fallen throughout the twentieth century as social class, rather than religion, has become the most important point of political cleavage throughout Britain. The British party system reflects the significance of class as the Labour Party has attracted most working-class support, and the Conservative Party that of the middle class. England is predominantly white and English-speaking. It is not, however, totally homogeneous; the nonwhite population has grown in recent decades and currently stands at nearly 5 percent of the total population. This diversity has spawned ethnic and racial tensions, particularly in urban areas where the nonwhite community is concentrated.

England's religious diversity and secularism are themes that we will return to later in this chapter. For now, it is important to understand the historical forces that have shaped contemporary church–state issues in Britain.

The Historical Background

When Pope Clement VII refused to grant Henry VIII an annulment from Catherine of Aragon, he broke from the Roman Catholic Church, married Anne Boleyn, and took political control of the English church. The formal establishment of the broadly Protestant Church of England came during Elizabeth I's reign with the Second Act of Supremacy in 1559. From the earliest days of the establishment, the Church of England enjoyed an unusual degree of autonomy in the power of appointments and in managing its own funds, but a close relationship developed between the state and the Anglican Church in which the institutions worked in concert for shared political and religious goals. The ideal envisioned by Richard Hooker, the sixteenth-century apologist for the Anglican establishment, was to unify church membership with membership in the political community so that there would be no division between the secular goals of the state and the sacred purposes of the church. Hooker provided a theological justification for this political arrangement; he believed that the church had a positive obligation to be involved in civil society and in the value of the state to the church. In terms of the law, this came to mean a state-supported and state-enforced religion with the imposition of various restrictions on religious dissenters.[8] The Corporation Act of 1661 and the Test Act of 1673, for example, effectively excluded Roman Catholics and Protestant nonconformists from participation in political affairs.

Religious pluralism and intense conflict among Anglicans, Roman Catholics, and Protestant nonconformists made it difficult to sustain Hooker's organic vision. The Treaty of Union with Scotland in 1707, for example, allowed for the establishment of the Presbyterian Church of Scotland. Driven by this division in the rest of Great Britain, the state grudgingly conceded freedom of worship to Protestant religious dissenters with the passage of the Toleration Act of 1689. The Toleration Act repealed some of the restrictions on Protestant nonconformists, such as those affecting their meeting and conducting acts of worship, but the Test and Corporation Acts were retained. It was not until the nineteenth century that the state finally lifted most of the disabilities attached to religious nonconformity. Protestant nonconformists and Roman Catholics won political emancipation in 1824 and 1829 respectively, in 1858 Jews were able to become members of Parliament, and in 1871 Parliament abolished religious tests for admission to universities. The Church of Wales was disestablished in 1920.[9]

The impetus for reform did not come from the Church of England, which opposed much of the legislation and used its power in the House of Lords to delay passage of various bills removing religious disabilities. The church feared that the reforms would de-Christianize the legislature and imperil the country's religion. The reforms also did not signal the supremacy of a liberal political philosophy with its commitment to church-state separation. Social and religious pluralism forced a more liberal policy on a state that had become weary of dealing with politicized religious conflict. The blunt realization by the state that it could not effectively force religious conformity on a recalcitrant nation led by necessity to the more liberal church-state policy. As Steve Bruce and Chris Wright note, "only when the fragmentation of the religious culture had gone so far as to be obviously irreversible and the price of trying to enforce religious orthodoxy became too great did the establishment accept that there could no longer be an effective state religion."[10]

There were also efforts to disestablish the Church of England. The Anti-State Church Association, founded in 1844, and the Liberation Society, 1853, led the disestablishment movement, but there was insufficient political and elite support for this effort. Ironically, the most earnest challenge to the status of the Church of England came not from religious dissenters, but from Catholic (Anglo-Catholics) and evangelical wings *within* the Anglican Church. Neither side opposed the religious establishment; both factions wanted the state to use its coercive powers to further the one "true" religion. Only when evangelicals and Anglo-Catholics realized by the end of the nineteenth century that they would be unable to take over the state church did they begin to question the wisdom of having a church so closely united with the state.[11]

The strong rivalry between the Church of England and nonconformist churches spilled over into party politics in the nineteenth century. The Liberal Party committed itself to state neutrality among religious groups and consolidated most nonconformist political support. Kenneth Wald, in an exhaustive study of voting patterns in the late nineteenth century, concludes that Protestant nonconformity was the best predictor of support for the Liberal Party.[12] The Conservative Party, on the other hand, defended the Established Church and attracted most Anglican votes. The education issue crystallized the religious division in British politics at this time. All the major churches founded schools in the early nineteenth century to propagate the faith and educate the children of church members, although Anglican schools were by far the most numerous. The state had very little role in providing public education until the passage of the Education Act of 1870 that created tax-supported schools under the control of local boards. The legislation assumed that religious schools would, with state financial aid, continue to provide education for members; the state's role was to fill the gaps where voluntary action by the churches could not meet the growing demand for education. State schools provided nonsectarian religious instruction, but there was less Christian content in the curriculum than in church schools.[13]

Protestant nonconformists and the Liberal Party opposed the bill on two grounds. First, some Liberals were religious voluntarists who opposed state aid to religious organizations because they felt it would compromise church autonomy. They also contended that public education should be free of church, i.e., Anglican, control. More radical elements of the Liberal Party, in the mold of Enlightenment liberalism, wanted a purely secular state educational system free of any religious influence whatsoever. Second, most Protestants opposed the Roman Catholic Church and did not want public money to aid what they termed an unorthodox religion. Anglicans and the Conservative Party, on the other hand, supported the bill and believed that it would achieve the best possible results for society and the church. The act would enable more children to receive a basic education, but would still allow the state to fund existing church schools, a majority of which were Anglican. In addition, Anglicans believed that religious instruction in state-supported schools benefited the nation as a whole. According to this establishment mindset, religious education would provide the basis for a common Christian morality for the nation's schoolchildren. The bill passed, but the education issue continued to divide religionists for the next three decades.[14]

The relaxation of restrictions on religious dissenters in the nineteenth century, coupled with the growing secularity of British society, helped to depoliticize religious disputes in the early twentieth century. The emerging Labour Party had roots in the nonconformist chapels, but it gradually became more closely associated with a socialist ideology as the twentieth century progressed. When the Labour Party displaced the Liberal Party as one of the two main parties in the 1920s, social class, rather than religious issues, became politically salient.[15] There was also a noticeable absence in Britain during this period of attempts to drive the churches from politics, as there was in other European countries. As Michael Fogarty notes, British churches did not face a direct challenge "in the form of state supremacy over the churches . . . or of sectarian liberalism."[16] It was not so much the power of the churches that explains the absence of this threat from Enlightenment liberalism, but the fact that religion had become politically unimportant. Because the state was neither hostile to nor excessively involved with religion, a Christian Democratic movement never developed in Britain. Without that threat, even from the socialist Labour Party that was more indifferent than hostile to religion, the churches did not feel compelled to defend and preserve their role in society with the formation of a Christian political party and other social organizations, as was the case in the Netherlands and Germany.

In practice, if not always in law, the Anglican Church that emerged from the sectarian rivalries of the late nineteenth and early twentieth centuries was far different from the one envisioned by Hooker two centuries earlier. The Church of England retained its establishment status, in contrast to the religious establishments in two former British colonies, America and Australia, but the nature of that establishment had radically shifted. The formal ties between church and state loosened as Parliament ceded greater control over the church's spiritual direction to ecclesiastical bodies, and the church's social and political role became more diffuse and ceremonial. In contrast to Hooker's model, the Church of England came to see itself as a comprehensive national institution that would guard and preserve the nation's shared cultural norms and serve as a religious counterpart to civil society. As religion became less socially significant, the Anglican Church became more ecumenical and accepting of pluralism. As a result, both church and state supported other denominations seeking the state's public acknowledgment, and politicized religious disputes largely disappeared from British politics in the twentieth century. The church continued to press for a political role, but it began to advocate an ecumenical Christian view of the nation's affairs, rather than a denominational one.

The debate around the Education Act of 1944 demonstrates the changing role of religion in Britain. The established Church of England and other Christian denominations fought one another on the education issue in the late nineteenth century, but religious animosities had been reduced by 1944 and the churches formed a powerful political coalition to protect the privileged position of their schools. Anglicans and Catholics, who had the largest stake in private religious schools, argued together that denominational schools deserved public funding because church schools provided a public good and gave parents the opportunity to exercise their right to direct the education of their children. Policy makers, who recognized the political power of these religious bodies and generally shared their view that religious education provided a public good, financed almost all the costs of existing church schools. The

Education Act created a dual system with state-run and religious schools sharing the responsibility for the education of British children.[17]

The act further stipulated that religious education be provided in all state-run schools and that each school day begin with an act of collective worship. It created a Standing Advisory Council for Religious Education (SACRE) to advise local educational authorities on the methods of teaching religious education. SACRE consisted of representatives from the Church of England, other religious denominations, the teachers unions, and the local council. All the existing churches, in short, could have a decisive influence on the content of religious education in state schools. The act forbade narrowly denominational teaching in state schools, but the clear intention was to make the religious dimension broadly Christian. Parents and teachers retained the right to opt out of religious instruction and worship, but it did not allow for religious instruction in other faiths.[18]

Policy makers self-consciously designed religious education as a way to further the goals of the state, and not simply as a way to placate church leaders. There was great optimism in the early years after the act passed that religious education could provide some unity of purpose for British schoolchildren. The hope was that it would nurture children in the dominant values and beliefs of British society, which were vaguely Christian. Religious education became, in Alan Storkey's words, "a part of the overall civil definition of religion . . . the Christian faith was seen to play a public cultural role as part of the national heritage."[19] Religious education in state-supported schools was consistent with a cultural consensus about the role of the established Church of England. In both instances, political elites viewed religion, the Christian religion specifically, as a significant influence on English culture, society, and history that could continue to play a useful role in shaping citizen's moral values.

Of the five countries in our study, England's establishment model lent itself most easily to a state promotion of "consensual" religious values. The established church had historically seen its role as working in concert with the state to promote common values, which it increasingly viewed in ecumenical and pluralistic terms. Religious education seemed ideally suited to this task as it could provide the moral framework necessary to inculcate British schoolchildren with norms that would bind society together. There was little appreciation, at this point, that religious diversity and secularization might introduce conflict and thereby challenge this civil religious model, or that religionists might oppose so utilitarian an understanding of the place of faith in public life. Developments in the latter half of the twentieth century challenged these assumptions and led, as we show in our review of current educational policy, to questions about the place of religion in state supported schools. For now, however, we want to turn to a review of the Church of England's legal status that continues to influence the resolution of church-state issues in Britain.

Britain's Partial Establishment

The Church of England lost most of its privileges by the end of the nineteenth century, but legal and cultural ramifications associated with Britain's religious establishment remained. Unlike some churches in the European community, the Church of England does not receive a direct state subsidy, but in many other respects the links between church and state are much closer. The Church of England is the established church in England, but not in the rest of Britain. The Presbyterian Church of Scotland has been the established church in Scotland since 1707, and the Church of Wales was disestablished in 1920.[20] The monarch is the head of the church and may not be nor marry a Roman Catholic. The church carries out the coronation and all other state functions where prayer or religious exercises may be required.

From a historical standpoint, the formal ties between Parliament and the Church of England have diminished, but from a comparative perspective the role of the government in church life is still remarkable. As an established church, the canon law of the Church of England is a part of English law, and until the early twentieth century Parliament passed much legislation affecting the church. Under the Enabling Act of 1919, the church's General Synod gained the authority to make changes in church liturgy and doctrine, although Parliament remains technically responsible for some matters of church law and can (but seldom does) reject a measure passed by the General Synod. In addition, the monarch, advised by the prime minister, has the power to appoint the archbishops and the diocesan bishops of the Church of England, although the choice is made from a field of candidates nominated by the church. In no other country in our study are the formal, legal ties between church and state as strong as in England and it is impossible even to imagine the state having this kind of authority over a church in them.[21]

The church continues to have a prominent political role, particularly in the House of Lords. The House of Lords has little effective political power; it occupies a subordinate position to the House of Commons and the government is ensured of the upper House's approval on any measure it proposes. What the House does do, however, is to provide a forum for discussion and debate about government bills and important public issues. The archbishops of Canterbury and York and the twenty-four senior diocesan bishops of the Church of England have seats in the House of Lords. Religious leaders of other churches have been appointed as peers in the Lords, but the Church of England is the only religious body with reserved seats. There is a widespread assumption that the Church of England and its bishops will have a role in major pieces of moral legislation. A recent divorce reform bill illustrates this point.

In 1995, the government introduced into the House of Commons the Family Law Bill that would allow no-fault divorces after a twelve-month waiting period. The bill ran into significant opposition when Lord Mackay introduced it into the House of Lords, particularly from the conservative wing of the Church of England. The archbishop of Canterbury, Dr. George Carey, backed the government's plan, but the archbishop of York, the Rt. Rev. Dr. David Hope, and several key bishops of the church rebelled against the bill on the ground that it violated the Christian idea that marriage is a lifelong commitment. There was little danger that the Lords would defeat the government bill, but they used their position to embarrass the government and introduce amendments to try to alter the government's position. The media reported on the opposition of these key Anglican church leaders in great detail and one paper concluded that it was a "significant blow" to the bill.[22] The bill eventually passed both houses of Parliament, but not before the government suffered a major defeat on an amendment introduced by the opposition in the Lords to require pensions to be split at the time of divorce, and accepted demands from backbench Tories in the Commons that spouses with strong religious views could claim additional hardship in their attempt to block a divorce.[23]

The nation's blasphemy laws also reflect the special legal status of the Church of England because they protect Christian or more specifically Anglican doctrines.[24] There have been some noteworthy blasphemy cases in recent years; currently there is a case before the European Court of Human Rights contesting the legality of Britain's law against blasphemy. The case challenges the decision of the British Board of Film Classification that banned Nigel Wingrove's video, Visions of Ecstasy, saying that its graphic scenes of Jesus having sex with a Carmelite nun violated Britain's law against blasphemy.[25] Non-Christian religions receive no protection against blasphemy, which caused considerable controversy in the British Muslim community following the *fatwa* delivered on Salman Rushdie for the blasphemies in his book *The Satanic Verses.*[26]

More important than the church's legal status, however, are the cultural assumptions that, as George Moyser notes, sustain the prominence of the Church of England.[27] We have already noted that church membership is low, only 5 percent of the British population are active members of an Anglican Church, but membership is concentrated in the middle class.[28] In addition, many of the nation's elite private schools, called "public" schools in Britain, are affiliated with the Anglican Church. Both of these facts help to explain how the Anglican Church has come to have significant representation in the upper echelons of the nation's political, legal, and cultural institutions.

The Church of England enjoys a level of social and political influence that cannot be explained simply by the number of people who are actively involved in church life. As two authors note, the established position of the Church of England "provides a prominent platform from which to contribute to the discussion of social and political issues."[29] The church generally receives considerable press coverage, particularly when it takes positions that are at odds with government policy. In 1982, the press reported extensively on a working party for the church's Board for Social Responsibility, *The Church and the Bomb*, which advocated unilateral nuclear disarmament. The publication of a report in 1985 by the archbishop of Canterbury's Commission on Urban Priority Areas, *Faith in the City*, also attracted much discussion in the press. The report focused on the social problems of urban areas, which the press interpreted as a repudiation by the church of Prime Minister Margaret Thatcher's economic policies. Dr. George Carey, the archbishop of Canterbury, created a significant stir in 1996 when he attacked the government's criminal justice policy that he claimed was motivated more by revenge than by justice.[30] The point is that the media, in looking for the "religious" response to government policy, focus on the views expressed by representatives of the Church of England. This partly reflects the fact that Anglican bishops have a platform in the House of Lords to make political pronouncements, but what is more important is that it shows there is still an assumption that the established Church of England is the nation's leading religious voice and that it is appropriate for the church to advocate a certain Christian view of the nation's affairs.

Finally, the public favors the religious establishment. Active membership in the church is low, but 60 percent of the population consider themselves members of the Anglican Church and are likely to use their local parish church for baptisms, weddings, or funerals. According to public opinion polls, the majority of these nominal Christians approve of the establishment and want their children taught religion in schools.[31]

There are periodic calls for the disestablishment of the Church of England, particularly from the Liberal Democratic Party, but these efforts have gone nowhere because there is little popular support for them.[32]

It is important to note that the establishment supported by the state and the public is, in historical terms, diminished. The legal advantages enjoyed by the Church of England are politically insignificant and there is no concerted effort by the state aggressively to promote the church or place restrictions or disabilities on non-Anglican churches. The state accommodates what we term a partial religious establishment that is quasi-Christian. The state pursues policies that are generally favorable toward organized religion as a whole because of a conviction shared by most political elites and the mass public that religion is morally and socially beneficial. Citizens perceive the religious establishment as, at best, a source of social cohesion and consensus and, at worst, as harmless. The fact that religion, outside of Northern Ireland, has not been a source of political conflict for most of the past century supports these assumptions.[33]

This establishment mindset also helps to explain why a majority of people in England consider themselves to be a Christian despite the fact that very few people actually go to church. Because the state offers a "free" religion—Anglican churches cannot easily turn away even inactive members of their parish if they want to be married in the church or have their children baptized by their local priest—people have less incentive formally to join and participate in church life. It is also possible, as Rodney Stark and Laurence Iannaccone have suggested, that state support for an established church, however minimal, impedes the development of competition from other churches and decreases the overall levels of religious participation.[34]

Non-Anglican churches do not generally question the religious establishment because government policies increasingly grant them treatment equal to that of the Church of England, and they generally support the idea that the government should recognize the public role of religion. In addition to state funding of church schools and religious education in state schools, the government provides churches as a whole with access to radio and television broadcasting. The British Broadcasting Corporation provides churches with hundreds of hours every year for religious broadcasting. The Central Religious Advisory Committee advises the BBC on religious broadcasting and in recent decades has become evenhanded among the various religious traditions in Britain.[35] This policy is consistent with an establishment model that views it as appropriate for the state to accommodate religious organizations, particularly in state-run institutions such as the media. This model affirms the idea that churches have an important cultural and social function to play, which the state should both recognize and support.

Non-Christian religious minorities pose a more serious challenge to this partial establishment because the state sometimes excludes them from the system. Religious minorities have not, however, actively tried to overturn the establishment. Muslims, for example, perceive the religious establishment as a less serious challenge to Islamic values than secularization. According to Tariq Modood, "the real division of opinion is not between a conservative element of the Church of England versus the rest of the country, but between those who think that religion has a place in secular public culture, that religious communities are part of the state, and those that do not."[36]

Modood's point is that secularization poses a more serious challenge to Islam than does the established church because secularism teaches that religion should not have a public role in a modern society. In contrast to secularism, the religious establishment preserves the idea that churches should be actively involved in social and political affairs, and that the state should accommodate that role. Muslims want the state to include them within the current system, as has been done for Roman Catholics and Protestant nonconformists in the past, particularly in the areas of religious free exercise rights and educational provisions. In order to analyze the extent to which religious minorities have won these concessions from the state, we turn now to a review of religious free exercise issues.

The Free Exercise of Religion

England, unlike the other countries in our study, does not have a codified constitution or a bill of rights and so there are no constitutional guarantees for religious freedom. There is no equivalent in England to the First Amendment to the U.S. Constitution, nor to the Civil Rights Act of 1964 that bars religious discrimination in employment, nor to the Religious Freedom Restoration Act, passed in 1993, that states government may not substantially burden one's free exercise of religion except in pursuance of a compelling governmental interest. Unlike Germany and the Netherlands, England lacks a strong theoretical commitment to religious free exercise. It is instructive, for example, that Britain does not view the issues of religion in state-run schools and public support for church schools as religious free exercise issues, as is the case in both the Netherlands and Germany. The absence of this kind of protection means that it is perfectly legal under British law to disqualify clergy of the Churches of England, Scotland, and Ireland and the Roman Catholic Church from sitting in the House of Commons. This practice would not be possible in any of the other countries of our study because each guarantees religious liberty in its constitution.

A combination of legal provisions, international law, and public opinion protects religious rights in Britain.[37] The most important legal assurances are the acts passed at the end of the nineteenth century that gave religious dissenters various rights, but these laws have limited application and the courts have not interpreted them as guaranteeing people a fundamental right of religious free exercise. The Race Relations Act of 1976 provides a legal framework for fighting against racial discrimination, but there is not a similar law barring religious discrimination.[38] As Modood notes, this act potentially contributes to a new form of religious inequality, "namely the inequality in law between those religious groups that the court recognizes as ethnic groups and those that they do not."[39] The courts have recently wrestled with the question of whether to define Sikhs as an ethnic group under the Race Relations Act, but generally speaking the courts have not included religious groups.

In theory, international law provides some form of protection against religious discrimination. Britain accepts the legal significance of the Universal Declaration of Human Rights, which includes an obligation for the state to protect religious liberty:

> Everyone has a right to freedom of thought, conscience and religion . . . freedom to manifest one's religion or beliefs may be subject only to such limitations as are prescribed by law and are necessary to protect public safety, order, health, or morals of the fundamental rights and freedoms of others.

In practice, there has been dispute about the implication and meaning of this principle and it has been difficult to transform this declaration on religious liberty into a convention that can be binding in British law.[40]

The absence of constitutional or significant legal protections means that citizens rely on public opinion and the political process for the protection of their religious rights. In most cases this is a sufficient guarantee, as the public has become more religiously tolerant in the past few decades and recognizes the validity of religious free exercise claims. In recent years, there has been a corresponding extension of various rights to religious groups that reflects this cultural value. Parents, for example, may withdraw their children from religious education and worship in state-run schools, and they can request that their children be sent to some other place for religious instruction provided it does not disrupt the running of the school. Policies related to other institutions, including prisons, labor unions, and hospitals, have also become more accommodating to religious minorities and the nonreligious.[41]

The immigration of non-Christian religious believers and the introduction of new religious movements, nevertheless, raised some religious tensions in Britain. A clear example of this is how Britain has dealt with religious practices that conflict with valid regulatory laws. The Employment Protection Act, for example, protects employees from losing their job because of their religious practice, unless the dismissal can be justified in law. British courts have consistently upheld dismissals, however, when the religious obligations of employees led them to violate the terms of their contract. The Court of Appeal sustained the firing of a member of the Seventh-Day Adventist Church who refused on religious grounds to work on Saturdays, as was required under his contract, and the dismissal of a Sikh who lost his job at an ice cream factory when he decided, in violation of hygiene rules, to grow a beard because of his religious beliefs. Similarly, in a case involving a Muslim who excused himself for part of Friday to attend prayers in the mosque, the court ruled that the employer's right to have him present at all times in the work day took precedence over his religious free exercise right.[42]

This is not to suggest that religious discrimination is widespread in Britain, because it is not. Discrimination exists, however, and the groups that have the most to fear from the absence of legal or constitutional protections are new religious movements whose practices are not as socially accepted as the older, more traditional religions. As Eileen Barker notes, "the longer a religious movement has been around, the greater the chance it has of being protected by the law."[43] Formerly excluded religious groups, such as Roman Catholics and Jews, have become integrated and respected members of the British community and they do not face religious discrimination. The public has come to accept and appreciate both of these religious traditions, and the increasingly generic, partial religious establishment has been able to incorporate their views. The same is true for public acceptance of those without a religious belief. According to a 1992 survey, only 9 percent of those polled in Britain believed that politicians who do not believe in God are unfit for public office, compared with 30 percent of Americans.[44] There is less public support, however, for Sikhs and Muslims, who face lingering discrimination from a public that questions the extent to which these religious groups can integrate into British society and into an essentially Judeo-

Christian religious establishment. Religious movements such as Rastaf-
arians, Black Muslims, Seventh-Day Adventists, and Scientologists face
the most persistent discrimination because society does not accept their
views and actions.

An obvious and important difference between England and the
United States is that members of minority faiths in Britain that suffer
because of their beliefs do not have the same recourse to the legal system
to protect their religious rights, as they do in the United States, although,
as seen earlier, the U.S. legal system is no sure guarantee of minority
religious freedoms. The fact that there is no constitutional guarantee of
religious freedom in England does affect the resolution of free exercise
issues. The state generally protects religious rights, for the religious and
the nonreligious, but it is a function more of elite and public opinion
and social reality than legal principles. Well-established churches have
less to fear from public opinion and the political process precisely because they have socially accepted values; religious minorities cannot always comfortably rely upon the political process to protect their rights.
Discrimination against minority religious groups is even more apparent
in the area of public aid to private religious schools.

Church, State, and Education

When applied to education, England's partial religious establishment promotes equality between religious and nonreligious educational
perspectives, but at the same time violates the norm of governmental
neutrality among religious traditions. The 1944 Education Act created
county schools under the control of Local Education Authorities (LEAs)
and two broad categories of church schools, the voluntary aided and the
voluntary controlled.[45] A church education trust owns a voluntary aided
school and a board of governors exercises full control over admissions
policy, religious education, school buildings, staff appointments, and in
secondary schools, curriculum. In a detailed study of Church of England
schools, Bernadette O'Keeffe found that the primary admissions criterion for most Church of England schools is the Christian faith of the
student's family, and most church schools give a preference in hiring to
fellow religionists.[46] In voluntary controlled schools, by contrast, church
governors are in a minority on the governing body, and the local authority is responsible for admissions and employing staff. A majority of
church schools are voluntary aided.

Religious elementary and secondary schools within the system receive a tuition grant from the state for each pupil who attends. In addition, the state covers 85 percent of capital costs for religious school buildings. Religious schools in Britain currently educate more than one out of four primary school students and one out of six secondary school pupils. Thirty-five percent of all primary schools and 16 percent of secondary schools are church related.[47] Church schools are very popular in England, both because they generally outperform state schools and because there is a strong desire on the part of parents, who may or may not be religiously active, for their children to have a religious education.[48]

Anglicans and Roman Catholics were the only churches with a large stake in education in 1944 and they quickly became partners with the state in terms of policy formation and planning for education. Both churches have powerful education boards that negotiate with government officials on issues of funding, curriculum, and school governance.[49] Together, these two churches now constitute over 95 percent of all publicly financed religious schools. There are a very small number of Methodist, Baptist, and Presbyterian schools. The state determines which new church schools to finance, and while the state has funded new church schools, often in consultation with Catholic and Anglican educational authorities, Jewish schools are the only religious newcomer to the denominational system since the passage of the 1944 Education Act to receive state aid.

Anglican, Roman Catholic, Methodist, and Jewish parents who want a religious education for their children can generally afford it. Together, these groups constitute over 95 percent of the country's religious population. This policy demonstrates a healthy neutrality on the part of the state between a religious and nonreligious perspective, and stands in stark contrast to policy in the United States that disadvantages those parents who desire an education for their children in the context of their religious beliefs.

Two factors influenced the development of religious education in the 1980s: immigration patterns and Prime Minister Thatcher's conservative educational policy. The immigration of non-Christian groups threatened the partnership between state-run and religious schools. Muslims have expressed a desire for their own denominational aided schools. Several dozen independent Islamic schools have formed but, as we shall examine below, none have received state funding. Because they do not receive state aid, the cost of these schools is high and less than 5 percent of the estimated 250,000 Islamic students attend a Muslim school.[50]

The second challenge to the current system came with the introduction of educational reforms by Thatcher. Her reforms followed from two main philosophical tenets: that individual choice ought to be expanded and that free markets are more efficient than public planning. In terms of educational policy, this led to the Education Reform Acts of 1980 and 1988. The Education Reform Act of 1980 introduced "parental choice" to the field of education. It entitled parents to state a preference for any school under the control of their local education authority and required schools to provide published information about test scores, admissions procedures, and educational philosophy. The act applied market pressures to schools who had to compete for students and face the possibility of being forced to close if they could not attract enough "consumers."[51]

The Education Reform Act of 1988 made even more fundamental changes in the laws relating to education. Several features of the act decentralized power from Local Education Authorities to individual schools and parents. Most significantly, it provided an opportunity for schools to opt out of the local authority and receive finance directly from the Department of Education and Science (DES). If there is a sufficient interest among parents, a ballot of all parents is held to decide if the school will "opt out" of local control and become "grant maintained" by the DES.[52] Under the new system, schools that have opted out receive a per pupil grant and money to cover capital costs directly from the state. Thatcher justified the new policy on the ground that the growth and power of government posed a threat to private action; county schools, she argued, could provide a better and less expensive education if they were free of control by their LEA. At the same time, the act centralized the power of the DES by introducing, for the first time, a national curriculum for primary and secondary schools.

The conservative aspects of the policy could potentially expand the number of religious schools in Britain that receive state aid. If the government wants to increase educational choice and consumer preferences, as it says it does, it should finance new schools, including religious ones, if there is consumer preference for those schools and the market will bear it. The problem is that there is no mechanism to increase the supply of popular schools to meet the demand for them and apparently the government is unwilling to finance religious schools for those churches not already within the system. On two separate occasions, the government has refused to grant voluntary aided status to an Islamic school in Brent that has a waiting list with a thousand names, a decision that contradicts the logic of the conservative approach to educational policy.[53] There are several hundred other religious schools, including evangelical

Christian and Orthodox Jewish ones, that have not yet applied for aid, but would probably do so if the process became more open.

The state has been unwilling to extend the denominational system to new church schools for several reasons. First, the government claims that separate religious schools for immigrant religious communities threatens the comprehensive state school model with its liberal assumptions about the role of education and religion in a democracy. In 1985 the government commissioned the Swann Report on education and ethnic communities. The report adopted a secular outlook that viewed religion as mainly a private matter and concluded that "separate schools would not be in the long term interest of ethnic minority communities."[54] The report recognized the need for a multicultural education that would expose students to the religious pluralism in Britain, but implied that state schools would better serve ethnic and religious minorities because they would more effectively integrate minorities into mainstream British culture.

Opponents of aid to new denominational schools also contend that religious schools are not in the best interests of society as a whole. They perceive religious schools to be socially divisive because they segregate children along religious lines, a process that militates against the development of the common bonds and values necessary in a liberal, pluralistic culture.[55] The implication is that the state can have greater control over the content of education in state-run schools and thereby ensure that ethnic and religious minorities learn the values necessary to sustain Britain's democracy. Among the most important of these liberal norms is tolerance, an idea that many believe is undermined in separate religious schools, particularly Islamic ones. The attack on Salman Rushdie's *Satanic Verses* by leaders of the British Islamic community, their failure to dissociate themselves from the Ayatollah Khomeini's *fatwa,* and subsequent street demonstrations against the book in Bradford reinforced a cultural stereotype of Muslims as an "illiberal" religious group. The Rushdie affair, coupled with a biased media image of British Muslims as religious fundamentalists, led many to conclude that the state should not support Islamic schools.[56]

Finally, there is the perception that some religions do not fit within the civil religious and religious establishment assumptions that support the current educational system. Many people assume that existing church schools—Anglican and Roman Catholic—are different from the so-called separate religious schools— particularly Islamic ones—because the former provide a service to the public as a whole and not just to church members. David Lanksheare, executive director of the Board of

Education for the Church of England, articulated this perspective to us in an interview: "In Church of England schools there is a clear understanding that the churches are in partnership with the state. Very many of our schools operate on the basis of a commitment to Christian service to the public."[57] To explain the idea of Christian service to the public, Lanksheare described a Church of England primary school with a majority of Islamic students. He claimed that these schools serve the public by teaching Islamic students the values necessary to help them assimilate into British society. Lanksheare implies that church schools serve the nation precisely because they are accepting of social and religious pluralism.

Muslim and evangelical Christian schools challenge these presuppositions because they make education within the context of a religious worldview the central feature of their curriculum and they reject the liberal, pluralistic aims of the state-run schools. A syllabus on Islamic education published by the Muslim Education Trust states: "Islamic education is a total and complete system which does not separate the mundane affairs of life from the moral and spiritual aspects. . . . The objective is to educate young people in Islam and to make them conscious and practicing Muslims and to prepare them for life."[58] Evangelical and fundamentalist school organizations make similar claims about the purpose of Christian education. Because they see their role as service to particular religious communities, and not the nation as a whole, evangelical Christian and Muslim schools would presumably be unable to fit into the presuppositions of the current educational system.

From the perspective of religionists outside the existing system, arguments against the expansion of the denominational system are faulty on various grounds. First, the system clearly benefits church members ahead of the general public when the main criterion for admission to a church school is the religious faith of the student's parents. O'Keeffe correctly points out that when oversubscribed schools restrict intake to Christian children, the message sent is "Christian education for Christian children. In this sense they become denominational because service to the nation is no longer a priority."[59] In an interview with us, Mughram Al Ghamdi of the Islamic Cultural Centre said it is unfair that Islamic schools do not receive state funding because "there are schools for Roman Catholics and for Anglicans."[60] From his perspective, church schools are for church members and the current policy is patently discriminatory, and it is hypocritical for leading policy makers to contend that "special arrangements for minorities may militate against the best interests of society as a whole," when the state has already made that compromise with other churches.[61] Anglican schools are more likely than state-run schools to be oversubscribed; 55 percent of primary schools and 82 percent of secondary schools are oversubscribed.[62] Because these schools are generally oversubscribed and give preference to church members, Muslims and other religious minorities have fewer opportunities than Anglicans or Roman Catholics to exercise choice in education.

Second, Islamic activists and scholars have questioned the secular assumptions of the current educational system. Syed Ali Ashraf writes, "their secularist policy is regarded by the Muslim community as an attempt to brainwash Muslim children and uproot them from their cultural moorings . . . and what is most dangerous for the upcoming generation, education does not provide children with certainty and a reliable, sustaining, and acceptable norm to fall back upon."[63] The conviction that the state system is secular and antireligious helps to explain the curious fact that Muslim parents consistently prefer Church of England schools to state-run schools. Muslims favor church schools, even Christian ones, because they believe they are more open than state schools to a religiously informed viewpoint.[64]

Muslims also question the assimilationist assumptions of the current system. For religionists who wish to retain distinctive religious and cultural beliefs, such as Muslims, Orthodox Jews, and Christian fundamentalists, assimilation to the values of a secular, liberal society is neither progressive nor in their interest. Integration becomes a defense for an educational policy that negates the values of a community outside the social and political mainstream.[65] A shared hostility toward the state-run system has created an unusual political coalition among Jews, Christians, and Muslims who want state aid for their religious schools. The state, on the other hand, legitimately wants to use schools to help integrate groups into British society, but simply assumes that Muslim and fundamentalist Christian schools would be unable to do this. It is conceivable, however, that these schools would, like their Anglican and Catholic counterparts before them, be able both to preserve a group's religious identity and to prepare their children for life in the broader British community.[66]

The current policy is clearly unequal among the various faiths in England. The growth of independent religious schools, particularly Islamic ones, indicates that there is a demand for new church schools, but the state has been reluctant to give financial support to these schools. England has historically incorporated a variety of "nonconformist" religious communities into its religious establishment, however, and it is quite possible that new religious groups will eventually be included within the system. This would also be consistent with England's tradition of political pragmatism that has usually brought incremental change to church-state issues.

The Education Reform Act of 1988 also raised tensions within the state-run system by strengthening the requirements for religious instruction and worship in state-run schools. In the face of mounting criticism from cultural conservatives, the government included requirements in the act for religious instruction to "reflect the fact that the religious traditions in Great Britain are in the main Christian whilst taking account of the teaching and practice of the other principal religions represented in Great Britain," and a daily act of worship of a "broadly Christian character."[67] Parents retained the right to withdraw their children from religious instruction. Those who supported these religious provisions claimed that most schools had neglected the requirements of the 1944 act, while those schools that did have worship and religious education promoted a "multifaith approach that relegated Christianity to a minority position."[68] It clearly was true that most schools had quietly been ignoring the religious conditions in the 1944 Education Act, which reflected the fact that Britain had become more secular and religiously pluralistic.

When the House of Lords debated the bill, the government minister, Baroness Hooper, argued that "such an act of collective worship can perform an important function in binding together members of a school and helping to develop their sense of community."[69] Hooper's comments are instructive of larger points about how Britain's religious establishment structures the debate on church-state issues. First, the fact that there is an established church, however minimal its legal powers currently are, helps to sustain a view that religion, of a particular kind, has a role to play in public institutions. While there has been some opposition to the new requirements, which we will review below, it has, from an American perspective, been surprisingly muted and limited to religious minorities and a few secular elites. Public support for religious education is high and parents rarely complain about the religious instruction and worship in state schools.[70] Seventy-two per cent of those surveyed in a 1992 poll believed that there should be daily prayers in the public schools, which was a higher percentage than the much more religiously active United States.[71] This establishment mindset made it possible for Hooper and others to argue that it made perfect sense for Parliament to require that the religious education and worship in state-run schools primarily be Christian because Britain was predominantly a Christian nation. It also followed that state officials, rather than church leaders, could and should establish a religious education curriculum for the state-run system in order to measure how effective schools were at reaching common goals.

Second, the religious establishment is not aggressively Christian. The idea affirmed is that religious education and worship can be the basis for cultural cohesion by inculcating students with shared values that are of service to society. The archbishop of York, Dr. John Habgood, contended that schools should give priority to religious education to avert the growth of a "morally bewildered generation."[72] In the context of a suddenly multifaith society, the intent of religious education was not so much to Christianize Britain as to provide children with a sense of moral and spiritual values and give them a greater understanding of the traditions of Britain's main religious groups. The Educational Research Trust, which led the movement for religion in the schools, argued that "a religious education would help to provide God-given moral absolutes for personal and social conduct."[73] This comment reflects an optimism about both the Anglican establishment and what a "generic" religious education can achieve. It implies that religious education, of a very general character and guided by an establishment, nonsectarian perspective, can provide moral absolutes for schoolchildren. What it fails to appreciate is that a school curriculum might be unable to provide a moral education for children if it is divorced from a specific faith community. It is also unequal for religionists and nonreligionists who do not accept "consensual" religious beliefs.

Teachers unions and Muslims have provided the most significant opposition to the bill. The main teachers union passed a resolution that called for an end to religious instruction and worship, while 79 percent of the members of the Head Teachers Union thought the government expectations on religious instruction and worship were unrealistic.[74] Muslim parents in Birmingham organized a boycott of religious lessons, but Muslim leaders have not called for a secular approach to education.[75] Instead, they want the opportunity to provide Islamic instruction in state-supported schools. Muslims contend that Islamic instruction can be as effective as Christian teaching if the purpose of religious education is to provide children with a sense of right and wrong. A few schools have liberalized their policies and allowed Islamic instruction, but most have not and the government has said that it has no intention of relaxing the laws requiring the schools to hold a broadly Christian religious assembly.[76]

In theory, the Education Reform Act of 1988 committed the state to providing religious instruction and worship in the schools, and the act has enabled parents at some schools to bring religion into the classroom in ways that would not be possible in the United States. In practice, however, a majority of the schools have failed to meet the requirements of the new legislation.[77] This is not surprising given the fact that Britain is a religiously pluralistic culture; there is a popular desire to have religious instruction, and even worship, in the schools but there is not a shared sense of what that education should entail. This has raised the larger issue of whether a common religious instruction can be the basis for cultural cohesion in a society increasingly divided by religion. The differences among the various religious traditions in England challenge the assumption of the establishment model that religion can perform this cultural function.

Religion in state-run schools demonstrates the power of an establishment model as the state provides religious worship and instruction geared toward a generic Christian perspective. However, the policy violates the principle of government neutrality among the various religions because the state shows a preference for a particular kind of Christian instruction and worship in its schools, does not incorporate religious groups that fall outside this perspective, and thereby limits the kind of religious instruction to which children can be exposed.

Church, State, and Nonprofit Service Organizations

As with education, British churches led the way in forming social service agencies in the late nineteenth century.[78] Religious values motivated the work of these early reform efforts in child care, poor relief, prison reform, and public health. Religious charities could not generate adequate resources to meet the growing demand for human services in the twentieth century, nor did they provide their services evenly. They practiced what Lester Salamon calls philanthropic particularism.[79] Religious philanthropy focused on specific subgroups of the population but often ignored others. Evangelical groups, who led the way in welfare reform in Britain, frequently made a distinction between the "deserving" and "undeserving" poor. As popular support for public welfare grew, government involvement increased to correct for "inherent shortcomings of the voluntary sector."[80]

Following World War II, legislation on health, housing, education, and income support formed the basis for a comprehensive British welfare state. As James Beckford notes, social welfare provision in Britain differed from that of many European countries in that it was never pillarized on the basis of religious differences. Religious philanthropy survived in the post-war period, but in the new statutory system the role of religious nonprofit agencies gradually diminished as the state assumed primary responsibility for the delivery and regulation of public welfare.[81] Religious agencies also faced increasing secularizing pressures from the emerging social work and health care professions that dominated public welfare. Social work professionals stressed "objective" and "scientific" criterion that they often believed excluded or made irrelevant a religiously informed point of view. Christian agencies, which in many cases shared the ideological presuppositions of the profession, fueled the secularization process by redefining their work in more "acceptable," i.e., nonreligious, terms.

Thatcher introduced considerable change to the voluntary sector, particularly in her third term of office. In keeping with her commitment to privatization, public choice, and reducing the government's role, Thatcher stressed the benefits of using voluntary organizations rather than the state to provide public services. She argued that voluntary agencies could expand consumer choice, reduce costs, and promote efficiency by introducing competition to public services. Contrary to popular imagination and her rhetoric, Thatcher did not reduce public spending on welfare; spending and public support for the welfare state remained high throughout her time in office.[82] Thatcher did, however, alter how the state provides public goods; her policies increased the role of voluntary agencies as service providers. A government publication of the Foreign and Commonwealth Office described the new arrangement in these terms: "Government departments and agencies and local authorities now enter into legal contracts with voluntary organizations for the delivery of particular services."[83] In 1990–91 direct grants paid by government departments to voluntary organizations stood at 2.6 billion pounds—a rise of 140.5 percent in real terms since 1980–81.[84]

Religious agencies remain an important part of the voluntary sector, although the importance of religion in these organizations varies a good deal. Agencies with a Christian basis provide one-third of the drug rehabilitation places in the United Kingdom, and one-half of the child care agencies have a religious orientation.[85] Many religiously based agencies have retained a distinctive perspective. Yeldall Christian Centres, for example, is an agency that runs drug and alcohol rehabilitation homes in Britain. Yeldall receives 30 percent of its 600,000–pound annual budget from the government and perceives a close link between its religious and social work. Yeldall describes its mission in this way: "The aim of the Yeldall Christian Centres is to give glory to God through offering healing and wholeness to people with broken lives . . . We see the best means of achieving true freedom for the drug dependent person is by rehabilitation through discipleship to Jesus Christ as Savior and Lord. However, we do not insist upon, or force, such a commitment upon anyone."[86]

All of the staff at Yeldall are Christian and must sign a statement of faith that is, in the words of the executive director, "Bible believing."[87] In addition to daily counseling sessions with professional social workers, residents—who volunteer for a spot at one of Yeldall's residential centers—are required to attend twice a week Bible studies and church services for the first fourteen weeks that they are in one of the centers.

The Salvation Army is the largest charitable organization in England with an annual budget of over 10 million pounds, close to two-thirds of which comes from the government. It employs 2,200 full-time workers and serves approximately 5,000 clients at any one time. Christine McMillan, associate director of London Homeless Shelters, told us the Salvation Army has a thousand hostel beds in London to serve the homeless; each hostel has religious symbols on the walls, spoken prayers at meals, voluntary religious services, and Bible studies. The government does require that all agencies that receive funding have an equal opportunities policy for hiring staff. In response to this legislation, the Salvation Army proposed its own equal opportunities policy that states that any managing position be filled by a practicing Christian. McMillan did not expect the government to challenge this policy.[88]

Policy makers seem mostly concerned about the quality of the services nonprofit groups provide; no one has questioned the legal system that allows religious agencies to receive state funding. Rab Rabindran, an official with the Department of Health, stated this view succinctly in an interview: "The government concern is that nonprofit agencies provide a service in the health and human social services field. We don't care who provides it, or really how they provide it, so long as they are providing what we think is the best service."[89] Religious agencies have questioned if the qualitative services they provide can be measured in purely instrumental ways, but there is no evidence that the state actively discriminates against them in favor of a more secular social work model. Not one of the religious agency heads we interviewed felt that the government more aggressively regulated their organization than a secular one that provided the same service.

A number of scholars have noted the risks nonprofit agencies face when they receive public funds.[90] Government funding puts pressure on agencies to maintain accountability, which is particularly a problem for religious agencies where, as Peter Dobkin Hall notes, "quality of service has tended to be defined in less than calculable ways."[91] There is an enormous amount of regulation and control of nonprofit organizations and many, if not most, religious agencies have secularized. Our in-depth interviews with agency heads suggest, however, that agencies can, and in many cases do, retain a distinctive religious orientation. Religious agencies face a number of questions about their service delivery, but at the same time there is a move toward a more pluralistic system that gives agencies greater flexibility.[92] The experience of Yeldall Christian Centres suggests that there is an opportunity for agencies to provide an alternative for clients who want services that represent religious values.

The government's use of religious agencies to provide social services has not led to the kinds of struggles that have occurred in public funding of denominational schools. Notably, the Church of England did not dominate the charity field in the late nineteenth century as most of the initial organizations were nondenominational. According to the most comprehensive guide to Christian religious agencies in Britain, there currently are one hundred twelve Christian social service and welfare organizations.[93] Over half of these agencies are interdenominational, a quarter are Roman Catholic only, 10 percent are Anglican, and the rest are affiliated with smaller churches. Anglicans and Roman Catholics never dominated the voluntary social service sector as they have in education, and the state has been more evenhanded in financing a wide variety of religious agencies. Jewish organizations receive extensive government aid; Muslim and Sikh agencies are in their infancy, but some of them have received government money as well.

Our interviews also suggest that the religious establishment does not disadvantage non-Anglican organizations. McMillan of the Salvation Army typified the reaction to questions about the establishment when she commented that the fact that her organization is not Anglican has not led to any overt or subtle discrimination by the state or its regulators. To the contrary, McMillan believes that the religious establishment helps the Salvation Army because "it creates a certain viewpoint that is accepting of state support for the religious activities of social service agencies."[94] We believe that there is much to this argument; the fact that there is an established church in Britain has helped to create a cultural assumption about the public role of religion. The state accommodates religious social service organizations because the state perceives them to be for the public good. Church-based agencies have worked in partnership with the state, and because virtually all religious agencies are eligible for public funds there has been none of the conflict that has occurred with state funding of religious schools.

Concluding Observations

England is the only country in our study that has retained a formal religious establishment, the second of our two church-state models. At first glance, it might appear to be a historical accident that England has an established church, a cultural relic of a bygone era that has little or no practical meaning today. It is certainly true that the partnership between church and state is not as strong as it once was, when the relationship between these two powerful institutions was seen as crucial for the nation's political stability and religious prosperity. We contend, however, that England's religious establishment continues to provide an alternative church-state model for pluralistic democracies, particularly in terms of the cultural assumptions and values it represents. The most important of these are the notions that religion and the churches have an important public role to perform and that it is appropriate for the state to take positive measures to recognize, accommodate, and support religion. The religious establishment serves as an acknowledgment by the state that faith has a public character to it. The inherent limits and opportunities of England's church-state policy follow from the values in its partial religious establishment.

The English church-state model does undermine, to some degree, the basic goal of governmental neutrality on matters of religion. The key limitations of the current system are that it does not provide religious freedom for all or equal treatment among religions, specifically in the field of education. The rights of religious minorities have gradually expanded since the formal establishment of the Church of England in the sixteenth century. There are, however, no statutory or constitutional provisions protecting religious rights and no theoretical commitment by the state to religious free exercise; in some cases government regulation discriminates against minority or unpopular faiths. When religionists suffer because of their faith, they do not have access to the legal system to secure their rights. Britain's educational system clearly denies equal treatment among religions because the state finances some religious schools but not others. The current system advantages those church schools funded under the 1944 Education Act, and disadvantages those schools not included in that original pact.

The state willingly accommodates religion, but only within "acceptable" limits. The boundary between "acceptable" and "unacceptable" religions is drawn according to a civil religion model whereby churches reinforce Britain's liberal social values and emphasize a generalized moral consensus. The effort to bring religion into the state-run schools demonstrates the limits of this model. The religion provided in the schools is generically Christian, which was a recognition on the part of policy makers that it would be unacceptable for the schools to teach the particularistic doctrines of the Church of England. This accommodation worked particularly well in a culture where most people shared similar values and few took religion seriously. Secularists and particularistic religious traditions, including fundamentalist Christian, Pentecostal, and Muslim schools, are outside this system because each of them, for different reasons, rejects the "consensual" religion taught in the public schools.

The paradox of England's partial religious establishment is that while it hinders the realization of governmental neutrality that we established as the basic standard by which to evaluate church-state practices, the system helps the state to achieve neutrality in other respects. The partial establishment disadvantages some churches, but those churches within the system receive public recognition and accommodation. The current educational system treats religions unequally, but it still expands choice for Jewish or Christian parents who want a school permeated by religious ideas. In this way, the system is more neutral between a religious and nonreligious educational perspective than in the United States. This is even more true for nonprofit social service organizations where the state provides funds for a wider variety of religious agencies to serve particular groups in the population. These nonprofit agencies achieve a diversity of service that would simply not be possible if the state provided the services by itself.

Religious pluralism in Britain has made it difficult to sustain this establishment model, as an increasing number of new religions want their rights secured and their schools financed. One way to solve the problem of pluralism is to stop funding religious schools and remove religious instruction and worship from state-run schools. Justice is best served, it could be argued, when the state is neutral among the various religious traditions, as the American strict separationist approach has done. Neutrality, in this view, means no state financial support or involvement with religious schools. In this way the state avoids favoring any particular faith, as it currently does with its partial support for church schools. The problem with this separationist approach, however, is that it is not truly neutral, but favors a nonreligious ethos over religious ones.

An alternative option that we believe is more genuinely neutral would be to expand the system of accommodation to include more religious traditions, along the lines of the Dutch or Australian model. The structure for such a provision already exists in education, with voluntary aided status for religious schools, and public funding of nonprofit organizations already realizes this goal. England has accommodated formerly excluded religious groups in the past, such as Protestant nonconformists and Jews, so there are reasons to believe that the state will expand its notion of a religious establishment to include Muslims and other faiths in the future. Given England's historical pragmatism this is the most likely outcome and would be, in our view, most consistent with the goal of neutrality among religious groups and between religious and nonreligious perspectives.

The limits to this expansion will come from three forces. First, there is a small segment of society that wants to get rid of the establishment and end state subsidies for church-related schools and religious organizations. Second, and more important, there are groups that want to defend a broadly Christian establishment model, as became apparent in the debate on the 1988 Education Reform Act, and have fought an expansion of the denominational system. In the short run, the immigration of significant numbers of non-Christian groups might strengthen the resolve and power of those who want a more clearly defined Christian religious establishment in Britain. Finally, the religious groups excluded from the benefits of the current system are not politically powerful so it will be difficult for them to use political pressure to win concessions from the state.

Notes

1. In 1991, the United Kingdom had a total population of 57.5 million. As noted in the text, England's population was 48 million, followed by Scotland (5 million), Wales (3 million), and Northern Ireland (1.5 million). Unless otherwise noted, all figures in this chapter are for England only.

2. For a good account of the British political system, see Philip Norton, *The British Polity*, 2nd ed. (New York: Longman, 1991).

3. Peter Brierley and David Longley, eds. *United Kingdom Christian Handbook 1992/93* (London: MARC Europe, 1993).

4. *The Public Perspective* (April/May 1995), 25.

5. *British Social Attitudes: Cumulative Sourcebook* (Brookfield, Vt.: Gower, 1992).

6. Paul Whiteley, Patrick Seyd, and Jeremy Richardson, *True Blues: The Politics of the Conservative Party* (Oxford: Clarendon Press, 1994).

7. Ruth Gledhill, "Church Turns into Liberal Democrats at Prayer," *The Times* (February 14, 1996).

8. For a good review of Hooker's influence, see Peter Cornwell, *Church and Nation* (Oxford: Basil Blackwell, 1983), chap. 1.

9. For a good review of this period, see John Madeley, "Politics and the Pulpit: The Case of Protestant Europe,"*West European Politics* 5 (April 1982): 149–71.

10. Steve Bruce and Chris Wright, "Law, Social Change, and Religious Toleration," *Journal of Church and State* 37 (Winter 1995), 110.

11. Kenneth Hylson Smith, *Evangelicals in the Church of England* (Edinburgh: T&T Clark, 1988).

12. Kenneth D. Wald, *Crosses on the Ballot* (Princeton: Princeton University Press, 1983).

13. For a review of this act, see Derek Beales, *From Castlereagh to Gladstone: 1815–1885* (New York: Norton, 1969), chap. 19.

14. D. W. Bebbington, *Evangelicalism in Modern Britain* (London: Unwin Hyman, 1989), chap. 4.

15. Samuel Beer, *Modern British Politics* (London: Faber and Faber, 1969), chap. 2.

16. Michael Fogarty, "The Churches and Public Policy in Britain," *Political Quarterly* 63 (July–September 1992), 302.

17. Bernadette O'Keeffe, *Faith, Culture and the Dual System* (London: Falmer Press, 1986).

18. Peter Mitchell, "Protestantism and Educational Provision," in Witold Tulasiewicz and Cho-Yee To, eds., *World Religions and Educational Practices*(London: Cassell, 1993), 125–43.

19. Alan Storkey, "The Case for Christian Schools," *Spectrum* 16 (Autumn 1983), 4–14.

20. For a review of the legal status of the Church of England, see Kenneth Medhurst and George Moyser, *Church and Politics in a Secular Age* (Oxford: Clarendon Press, 1988), and Kenneth Medhurst, "Reflections on the Church of England and Politics at a Moment of Transition," *Parliamentary Affairs* 44 (April 1991), 240–61.

21. David McClean, "State and Church in the United Kingdom," In Gerhard Robbers, ed., *State and Church in the European Union* (Baden-Baden: European Consortium of Church and State Research, 1996), 307–22.

22. Anthony Doran, "Divorce Bill Is Against God's Will, Says Bishop," *The Daily Mail* (January 11, 1996).

23. Arthur Leathley and Alice Thomson, "Pension Split Deal Saves Divorce Reform Bill," *The Times* (June 18, 1996).

24. Eileen Barker, "The British Right to Discriminate," in Thomas Robbins and Roland Robertson, eds., *Church-State Relations: Tensions and Transitions* (New Brunswick, N.J.: Transaction Books, 1987), 273.

25. Sarah Lyall, "Rights Panel for Europe Stirs Anger in Britain," *New York Times* (May 6, 1996). The most noteworthy blasphemy case involved Mrs. Mary Whitehouse, a well-known British conservative activist, who successfully initiated a private prosecution of *Gay News* when it published a poem in which a Roman soldier expressed a homosexual love for Jesus.

26. Tariq Modood, "British Asian Muslims and the Rushdie Affair," *Political Quarterly* 61 (April-June 1990), 143–60.

27. George Moyser, ed., *Church and Politics Today* (Edinburgh: T&T Clark, 1985), 7.

28. David Martin, "Great Britain," in Hans Mol, ed., *Western Religions: A Country by Country Sociological Study* (The Hague: Mouten, 1972), 229–45.

29. Medhurst and Moyser, *Church and Politics in a Secular Age*, 316.

30. Ruth Gledhill and Jill Sherman, "Carey Attacks Howard over Wild Frontier Policy of Revenge," *The Times* (May 10, 1996).

31. Peter Brierley, ed., *United Kingdom Christian Handbook: 1987/88* (London: MARC Europe, 1989).

32. David McClean, "Church and State in England, 1993," *European Journal of Church and State Research* 1 (1994), 19–22.

33. For a similar argument about support for religious accommodation in the United States, see Ted G. Jelen and Clyde Wilcox, *Public Attitudes Toward Church and State* (Armonk, N.Y.: Sharpe, 1995).

34. Rodney Stark and Laurence R. Iannaccone, "A Supply Side Reinterpretation of the 'Secularization' of Europe," *Journal for the Scientific Study of Religion* 33 (1994), 230–52.

35. David Winter, *Battered Bride* (Eastbourne: Monarch, 1988), chap. 13.

36. Tariq Modood, "Establishment, Multiculturalism and British Citizenship," *Political Quarterly* 65 (January-March 1994), 53–73.

37. St. John A. Robilliard, "Religious Freedom as a Human Right Within the United Kingdom," *Human Rights Review* 4 (Spring 1981), 90–111.

38. Muhammad Anwar, *Race Relation Policies in Britain* (Warwick: Centre for Research in Ethnic Relations, 1991).

39. Modood, "Establishment, Multiculturalism and British Citizenship," 57.

40. Barker, "The British Right to Discriminate, 270–1.

41. Robilliard, "Religious Freedom as a Human Right Within the United Kingdom," 98–100.

42. McClean, "State and Church in the United Kingdom," 319.

43. Barker, "The British Right to Discriminate, 279.

44. *The Public Perspective*, November/December 1992, 9.

45. For a good description of the difference between voluntary aided and voluntary controlled schools, see David W. Lanksheare, *A Shared Vision: Education in Church Schools* (London: Church House, 1992).

46. Bernadette O'Keeffe, *Faith, Culture and the Dual System*, 152.

47. Robert Burgess, "Five Items for the Policy Agenda in Church Schools," in Bernadette O'Keeffe, ed., *Schools for Tomorrow: Building Walls or Building Bridges* (London: Falmer Press, 1988), 162–81.

48. "UK Education—Further Blessings of a Religious Schooling," *Daily Telegraph* (January 4, 1995).

49. Robert Waddington, "The Church and Educational Policy," in Moyser, ed. *Church and Politics Today* , 221–55.

50. Mark Halstead, "Educating Muslim Minorities: Some Western European Approaches," in Tulasiewicz and To, eds., *World Religions and Educational Practices*, 168.

51. For a discussion of these educational reforms, see Mike Feintuck, *Accountability and Choice in Schooling* (Philadelphia: Open University Press, 1994).

52. Malcolm McVicar, "Education Policy: Education as a Business?" in Stephen P. Savage and Lyton Robins, eds., *Public Policy Under Thatcher* (London: Macmillan, 1990), 131–44.

53. Geraldine Hackett, "The Scramble for State Funding," *Times Educational Supplement* 3971 (August 7, 1992), 8, and "Religion and Education," *New Statesman and Society* (August 27, 1993), 5.

54. Bernadette O'Keeffe, *Schools for Tomorrow*, chap. 1.

55. Patricia White, "The New Right and Parental Choice," *Journal of Philosophy of Education* 22 (1988), 195–99.

56. Modood, "British Asian Muslims and the Rushdie Affair," *Political Quarterly*, 143–60.

57. Interview with David Lanksheare (May 13, 1994).

58. *Syllabus and Guidelines for Islamic Teaching* (London: Muslim Educational Trust, 1984), 1.

59. O'Keeffe, *Faith, Culture and the Dual System*, 152.

60. Interview with Mughram Al Ghamdi of the Islamic Cultural Centre (May 17, 1994).

61. Edward Hulmes, "Christian Education in a Multi-Cultural Society," in V. Alan McClelland, ed., *Christian Education in a Pluralistic Society* (London: Routledge, 1988), 93.

62. O'Keeffe, *Faith, Culture and the Dual System*, chap. 1.

63. Syed Ali Ashraf, "A View of Education—An Islamic Perspective," in O'Keeffe, ed., *Schools for Tomorrow*, 5.

64. Modood, "Establishment, Multiculturalism and British Citizenship," 62.

65. See Owen Cole, "Religious Education after Swann," in O'Keeffe, ed., *Schools for Tomorrow*, 125–44.

66. See Halstead, "Educating Muslim Minorities: Some Western European Approaches."

67. For a review of the religious provisions of the act, see Ralph Gower, *Religious Education at the Primary Stage* (Oxford: Lion Educational Trust, 1990).

68. John Burn and Colin Hart, *The Crisis in Religious Education* (London: Education Research Trust, 1988).

69. Paul Vallely, "UK Keeping Faith in the System," *The Independent* (January 7, 1995).

70. Fran Abrams, "Education—Breaking the Government Commandments," *The Independent* (October 6, 1994).

71. *The Public Perspective* (November/December 1992).

72. Ben Preston, "Habgood Urges Support for Religious Education," *The Times* (March 9, 1995).

73. Burn and Hart, *The Crisis in Religious Education*.

74. Lesley Gerard, "Delegates Demand an End to Law on Daily Prayers," *The Independent* (April 13, 1995), and Paul Vallely, "Keeping Faith in the System," *The Independent* (January 7, 1995).

75. Madeleine Bunting and Martin Wainright, "Muslims to Step up Boycott of Religious Lessons," *The Guardian* (April 12, 1996).

76. Paul Vallely, "How Much Tolerance Can We Tolerate," *The Independent* (March 4, 1996).

77. *Religious Education and Collective Worship: A Report from the Office of Her Majesty's Chief Inspector of Schools* (London: HMSO, 1994).

78. For a review of this activism, see D. W. Bebbington, *Evangelicals in Modern Britain*, chap. 4, and June Rose, *For the Sake of the Children: Inside Dr. Barnardo's* (London: Hodder and Stoughton, 1987).

79. Lester Salamon, "Partners in Public Service: The Scope and Theory of Government-Nonprofit Relations," in Walter M. Powell, ed., *The Nonprofit Sector: A Research Handbook* (New Haven: Yale University Press, 1987), 99–117.

80. Salamon, "Partners in Public Service," 111.

81. James A. Beckford, "Great Britain: Voluntarism and Sectional Interests," in Robert Wuthnow, ed. *Between States and Markets* (Princeton: Princeton University Press, 1991), 30–63.

82. Ivor Crewe, "The Thatcher Legacy," in Anthony King, ed., *Britain at the Polls: 1992* (Chatham, N.J.: Chatham House, 1993), 1–28.

83. *Britain's Voluntary Organizations* (London: Foreign and Commonwealth Office, 1993).

84. *Britain's Voluntary Organizations*, and Perri 6 and Penny Fieldgrass, *Snapshots of the Voluntary Sector* (London: NCVO Publications, 1992).

85. These estimates were provided to us in a personal correspondence by Rachel Westall, of the Evangelical Coalition on Drugs, and in an interview with Tom White, executive director, National Children's Home (May 10, 1994).

86. Statements taken from "Yeldall Christian Centres: A Christian Response to Addiction and Homelessness" and "Yeldall Manor Care Plan." Undated publications of Yeldall Christian Centres.

87. Interview with David Partington, executive director, and Jeremy Parr, Centre director, Yeldall Christian Centres (May 12, 1994).

88. Interview with Christine McMillan, associate director, London Homeless Shelters for the Salvation Army (May 13, 1994).

89. Interview with Rab Rabidran, Department of Health (May 16, 1994).

90. See Micheal Lipsky and Steven Rathgeb Smith, "Nonprofit Organizations, Government, and the Welfare State," *Political Science Quarterly* 104 (1989–90), 626.

91. Peter Dobkin Hall, "The History of Religious Philanthropy in America," in Robert Wuthnow and Virginia A. Hodgkinson, eds., *Faith and Philanthropy in America* (San Francisco: Jossey-Bass, 1990), 56.

92. Marilyn Taylor, "The Changing Role of the Nonprofit Sector in Britain: Moving Toward the Market," in Benjamin Gidrow, Ralph M. Kramer, and Lester Salamon, eds., *Government and the Third Sector: Emerging Relationships in Welfare States* (San Francisco: Jossey-Bass, 1992), 147–75.

93. Brierley and Longley, *United Kingdom Christian Handbook 1992/93*.

94. Interview with Christine McMillan, associate director, London Homeless Shelters for the Salvation Army (May 13, 1994).

Chapter 6

GERMANY: PARTNERSHIP AND AUTONOMY

$\mathcal{D}$iscussions of church-state relations in Germany frequently invoke two basic principles: partnership and autonomy. Germans typically see church and state, not as mutually exclusive, separate spheres of human endeavor, but as cooperative partners, both of whom have a role to play in contributing to a prosperous, stable German society. Somewhat in tension with this principle—or at the least serving as a balance to it—is the principle of autonomy or self-determination. The German mindset sees churches and other religious organizations as possessing a basic right to an independence that leaves them in control of their own destiny and nature; they possess an autonomy on which the state is not to infringe.

Two additional values or principles supplement these two principles: neutrality and freedom of religion as a positive freedom. Neutrality, as one German authority on church-state relations has noted, means "the State [is] not to be identified with a Church; there is to be no Established Church. The State is not allowed to have any special inclination to a particular religious congregation. . . . On the other hand, religious institutions must not be placed in a more disadvantageous position than societal groups; this forbids a decision for State atheism."[1] Among all religious groups and between the religious and the nonreligious the state is to be neutral, not favoring one over another. Freedom of religion as a positive freedom insists that freedom of religion is more than a negative freedom; it extends beyond freedom from government restrictions on one's religious beliefs or practices to include positive efforts by the government to ensure that the religious are in a position actually to exercise the freedoms assured them. Donald Kommers has put it well: "Freedom of religion in the positive sense implies an obligation on the part of the state to create a social order in which it is possible for the religious personality to develop and flourish conveniently and easily."[2]

These four principles work together to create an approach to church-state relations that to most Americans appears puzzling. The German Constitution clearly commands that "There shall be no state church," and Germans often speak of church-state separation and state neutrality on matters of religion. Yet Germany's equal emphasis on a church-state partnership and religious freedom as a positive freedom has led to practices many Americans would find in violation of church-state separation and neutrality. Paradoxically, Germany's church-state thinking and practices have some parallels with both the principled pluralism of the Netherlands and the partial establishment of England.

In seeking to understand German church-state principles and practices, we first consider a few salient facts concerning Germany. The next section considers the historical background to contemporary church-state practices, paying special attention to how it has shaped the four principles already mentioned. The next four sections consider how in practice these principles and other forces have worked to mold the German approach to free exercise issues, to various forms of direct government cooperation with the churches, to religion and education, and to government policies toward religiously based social service programs. The final section presents some concluding observations.

The Nation

Germany is a country of eighty-one million people and 137,000 square miles, making it second to Russia as the most populous country of Europe. It has risen from the ashes of World War II to become a European—even a world—economic and political powerhouse. Some have argued that the "economic miracle" of the 1950s, as it was often called, has been exceeded by the political miracle that has transformed a nation that had been marked by authoritarian government and political instability into a model of stability and liberal democracy for fifty years. Not only do democratic institutions and practices mark German government and politics, but survey research demonstrates that the attitudes and values of the German people have changed to become more compatible with democratic norms. One researcher, for example, found when American and German schoolchildren were tested for authoritarianism in 1945 the American children were significantly less authoritarian; when they were tested in the late 1970s the German children were as nonauthoritarian as the American children and were even less authoritarian by several measures.[3]

Ninety-three percent of the population is ethnically German, with the remaining 7 percent consisting of guest workers from Turkey, the countries of the former Yugoslavia, Italy, and a scattering of other countries. Religiously, 29 million (38 percent) are members of the Evangelical, or Protestant, Church, 28 million (36 percent) are members of the Catholic Church, 2.5 million (3 percent) are Muslims, 47,000 are Jewish (less than 1 percent), and 16 million (21 percent) are without a religious affiliation.[4] The Evangelical Church in Germany (EKD) is a federation of twenty-four regional Protestant churches, which are mostly Lutheran in background, while some come out of the Reformed (that is, Calvinist) tradition and some are products of a union between Lutheran and Reformed churches.[5] The regional churches enjoy a significant amount of autonomy.

The churches came out of the Nazi era with their reputations largely intact and perhaps even enhanced as one of the few German social structures that offered any significant opposition to the Nazi regime. The churches and the closely related Christian Democratic movement played major roles in the rise of Germany from the devastation of World War II during the 1945–60 period. However, by 1973 already one commentator wrote that "the church [has] lost a controlling influence over popular attitudes and with that its commanding position in society."[6] The Evangelical Church reports that as of 1987 about 9 percent of their members regularly attend meetings of various church groups,[7] which is actually higher than the estimate of one historian that Protestant church attendance a hundred years ago was only 3 percent of its membership.[8] But this low level of church activity can be misleading. There continues to be broad support and respect for both the Evangelical and Catholic churches. A 1991 survey showed that 28 percent of the population of West Germany reported they had much confidence in churches and religious organizations, and another 36 percent reported they had some confidence in them.[9] The Christian Democrats have been the dominant party throughout most of the postwar era. A 1995 Constitutional Court decision ruling that crucifixes may not be displayed in public school classrooms if any student objects on religious grounds was greeted by a storm of denunciation and protest throughout Germany.

Politically, Germany has a federal system with sixteen states (Länder). More power is centralized in the national government than is the case in the United States, but significant powers are assigned to the states. Germany has a parliamentary system of government, with a lower house, the Bundestag, directly elected by the people and an upper house, the Bundesrat, composed of representative of the states. Its approval is generally needed for legislation affecting the states, but on other legislation the Bundestag can override a negative vote by the Bundesrat by a simple majority. The chancellor is elected by the Bundestag. Germany has two major parties, the Christian Democratic Union (the Christian Social Union in Bavaria) and the Social Democratic Party. Following the 1994 elections the Christian Democrats had 42 percent of the seats in the Bundestag and the Social Democrats had 36 percent. The most important smaller parties are the Free Democratic Party (a liberal business-oriented party), the Greens (a reform-minded environmental party), and the Party of Democratic Socialism (the recast Communist Party). The current government is headed by Chancellor Helmut Kohl, who has served as chancellor since 1982 and heads a Christian Democrats-Free Democrats coalition.

It is also important to note the role of the Constitutional Court, since it has the power of judicial review. This is a court created by the 1949 Constitution to decide questions of constitutional interpretation.[10] It is divided into two Senates, as they are called, each composed of eight justices, and cases considered by the Constitutional Court are considered by one Senate or the other (referred to simply as the First Senate or the Second Senate). Half the justices are elected by the Bundestag and half by the Bundesrat. All serve twelve-year terms and are not allowed to serve more than one term. As we shall shortly see, the Constitutional Court has dealt with a number of crucial church-state issues.

Historical Background

There are five historical periods that are important in giving insight into German church-state practices and the origins of the four principles relevant to church-state relations mentioned in the introduction to the chapter. The first period is that of the Middle Ages and the Protestant Reformation. Throughout this era what is Germany today was a host of kingdoms and principalities very loosely tied together in the Holy Roman Empire; Germany as a nation-state did not exist. During the Middle Ages the concept of the "two-swords" or two authorities—church and civil rulers—took deep root in the German territories, as it did through most of Christendom. Under this concept the people were under two rulers, the prince and the church, and both worked for the stability and prosperity of society. This concept left undefined exactly which authority was responsible for what and led to many conflicts between the papacy and the Holy Roman Emperors, such as that between Pope Gregory VII and King Henry IV.

The Reformation shattered the unity of European Christendom. The German territories followed the practice of *cuius regio, eius religio* (the religion of the ruler is the religion of the state). The 1648 Peace of Westphalia, which ended the devastating Thirty Years War, reaffirmed the right of rulers to determine the religion to be followed in their territories, but also provided for the rights of dissenters. In each region, the prince determined whether his people were to be Catholic, Lutheran, or Calvinist. Given the relatively small size of many of the German principalities, this practice created areas almost totally committed to one of these religious traditions within Christianity. Up until the post-World War II era with its increasing prosperity and greater mobility many areas of Germany remained overwhelmingly Catholic or Protestant. Even today this is still the case to a significant degree in some areas. The practice of *cuius regio, eius religio* also perpetuated the "two swords" concept, although in practice the secular authority came to dominate the spiritual authority. With the church (Protestant or Catholic) usually dependent on the civil rulers for its existence, this is not surprising.

It was from out of this time period that the tradition of a church-state partnership emerged. The well-being of society rested on the two pillars of church and state, or throne and altar, as it is often put. They were seen as united in a common cause. Thus cooperation and mutual support came to be the norm. The religious uniformity within the separate principalities made church-state cooperation and mutual support possible, for the most part, without raising charges of religious discrimination and favoritism. Paradoxically, the German tradition of church autonomy can also be traced to this same time period. The "two swords" doctrine held in theory—even if it was often not followed in practice—that the church and the state, the two swords, were coequal institutions, each with rights and responsibilities. The church was not an arm of or subservient to the state.

The second time period of importance for understanding the development of church-state relations in Germany is the era stretching from the Congress of Vienna in 1815 through World War I. At the close of the Napoleonic era the degree of unity that Napoleon had imposed dissipated. Germany reverted to a series of small principalities united into a very weak confederation and with conservative, nondemocratic forces in control. From 1815 to 1871 weak, usually outmaneuvered liberal movements failed to gain ascendancy. Prussia gradually arose as a dominant force, and by 1871—with the help of military victories over Denmark, Austria, and France—had united Germany in a true nation-state. Prussia thereby established the second German empire, which lasted until the end of World War I. It was a conservative regime, with a monarch (first William I, then Frederick III for a few months, followed by William I's grandson William II in 1888), a weak parliament, and a powerful chancellor responsible to the monarch. Otto von Bismarck engineered the unification of Germany and served as its chancellor until 1890.

Three marks of this period are important to note for understanding subsequent church-state developments and patterns. One is the relative weakness of the liberal movement. Enlightenment liberalism never became the powerful force it did in the other countries considered in this book. It had a brief ascendancy following the revolutions of 1848, but within a year the conservative landowning and titled classes had again asserted themselves. This meant that the Catholics and Protestants did not face a strong liberal movement that might have forced them into cooperative efforts, as had occurred in the neighboring Netherlands; instead the Catholics were overshadowed by the Protestant leadership of the empire, who made common cause with the conservative, antiliberal forces.

The second point to be noted is that the second empire was marked by a very strong alliance between the Evangelical Church and the newly formed German state. The state provided direct financial subsidies to the church, and "the church and its liturgical ceremonies became an important unifying force, binding the nation to the ruling dynasty and securing it through a providential interpretation of German history."[11] The close alliance between church and state that had existed from the Medieval and Reformation eras was maintained during the second empire.

A third important point is that it was during this era that the Catholics developed a significant political movement. At the time of German unification the new nation was clearly a Protestant nation. Its moving force was Prussia, which was strongly Protestant. For a period of time in the 1870s Bismarck launched what came to be called *Kulturkamf* (culture war), a series of oppressive and discriminatory measures against the Catholics. Doing so had the opposite effect of what was intended, as Catholics rallied behind their leaders and the Catholic Center Party developed into a political force that had to be reckoned with. Most of the discriminatory measures were repealed in the early 1880s, but the Center Party remained a political force.

Following the defeat of Germany in World War I the second empire came to an end and was replaced by the Weimar Republic, named after the city of Weimar where the new constitution was written. This is the third historical period to be noted here. Given the crisis created by the German defeat, the spirit of revolution that was in the air, and the generally liberal nature of the new constitution, one might suppose that the Weimar Constitution would have made a larger break with past church-state practices than what it did. Historian Paul Means has noted that "the revolution was not as complete with respect to the church as its enemies had hoped and its friends had feared."[12] A variety of subsidies and privileges were kept by the Catholic and Evangelical churches. Nevertheless, the Weimar Constitution for the first time formally adopted the principle of church-state separation, declared there was to be no state church, and provided that "civil and political rights and duties shall be neither dependent on nor restricted by the exercise of religious freedom."[13] It thereby recognized the basic principle of governmental neutrality on matters of religion, as well as the earlier principle of autonomy. The significance of the Weimar Constitution for religious freedom can be seen by the fact that the current Constitution incorporated by reference the basic articles establishing religious freedom found in the Weimar Constitution when it was adopted after World War II.

The Nazi era is the fourth era of significance for present-day German church-state relations to be noted here. Most of the Evangelical and Catholic church leadership had remained largely negative toward the Weimar Constitution, attitudes that seemed to be vindicated when Germany experienced a series of severe economic reversals and political difficulties. Thus when Adolf Hitler and his National Socialists promised stability, prosperity, freedom to the churches, and greatness for the Fatherland, the churches, for the most part, initially rallied in support. The Catholic Center Party unanimously supported the Enabling Act in 1933 that gave Hitler dictatorial powers. In the same year the Vatican signed the famous Reichskonkordat with the Nazi regime, which assured the Catholic Church certain rights but also helped the Nazis consolidate their power. Within the Evangelical Church, a "German Christian" movement emerged that enthusiastically supported Hitler's rise to power and thoroughly wedded German discipline and greatness with Christianity.

On the other hand, the Catholic Church never truly supported the Nazi regime. It was more concerned with protecting its own institutional autonomy and maintaining a semblance of normal church life in the midst of political upheaval and war than either supporting or opposing Nazism. It should be noted, however, that many individual Catholic leaders, such as Cardinal Graf Galen of Munich, courageously opposed the Nazi regime. Within the more culturally powerful Evangelical Church—after an initial enthusiasm for Hitler—opposition to him quickly arose as the true nature of Nazism became evident. Frederic Spotts reports that by May 1934 already "anti-Nazi resistance had sufficiently crystallized for a Reich Synod of the opponents to be held in the Rhineland town of Barmen. Here, largely under the influence of Karl Barth, a 'Confessing Church' . . . was organized, based upon a confession of faith in the supremacy of Scripture which might not be changed to suit prevailing ideological or political convictions."[14] This Confessing Church gained wide support and successfully opposed the pro-Nazi "German Evangelical Church." During the Hitler regime, 3,000 pastors were arrested, at least 125 were sent to concentration camps, and 22 were executed, including the famous pastor and theologian Dietrich Bonhoeffer.[15] After the war the newly constituted Evangelical Church— under the leadership, among others, of Martin Niemöller, who had recently been released from seven years in a concentration camp—adopted the Stuttgart Declaration, which acknowledged the churches' and the nation's guilt:

> We know ourselves to be with our nation not only in a great community of suffering but also in a solidarity of guilt. With great pain we say: because of us, infinite suffering has been brought to many peoples and countries. . . . We condemn ourselves because we did not believe more courageously, did not pray more devotedly, did not believe more joyously, and did not love more deeply. Now a fresh start is to be made in our churches.[16]

As a result of this highly traumatic era two lessons with lasting implications for church-state relations have been burned into German thinking. One is that the church often courts enormous danger when it is too subservient to the state. The church up to that point in German history was suddenly seen as being too subservient to the state, too ready to make common cause with the state, and too quick to advance whatever policies the state was supporting. The principle of church autonomy, already present in the German tradition, received a new and urgent reemphasis. A second lesson was that the church must play a role in the political and social life of the nation. The big error of the church was not seen as being its active support of Hitler—which had been brief and limited—but its silence and acquiescence. Both the Catholic and Evangelical churches emerged from the era of National Socialism with a greatly strengthened resolve to be active, positive forces in society. The concept of strict church–state separation even today is seen as a dangerous doctrine, one that implies the political realm is to be secularized, with religion's influence muted or nonexistent.

The postwar era is the fifth of the historical time periods to be noted. It saw the rise of the Christian Democratic movement, the most powerful political force in the postwar era.

> Christian Democracy was created by a few men—many of whom, being under death sentence for anti-Nazi activities, had no right to be alive in 1945—who confounded some of the elementary rules of society and politics. This small group of persons . . . succeeded in establishing an inter-confessional political party in Berlin within a month of the collapse of the Third Reich and in most other parts of Germany within six months after that.[17]

This new party was interconfessional—including both Catholics and Protestants—and was firmly committed to liberal democracy and to learning from the bitter experiences under the Weimar Republic and the Third Reich. By firmly linking Christianity—both Protestant and Catholic—to the powerful democratic impulses sweeping postwar Germany, it made possible the continued cooperation or partnership of the state with religion. Religion and Christianity came to be seen as positive, democratizing forces and as bulwarks against the reemergence of Nazism. Church-state cooperation was thereby seen not as a danger to be avoided, but as an asset to be used in the search for democracy.

In 1948 the western allies decided it was time to move ahead with a constitution for the three zones of Germany under their jurisdiction. The parliaments of the eleven German states that had been previously set up elected a Parliamentary Council to write the constitution. Working from a draft that a conference of experts had put together, the council wrote a new constitution.[18] It was approved by the Allies and the state parliaments, and went into effect in May 1949. Its preamble begins with a recognition of God: "Conscious of their responsibility before God and Humankind. . . ."[19] The first nineteen articles constitute a bill of rights, with Article 4 assuring that "(1) Freedom of faith and conscience as well as freedom of creed, religious or ideological, are inviolable," and "(2) The undisturbed practice of religion shall be guaranteed." Its third section provides for conscientious objectors to be relieved from military service. It is helpful to note that ideological as well as religious freedom and the practice as well as the freedom of conscience are safeguarded. Article 3 is also relevant to church-state issues. It provides that "All people are equal before the law" and "Nobody shall be prejudiced or favoured because of their sex, birth, race, language, national or social origin, faith, religion or political opinions." The basic principle of neutrality is seen in these provisions. Article 7 of the Constitution deals with education and, as will be seen later, contains several provisions crucial for church-state relations. The provisions of Articles 3 and 4 are supplemented by Article 140, which incorporates the basic religious freedom provisions of the old Weimar Constitution into the current Basic Law. Among the provisions thereby included in the Basic Law are a ban on the existence of a state church and—as we will see later—several provisions with implications for religious establishment issues.

In the German Democratic Republic (GDR) the churches faced enormous pressures for over forty years.[20] Although the outright opposition of the communist authorities waxed and waned over the forty years of their rule, even in the best of times parents were pressured not to baptize their children, church-going young people were often unable to obtain a college education, and active Christians were often denied government and business promotions. The church suffered as a result of such pressures. Just before the fall of the Berlin Wall in 1989, John Burgess reported that "by all measures of participation in traditional religious life, East Germany today is one of the world's most secularized societies."[21] From 1961 to 1989 the West German Evangelical Church lost 15 percent of its membership, but the East German Evangelical Church lost over 50 percent.[22] By several measures the population of the former GDR exhibits significantly more secularist attitudes than does the population of the old West Germany.[23]

Thus the unification of Germany in 1990 meant that German society as a whole became more secular than what it had been when West Germany existed as a separate state. Also, the church leadership from the old GDR has a more cautious, suspicious outlook toward the government than is the case for the West German church leadership. For the East Germans, over forty years under communist rule reinforced the lessons learned from Hitler's subversion and persecution of the churches.

Free Exercise Issues

In Germany, the free exercise of religion is seen as a basic, fundamental right that has been interpreted broadly by the courts. The free exercise of religion trumps, so to speak, concerns over the establishment of religion. This is a point explicitly made by Axel von Campenhausen, an Evangelical Church expert on church-state relations: "This is the main question. Is there religious liberty for everyone or not? The old democracies in Europe say this is the main purpose [of religious freedom]. Whether the church as an institution is independent from the state or not, whether the Queen of England is head of the church or of the Church of Scotland . . . is not so important if people are free to worship as they wish."[24]

The fact that Germany's Constitutional Court has interpreted free exercise rights more broadly than has the U. S. Supreme Court can be seen in the Constitutional Court's unambiguous holding that the free exercise of religion includes not only the right to believe, but also the right to act on one's beliefs. In a case dealing with a pastor who refused to take an oath when called to testify as a witness in a criminal trial, the Constitutional Court stated: "Religious freedom under Article 4(1) of the Basic Law . . . encompasses not only the (internal) freedom to believe or not to believe but also the individual's right to align his behavior with the precepts of his faith and to act in accordance with his internal convictions."[25]

The strong emphasis on the free exercise of religion can also be seen in the tendency of the German courts to decide cases on free exercise grounds that in the United States would be seen as establishment of religion cases. This is due to the German courts' seeing religious freedom as having a positive as well as a negative aspect to it. In a 1979 decision finding the use of general prayers in the public schools constitutional, for example, the Constitutional Court based its decision on the concept of positive religious freedom: "To be sure, the state must balance this affirmative freedom to worship as expressed by permitting school prayer with the negative freedom of confession of other parents and pupils opposed to school prayer. Basically, [schools] may achieve this balance by guaranteeing that participation be voluntary for pupils and teachers."[26] The Constitutional Court saw allowing prayers in schools as making room for children who wanted to pray and disallowing such prayers as being a violation of their freedom to pray.

The expansive nature of religious freedom rights in Germany can also be seen in the commitment to including the charitable activities of churches and the organizations they sponsor within the scope of the religious freedom language of the Basic Law. A 1968 case that came before the Constitutional Court involved a Catholic youth association that was having a drive to collect old clothes and other used goods for use in helping needy persons overseas. A scrap dealer challenged the right of the youth association to hold such a drive, arguing it constituted unfair competition. The Court ruled in favor of the youth association and its right to collect used goods. One of the issues it settled was that the free exercise rights enjoyed by churches extended to associated charitable associations such as the youth association.

> The basic right secured by Article 4(1) and (2) of the Basic Law is accorded . . . to associations only partially devoted to fostering the religious or ideological life of their members. It is essential only that the organization be directed toward the attainment of a religious goal. . . . [The youth association's] articles of association expressly provide that the association is to serve the living church in its mission of alleviating through material support the spiritual and corporal needs of people throughout the world. The fundamental right to the free exercise of religion pertains, therefore, to this association.[27]

In contrast, the U. S. Supreme Court has tended to see organizations such as this engaged in both religious and secular activities and to extend free exercise rights only to their religious activities.

The strong emphasis on the free exercise of religion is rooted in the twin emphases on religious liberty as a positive right and the principle of neutrality. The Constitutional Court has frequently referred to neutrality as an important component of its free exercise decisions. Free exercise rights extend to people of all religious faiths and of none. In one of its decisions the Court declared: "The right to free exercise extends not only to Christian Churches but also to other religious creeds and ideological associations. This is a consequence of the ideological-religious neutrality to which the state is bound and the principle of equality with respect to churches and denominations."[28] In the case dealing with the pastor who had refused to take an oath in a criminal proceeding, the Court referred to "the command of ideological-religious neutrality that binds the state"[29] and gave a ringing endorsement of basic religious liberty: "The state may neither favor certain creeds nor evaluate the beliefs or lack of faith of its citizens. . . . The state may not evaluate its citizens' religious convictions or characterize these beliefs as right or wrong."[30] It upheld the right of the clergyman to refuse to take the oath.

Religious freedom as a positive right is also important in free exercise protections since freedom is seen as including the opportunity to exercise that freedom. In an interview with us Gerhard Robbers of Trier University's law faculty made clear that positive religious freedom is fully in keeping with religious neutrality: "Positive religious freedom means that government actively creates room for religious behavior, for religious life. . . . This is not promoting religion. That would be against neutrality. Atheists would object if government would promote religion.

. . . It is making room for religion. It is just that there needs to be a basis, if people are religious, for them to practice their religion."[31]

The expansive and strong concept of free exercise does not mean it is unlimited. The Constitutional Court and German commentators have frequently stressed that when the free exercise of religion infringes on human dignity or public health and safety a certain balancing or weighing process must take place. In one decision the Court wrote that the church-state provisions of the Constitution require the courts "to balance and weigh the different interests and values at stake in the relationship between the freedom of the churches and the limits imposed on this freedom."[32]

The *Tobacco Atheist Case* illustrates this balancing process. It was a strange case that involved a prison inmate who was denied parole because, while in prison, he had sought to entice his fellow inmates to renounce the church by offering them tobacco. The Constitutional Court upheld the denial of parole on the basis of there being limits on one's freedom of religion, or—in this case—nonreligion:

> The religiously neutral state . . . must prevent misuse of this [religious] freedom. . . . It follows from the Basic Law's order of values, especially from the dignity of the human being, that a misuse is especially apparent whenever the dignity of another person is violated. Recruiting for a belief and convincing someone to turn from another belief, normally legal activities, become misuses of the basic right if a person tries, directly or indirectly, to use a base or immoral instrument to lure other persons from their beliefs."[33]

The order of values mentioned here refers to the concept of there being a hierarchy of values in the Constitution so that one value can trump another one. Here the Court held that the very basic value of human dignity (Article 1: "The dignity of man is inviolable. To respect and protect it shall be the duty of all public authority") trumped the right to influence the religious opinions of others, given the "special circumstances of penal servitude."[34]

In an interview von Campenhausen stressed that in protecting public health or safety religious liberty can be infringed. He gave as an example the inappropriateness of a church cemetery being located near a town's water supply. "In the name of the sanitation of the water the state is able to reduce self-determination of the churches, even when the state is not antireligious, but friendly, neutral. Living together makes it necessary."[35] Then he cited a second example, "Of course, it is possible to have a demonstration or procession on the streets—a religious procession—but the traffic has its rights too. . . . You must compromise. So it is a balance."[36] The German approach is similar to the "compelling state interest" test the U. S. Supreme Court has sometimes followed and was reinforced by the 1993 Religious Freedom Restoration Act passed by Congress.

Some of the principles discussed thus far can be illustrated by reference to a particularly dramatic free exercise case that came before the Constitutional Court. A married couple, both of whom were members of the Association of Evangelical Brotherhood, held to a religious faith that believed it was inappropriate to make use of blood transfusions to solve medical problems. The wife suffered complications in the birth of the couple's fourth child, and the doctors thought a blood transfusion was essential. The wife, with the support of her husband, refused the blood transfusion and died. The husband was subsequently prosecuted and convicted for failure to provide his wife with necessary assistance. On appeal, the Court overturned the decisions of the lower courts of the basis of the free exercise provision of Article 4 of the Basic Law.

Three aspects of the Constitutional Court's decision in this case are instructive. First, the Court made a clear affirmation of religious liberty: "In a state in which human dignity is the highest value, and in which the free self-determination of the individual is also recognized as an important community value, freedom of belief affords the individual a legal realm free of state interference in which a person may live his life according to his convictions."[37]

Second, the Court went on to note that in this case personal religious freedom was clashing with a person's obligation to obey the law, but in this case the law must yield.

> The duty of all public authority to respect serious religious convictions, [as] contained in Article 4(1) of the Basic Law, must lead to a relaxation of criminal laws when an actual conflict between a generally accepted legal duty and a dictate of faith results in a spiritual crisis for the offender that, in view of the punishment labeling him a criminal, would represent an excessive social reaction violative of his human dignity.[38]

Thus the Court decided even a law that was not aimed at constricting certain religious practices, but was a law of general applicability that met certain legitimate, appropriate public purposes, was overruled by the free exercise protections of Article 4. This is a position that the U. S. Supreme Court, as seen in Chapter 2, has for the most part refused to adopt.

Third—and perhaps most importantly—there runs through the Court's decision a basic respect for the sincerity and importance of the religious beliefs of the husband whom most would judge helped cause his wife's death.

> The duties which the complainant owed to his children would lead to a different conclusion if, under the pretext of his own convictions, the complainant had allowed his wife to die, thus depriving his children of their mother. This is exactly what the complainant did not want. He was certain that prayer was the most effective way of saving his wife. His duties to the children do not extend so far . . . that he would have had to abandon what he thought was a more promising aid in favor of medical treatment which he believed would be ineffectual without God's help. Admittedly, society's moral standards would dictate that the complainant follow both paths simultaneously. However, because his religious convictions would not permit him [to use both ways to save his wife], imposing criminal sanctions against him was not justified.[39]

Two continuing free exercise controversies involve the immigrant Muslim population and the Church of Scientology. In regard to the sizable Muslim population in Germany, ways have not yet been found to integrate them fully into the German concept of religious liberty. Muslims constitute 3 percent of the population, making them the third largest religious community in Germany. Their fairly recent arrival in Germany, their lack of a centralized organizational structure, and their often distinctive religious practices have created religious freedom problems. Most forms of cooperation between church and state to be documented in the following sections have not been fully extended to Muslims. A key problem has been described by Joseph Listl:

> There is in Germany a rather big number of Moslem societies. Yet, they are not united in one coherent association or in one religious community and they do not have one direction. . . . [T]here is so far in Germany not one Moslem organization that meets the requirements to obtain the status of a corporation of public law [as do the large Catholic and Evangelical churches]. The main obstacle is situated in the fact that at least nowadays Moslem communities still lack a "constitution" "that would enable them to develop a relationship with the state based on partnership and lasting collaboration."[40]

The entire German church-state system developed out of a situation where there were only two large churches—the Catholic and the Evangelical. Thus many of the laws and practices being followed do not fit the situation posed by the Muslims, with their many divisions and frequent lack of a formal structure. Some immigrant Muslims have been the subject of hate attacks by neo-Nazi groups, but the official German authorities have done all they can to condemn and discourage such attacks. The more contentious problems are, first, accommodating the Muslim communities into the day-to-day German church-state practices, such as the church tax, religious instruction in the schools, and other such practices to be discussed shortly, and, second, safeguarding the free exercise of the Muslim faith when it comes to certain distinctive, nonmainstream practices.

In regard to the second of these problems, two Muslim leaders we interviewed stated that a serious religious freedom concern of German Muslims was the failure to obtain official approval for the ritual slaughter of animals in keeping with Muslim law. It is now believed that such slaughter is inhumane and thus is forbidden, even though both Muslim leaders insisted it is really no different from the Jewish kosher slaughter of animals, which is allowed. Similarly, problems have occasionally arisen over issues such as coeducational physical education classes in elementary schools in which young girls have sometimes been required to participate in clothing considered immodest, Muslim calls to prayers that have often been banned by local authorities, the right of Muslim women to wear head coverings in their passport photos, and the right of workers and schoolchildren to have time off on Muslim holy days. Issues such as these are being dealt with. Recently the Federal Administrative Court in Berlin, the highest administrative court in Germany, ruled that Muslim girls in elementary schools would be excused from having to participate in coeducation physical education classes.[41] Muslim women are now allowed to wear head coverings in their passport photos, and workers and children are generally allowed time off for holy days if advance permission is obtained. German government and society appears to be making the sorts of adjustments it needs to make to assure that its Muslim population is able to freely practice its faith. There are still areas of tension—as we saw earlier is also the case in the Netherlands and Britain—but progress is being made.

A second continuing free exercise issue concerns the Church of Scientology, which has about 30,000 members in Germany, mainly around Hamburg and a few other large cities.[42] It is openly involved in many commercial enterprises and charges its members high fees for its counseling sessions and other services. The problem in Germany is that the group claims to be a church and thereby eligible for all the recognitions and protections offered religious associations; German authorities claim it is not a church but an economic organization. There is much popular animosity toward Scientology, and the German news media have given wide coverage to former members who now charge brainwashing and economic fleecing. The state of Bavaria refuses to hire Scientologists for civil service jobs, and they experience other forms of economic discrimination. Almost all court decisions have gone against the Church of Scientology. The Federal Administrative Court has ruled that its sale of books and its courses and seminars are a business and the Federal Labor Court in Kassel formally ruled in 1995 that Scientology is not a church, "but an organisation that pursues economic interests under an ecclesiastical cover."[43] Scientology has responded with charges that they are being persecuted as were the Jews during the Nazi era. Feelings run strong on both sides. Scientology has aroused great controversy in many other countries throughout Europe. In the United States it took Scientology 39 years of legal struggles before it won tax-exempt status from the Internal Revenue Service. Acts of discrimination against individual Scientologists appear to violate basic free exercise rights and one hopes that in time they will be dealt with by the Constitutional Court. However, given the borderline religious nature most outside observers ascribe to Scientology, it does not seem fair to hold Germany's refusal to recognize it as bona fide church as a clear case of violating religious free exercise rights.

State Support for Churches

The concept of a church-state partnership has done much to frame questions related to various forms of state cooperation with or support for religion. A booklet put out by the Evangelical Church clearly makes this point: "State and Church, which consider themselves to bear responsibility for the same people in one and the same society, are thus obliged to strive for intelligent cooperation."[44] Robbers has expressed a similar outlook: "It is part of the special position of the Churches that they have in a special way a public mandate."[45] In an interview he stated: "Once you accept that religion is something public, government should also have something to do with it, the community as such should have something to do with it."[46] Church and state—throne and altar—are seen as having different responsibilities, but they both have public responsibilities, they are both important for society as a whole and its welfare, and thus cooperation between the two works to the benefit of society as a whole.

The result is a system that is far from a total separation of church and state, but one that the Constitutional Court has described as a "limping" (*hinkende*) separation.[47] In fact, von Campenhausen has written, "Religious freedom and complete separation of church and state are in a certain sense mutually exclusive."[48] When asked about this statement von Campenhausen answered:

> This is true. If the citizen has the right of religious freedom, the state is not allowed to say, "I will place your children in compulsory school. All their life I will occupy with my state school. You have liberty, but I occupy the life of the children." It can't be. That's contradictory. . . . Separation and religious liberty cannot be combined if you have an entire separation. The State has a responsibility not to prevent its citizens from being religious.[49]

One is back to the concept of religious liberty as a positive as well as a negative freedom. This is not to say that the state should favor any one religious group over another, or should even favor the religious over the nonreligious. One German observer after another whom we interviewed made this point. But it does mean that the state should cooperate with the church and should seek to create space or room for it to fulfill its responsibilities.

This mindset results in government supporting and helping the churches in a number of their activities. One way it does this is by granting the three main, historical religious communities—Evangelical, Catholic, and Jewish—status as public corporations.[50] This status helps assure these religious bodies of their legal autonomy. It means ecclesiastical law has the status of public administrative law, allows the churches to make treaties with the government in which they come to agreement on matters of mutual concern, and grants them several other privileges. Probably its greatest significance is the mindset that it reveals, one that sees the major religious bodies as having a public, or societal, significance. Religion is seen as being more than a purely private concern. Other religious bodies than the three that are now recognized as public corporations potentially can also attain that status by meeting certain requirements, but none has thus far done so.

The failure of the Muslim community to attain public corporation status, given the fact it is the third largest religious community in Germany, is especially noteworthy. This failure is due, not primarily to overt discrimination against Islam, but to the fact that the Muslim organizational structure does not fit the prevailing German pattern. Both the Catholic and Evangelical churches are hierarchical in nature and thus they have centralized councils and leaders who can deal with centralized governmental bureaucratic bodies and leaders. But Islam is not hierarchical in nature; instead, there are a host of decentralized leaders and communities. This has led to an impasse, with German authorities for the most part saying the Muslims need to organize themselves in such a way that they can qualify for public corporation status and many Muslims saying the Germans need to make allowance for their organizational structures. The deputy chairman of the Central Council of Muslims in Germany has described the situation this way: "It is not easy to qualify as a public corporation and Muslim efforts to qualify have thus far been unsuccessful. And the German authorities have not been too keen to do so. They say there is no central organization. . . . But to be fair, the failure to obtain public corporation status is as much the fault of Muslims themselves as of the German authorities."[51]

Best known and most important of the privileges granted to churches that have qualified as public corporations is the church tax (*Kirchensteuer*).[52] Under the church tax all members of the Catholic and Evangelical churches and of Jewish congregations are assessed a fee set by the churches that amounts to about 8 or 9 percent of what is owed the federal government in income taxes. This money is added to one's income tax bill—in fact, it is deducted from one's paychecks by employers along with the income taxes that are owed—and is forwarded to the churches by the government, after the government deducts a small fee (about 3 to 5 percent of the money collected) for collection expenses. People who do not pay are subject to the same penalties and means of collection as are taxes that are owed. The only way a member can escape the church tax is to resign his or her membership in the church, which, due to the public corporation nature of the churches, involves a formal, legal process and an appearance before the civil authorities.

In 1992 the church tax provided over 17 billion deutsche marks (about $12 billion) to the Catholic and Evangelical churches, which amounted to about 80 percent of their total income.[53] It clearly is their major source of income and has made the German churches among the wealthiest in Europe. The money is used to finance both core church activities and wide-ranging charitable and educational activities.

The legal basis for the church tax is found in Article 137(6) of the Weimar Constitution, which has been incorporated into the current Constitution. It reads: "Religious communities that are public corporations shall be entitled to levy taxes in accordance with Land [state] law on the basis of the civil taxation." In a series of decisions the Constitutional Court has upheld the legality of the church tax system, but has also insisted—contrary to practices sometimes followed in the past—that it may only be applied to actual members of the religious bodies. In one case the Court ruled that a husband's wages, who himself was not a church member, could not be subjected to the church tax because his wife was a member: "[A] law may not be viewed as part of the constitutional order if it obligates a person to pay financial benefits to a religious association of which he or she is not a member. . . . [O]ne partner's connection with a church does not obligate the other partner."[54]

The origins of the church tax system go back to the early nineteenth century, when the state confiscated church property in most areas of Germany, and as compensation, the civil governments agreed to make annual payments to the churches. In time these cash payments were transferred into the right of the churches to tax their members, with the civil authorities cooperating in collecting the taxes.

It is important to be clear on what the church tax is and is not. It is not simply a matter of general tax revenues being turned over to the churches. It is a cooperative venture by the churches and the civil authorities, in which the churches levy certain fees on their own members and the civil authorities collect those fees and are reimbursed for their expenses in doing so. Thus one can argue that the church tax does not violate the norm of governmental neutrality—funds are collected only from the church's own members with the amount set by the church, the government is reimbursed for its expenses, and one can avoid their payment by simply leaving the church. Jewish as well as Christian congregations are beneficiaries of it. On the other hand, one can argue that the principle of neutrality is being violated since the coercive power of the state is being put at the disposal of the churches, a service that is not available to nonreligious ideological organizations and smaller religious groups, such as the free churches and the many Muslim groups that have not yet qualified as public corporations.

To the non-German observer the wide acceptance of the church tax system is surprising, especially given the apparent lack of religious zeal on the part of most church members. Most German church members are sporadic in their church involvements, yet they pay the church tax with little complaint. The Greens and the Party of Democratic Socialism (the old East German Communist Party) have come out against the church tax system, but neither of the two largest parties—the CDU/CSU and SPD—have opposed it, and the Free Democratic Party, after coming out against it in the 1970s, has tacitly abandoned its opposition to it. The church tax and its general acceptance, more than anything else, helps demonstrate that the concept of church-state partnership in

German society is a concept that has permeated German society and is not merely a theoretical or elite principle. None of the persons we interviewed made an explicit comparison between the church tax and the United Way charitable contribution system in the United States, but we made that connection several times after listening to Germans explain the church tax and its acceptance. The churches are generally seen as socially important institutions; they strengthen German society, symbolize German culture, and ably provide many charitable and educational services. The church tax is one means by which one can relatively painlessly—because of the wage deductions—fulfill one's financial obligation to these all-important cultural, charitable, and educational institutions.

This is not to say that the church tax is without criticism or controversy. A Catholic journalist whom we interviewed and who has had his differences with the church hierarchy complained strongly that the church tax greatly strengthens the power of the central church hierarchy, since the money goes to the regional church offices and is distributed downward from there. Others have felt that the church tax has made the churches overly complacent. One person we interviewed compared the situation to one that is frequently alleged to occur when a developed nation gives too much money too freely to an underdeveloped nation: complacency, a strengthening of forces defending the status quo, and a sapping of initiative and creativity.

The unification of Germany in 1990 has posed some special problems for the church tax system. One is that unification led to the imposition of an income tax surcharge of 7.5 percent to help pay for needed economic support to the former East German territories. This is about the same amount that the church tax adds to one's income tax, and has led some people to think they were being taxed twice for more altruistic or Germanwide purposes. Thus there has been a recent increase in church leavings. A second factor is based on the fact that the residents of the former German Democratic Republic were not accustomed to paying the church tax and suddenly were subjected to it. In the GDR the churches had continued to impose a church tax, but the state did not cooperate in collecting it, and thus in practice it had become a voluntary contribution. The resignation of church memberships has been especially high in the area of the old GDR. But one must be careful not to overstate the extent of church membership loss. The head of the internal research office for the Evangelical Church estimates the churches are losing about 1 percent of their membership a year, a trend he believes will continue.[55] He indicated, however, evidence demonstrates that about two-thirds of this loss is due to demographic factors such as a low

birth rate and only about one-third is due to people leaving the church
(and among those it is unknown how many are leaving because of the
church tax).

In addition to the church tax, there are some other forms of direct
governmental support for the churches, usually at the state or local level.
Some state or local governments help subsidize the salaries of certain
church officials or help fund the construction or upkeep of church
buildings. Such supports are largely holdovers from an earlier age when
there were many such financial supports for the churches, and today are
usually justified on the basis that non-religious organizations often receive such help. As Robbers has expressed it: "Further, many churches
receive allocations from the State for activities in the same way as other
publicly funded events; it is a part of the idea of State neutrality that
Church activities are not to be put in a worse position than that of State
funded local athletic clubs."[56]

This section has outlined several forms of direct government cooperation with churches in their wide range of activities, including their
core religious activities such as worship. There is no legally, formally
established church, yet the Evangelical, Catholic, and Jewish faiths have
certain advantages that other religious bodies and competing secular ideologies do not fully share.

Church, State, and Education

The distinguishing mark of Germany regarding religion and education was, until very recently, the domination of public education by
confessional schools (that is, schools that were public in the sense of
being financed, owned, and controlled by government, and confessional
in the sense of being marked by either Catholic or Evangelical religious
exercises and teachings). At the time of the writing of the Weimar Constitution there was a strong movement to develop secular schools that
would be committed to teaching loyalty to the new liberal, political
order, but the Catholic Center Party, with the help of conservative
Evangelicals, was strong enough to force a compromise that made room
for the continued existence of confessional schools.[57] As a result, confessional schools dominated public education in the interwar period. Of
the 53,000 public schools, 55 percent were confessional Evangelical
schools, 28 percent were confessional Catholic schools, 15 percent were
interdenominational (that is, of a broadly Christian, nonsectarian na-

ture), and a handful were either confessional Jewish schools (97) or secular (295).[58]

There was a strong effort during the Nazi era to undermine the diversity of the school system in favor of schools uniformly supportive of the regime. As one Nazi leader bragged, "The curriculum of all categories in our schools has already been so far reformed in an anti-Christian and anti-Jewish spirit that the generation which is growing up will be protected from the black [that is, clerical] swindle."[59]

Following World War II the occupying powers generally favored doing away with confessional schools in favor of unified, secular schools.[60] Again, this was resisted by church authorities, especially by the Catholic Church. In the western zone, therefore, the occupying authorities allowed local areas to decide whether they wished interdenominational schools or confessional schools. The 1949 Basic Law placed the responsibility for education with the state governments, not the national government. Initially, most Catholic areas opted for confessional schools and most Protestant areas for interdenominational schools. As recently as 1967, 40 percent of all schools in Germany were public Catholic schools, 17 percent were public Evangelical schools, 40 percent were interdenominational (or nonconfessional, sometimes referred to as "Christian") public schools, and 3 percent were private schools.[61] But things have changed. Protestants had for some time not seen the need for separate confessional schools, and starting in the 1960s the often inferior quality of the public Catholic schools—many of which were very small—drew public attention.[62] As a result many Catholic areas opted for interdenominational Christian schools. (The terminology here is confusing for Americans, since even the interdenominational or "Christian" schools are public schools.) In 1968, for example, Bavaria—a heavily Catholic area—voted by referendum to do away with Catholic schools in favor of interdenominational Christian schools. The religious nature of interdenominational schools is largely confined to prayers, separate voluntary classes in the religion of one's choice, and a general emphasis on the historical or cultural role of religion in Germany society.

Today four types of schools are found in Germany. The most common type is the interdenominational Christian public school, followed by the confessional public school (usually Catholic in nature, but sometimes Evangelical). There are also secular (or nondenominational) public schools—most often found in northern cities such as Bremen and Berlin—and private confessional schools.

The legal, constitutional basis for public schools that have confessional or religious exercises and instruction as an integral part of them—

practices that would be clearly unconstitutional in the United States under current Supreme Court interpretations—is found in subsections 2 through 4 of Article 7 of the Basic Law:

2. Parents and guardians have the right to decide whether children receive religious instruction.
3. Religious instruction shall form part of the curriculum in state schools except non-denominational schools. Without prejudice to the state's right of supervision, religious instruction shall be given in accordance with the doctrine of the religious community concerned. Teachers may not be obligated to give religious instruction against their will.
4. The right to establish private schools shall be guaranteed. Private schools as alternatives to state schools shall require the approval of the state and be subject to Land legislation.

A 1975 case decided by the Constitutional Court dealt directly with the issue of religious instruction in public schools. The state of Baden-Württenberg had decided in 1967 to establish interdenominational Christian schools. Some nonreligious parents objected to the religious education their children were receiving. The Court ruled in favor of the interdenominational school, and its reasoning in doing so reveals much about the German approach to this issue and how it differs from the American one. The Court first noted that "the complainants' request to keep the education of their children free from all religious influences . . . must inevitably conflict with the desire of other citizens to afford their children a religious education. . . ."[63] It then went on to make a crucial observation that the U. S. Supreme Court has never accepted: "The elimination of all ideological and religious references would not neutralize the existing ideological tensions and conflicts, but would disadvantage parents who desire a Christian education for their children and would result in compelling them to send their children to a lay school that would roughly correspond with the complainants' wishes."[64] The key point made by the Court—and one that is hard to deny—is that a school stripped of all religious elements is not in a zone of neutrality between the religious and the secular, but is implicitly secular in nature. In such a school the children of the nonreligious parents would receive the exact sort of education their parents desire; the children of religious parents would not. Given this fact and the resulting necessity for compromise, the Court ruled that the state should be given the latitude to make the policy decision that it had. "As a result, the state legislature is not absolutely prohibited from incorporating Christian references when it establishes a state elementary school, even though a minority of parents have no choice but to send their children."[65] It then went on to state that the school may not proselytize, that no one may be forced to attend religion classes, and that Christianity in secular disciplines should be limited to references to it as a formative cultural force in western civilization.

Article 7(3) requires the government to assure the presence of religious instruction in state-run schools: "Religious instruction shall form part of the curriculum in state schools. . . ." The operative word here is "shall," not "may." Also important is the fact that religious instruction is to be a part of the standard curriculum, not an extracurricular or ancillary course of study. It is, however, to be voluntary. For children up to the age of fourteen, parents may choose the nature of the religious instruction they are to receive or decide they are to receive no religious instruction at all. At the age of fourteen, the decision rests with the students, not their parents. Thus the religious instruction made available in most German schools is similar to the in-school released time programs the U. S. Supreme Court rejected as violating the First Amendment in a 1948 decision.[66]

It is also important to note that the religious bodies themselves, not the public school authorities, control the content of the religious courses of study. One sees here the concept of church autonomy entering in. One Evangelical church official explained to us that this helps assure the religious neutrality of the state.[67] He made clear it is the parents'—not the state's—responsibility to teach religion, values, and worldviews. This they accomplish by choosing what religious instruction their children are to receive and, through their religious community, determining the content of that instruction. The state neither assigns children to the religious instruction classes nor controls their content.

In practice these classes are for two or three hours a week, and are taught by regular public school teachers (although under Article 7(3) of the Constitution no teacher can be forced to teach a class in religion against his or her will) or by pastors specially appointed to this role. This system poses a problem for small Christian religious groups, Jews, and Muslims. Given the overwhelming number of Germans that belong to either the Catholic or Evangelical churches, it is difficult for this system to accommodate small religious communities. Almost all the classes now are in the Catholic or Evangelical religious traditions. Normally there need to be six to eight students to justify a special class for them, and given the role of the religious communities themselves in developing the actual courses of study to be followed, the religious communities need to be large enough and sufficiently organized to come together in agreement on a course of study the public schools can then implement. With only 47,000 Jews out of a population of 81 million, they almost invariably do not have enough students in any given school to qualify for a separate class. The same is true of small Christian groups. The Muslims often have enough numbers, but they do not have the tradition of a centralized, hierarchical organization. As is the case with public corporation status, difficulties have arisen because the current German system was developed to accommodate the more structured, bureaucratized Catholic and Evangelical churches and does not accommodate the prevailing situation among the Muslims. Interviews with Muslim leaders indicated that this situation is viewed among Muslims as a more serious problem than either certain free exercise problems or difficulties in obtaining public corporation status. M. A. H. Hobohm, deputy chairman of the Central Council of Muslims in Germany and managing director of the King Fahad Academy in Bonn, when asked if he thought this situation would be resolved in the next four or five years, gave evidence of both the hope and the frustration of Muslims on this issue:

> We hope it will happen earlier, of course we are aware this cannot be done overnight. One cannot overnight start religious instruction classes at all German public schools where there are Muslim children. But we have to start with three or four schools in one or two of the states, and then gradually, year by year, increase the schools where such instruction takes place. . . . It is a rather cumbersome and difficult process. The German authorities are not in principle against it. But they are also not very understanding, and not very helpful. And very often we have to face a situation where the German authorities tell us, "We do not know with whom to talk in such matters because there are so many Islamic communities and even Islamic faith organizations." They either do not really understand that in Islam there is no hierarchical order, no organization with a center, or they don't want to understand it. Sometimes I have the feeling we have stated this to them so often that if they really don't understand it, it is because they lack the will to understand it.[68]

For both practical and theoretical reasons most schools in the states of the former GDR are not offering religious instruction.[69] Practically, there are often not enough teachers with the background and interest to teach classes in religion. More theoretically, some of the more thoroughly secular states, such as Brandenburg, object in principle to offering religious instruction in the public schools. Brandenburg now offers optional instruction in ethics and religion, but of a common nature, without dividing students into Catholics, Evangelicals, and nonbelievers. Others believe—reacting to the often propagandizing nature of the schools under communism—that the schools ought not to be involved at all in teaching values, religion, or worldviews. There is also a growing movement among the deeply religious toward private religiously based schools.

In regard to religious exercises in the public schools, most confessional and interdenominational schools have prayers at the beginning of the school day and sometimes at the end. As Kommers has written, "The predominant German view is that such practices constitute an important aspect of religious liberty so long as freedom of choice prevails."[70] As seen earlier, in 1979 the Constitutional Court considered the question of the constitutionality of such prayers and ruled in favor of their constitutionality based on the positive right of religious parents to have their children pray in school, as long as the voluntary nature of the prayers is maintained.

The church-state issue that stirred up the most controversy in Germany in recent years concerned a Bavarian law that required a crucifix to be displayed in every public school classroom. In 1995 the Constitutional Court ruled that if any student objected to having a crucifix in the classroom, it would have to be removed. At the heart of its decision was the Court's conclusion that "freedom of faith as guaranteed by Article 4(1) of the Basic Law requires the state to remain neutral in matters of faith and religion."[71] The Court then went on to weigh the positive freedom of religious parents to have a religious symbol such as a cross present in their children's classrooms against the negative freedom of nonreligious or non-Christian parents to have their children's classrooms free of a Christian religious symbol. It concluded: "Parents and pupils who adhere to the Christian faith cannot justify the display of the cross by invoking their positive freedom of religious liberty. All parents and pupils are equally entitled to the positive freedom of faith, not just Christian parents and pupils."[72] It then pointed out that the key distinction it saw between the display of the crucifix in the classrooms and prayer and other Christian religious aspects in the public schools was the element of voluntarism.

> In as much as schools heed the Constitution, leaving room for religious instruction, school prayer, and other religious events, all of these activities must be conducted on a voluntary basis and the school must ensure that students who do not wish to participate in these activities are excused from them and suffer no discrimination because of their decision not to participate. The situation is different with respect to

the display of the cross. Students who do not share the same faith are unable to remove themselves from its presence and message.[73]

The dissenting justices argued that "the negative freedom of religion must not be allowed to negate the positive right to manifest one's religious freedom in the event the two conflict."[74] In taking this stand they stressed that the cross did not have a proselytizing purpose and did not require any overt acts of recognition or acceptance from the non-Christian students.

This decision unleashed a storm of criticism throughout Germany. Chancellor Kohl condemned it. Newspapers and radio call-in shows debated it, with the clear preponderance of opinion indicating opposition to it. In fact, the criticism grew so intense and the calls for ignoring the Court's decision so frequent that there were fears for the constitutional order and the legitimacy of the Court. Justice Dieter Grimm, one of the Constitutional Court justices who had been in the majority, felt compelled to write a major statement in which he argued for the rule of law and called for obedience to the Court's decision, even by those who strongly disagree with it.[75] The furor began to die down only when the Court made clear it had not ruled that all crucifixes in Bavarian classrooms must come down, but only that they must come down if students in a particular classroom register a complaint. The vast majority stay on the classroom walls.

This decision and the reactions to it illustrate several key points. First, to an American observer—coming from a political system where even the posting of the Ten Commandments in classrooms and the presence of a cross in a city's seal have been held unconstitutional[76]—it is surprising that the question of crucifixes in public school classrooms is even being debated. That this issue is at the cutting edge of church-state debate in Germany today illustrates the extent to which church and state are in a cooperative relationship. The uproar the decision created in the nation reveals the strong support that still exists for this relationship. Second, this case illustrates the broad acceptance of the concepts of neutrality and positive religious freedom. The reasoning of both the majority and dissenting justices revolved around these concepts. They were accepted by both sides in this case; they differed only on how they were to be applied in this instance. Both sides agreed the state should be neutral on matters of religion, neither favoring nor discriminating against any religious or ideological perspective, and in interpreting this neutrality, both agreed that a genuine neutrality sometimes requires the state to take certain positive steps in order to create the possibility or the space people of faith need to live their faith.

There are—compared to the other countries studied in this book—few private schools in Germany, either religiously or secularly based. Only about 5 percent of students attend private schools.[77] Of these about 80 percent attend church-related schools, and of these about three-fourths attend Catholic schools and one-fourth Evangelical schools.[78] Private schools receive most of their current expenses—but not their capital expenses—from public funds, although the exact amount they receive can vary from 75 to 90 percent of their costs.[79]

The Constitution assures in Article 7(4) the right to establish private schools, but they must be approved by the state government and obtaining that approval can be a difficult, time-consuming process. The basic requirement for approval is a school's ability to demonstrate that it is equivalent to the public schools in terms of educational quality and that it does not discriminate in its acceptance of pupils on the basis of the economic means of their parents. But once such standards have been met, the Constitutional Court ruled in 1987, private schools must receive public funding. The Court did so largely on the basis that educational freedom requires that parents be able to choose for their children the school with the religious or ideological worldview with which they are in agreement. Without state subsidies this freedom would be only available to parents with wealth. "Only when [private schooling] is fundamentally available to all citizens without regard to the personal financial situation can the [constitutionally] protected educational freedom actually be realized and claimed on an equal basis by all parents and students. . . . This constitutional norm must thus be considered as a mandate to lawmakers to protect and promote private schools."[80]

There are two private Muslim schools, in Berlin and Munich, that follow the normal German curriculum in additional to providing Islamic instruction.[81] They—in distinction from the experience of Muslim schools in Britain—have qualified for government funding, on the same basis as have other private confessional schools in the Catholic and Evangelical Christian traditions. Other Muslim schools that do not follow the German curriculum, but place a heavy emphasis on distinctive Muslim lessons and practices, do not receive government funds since they have been unable to demonstrate that they offer an education equivalent to that of the public schools.

Given the amount of religion that is allowed in the German public schools, it is not surprising that religiously based schools, once they receive official state recognition, find few, if any, restrictions placed on their ability to integrate religious elements into their programs. They are free, for example, to appoint teachers on the basis of their church membership.[82] The key requirements are that they must meet the state-established curriculum standards and their students must be able to do well in the comprehensive exams that are an integral part of the German educational system.

One final note on private church-related education involves the widespread church-sponsored kindergartens. German children typically start school at the age of six and the regular school system does not contain kindergartens as in the United States. A majority of families send their children from three to five years of age to kindergartens, which are sponsored by churches or independent societies created for that purpose. The official in charge of kindergarten programs for the Evangelical Church in the Rhineland region told us that roughly one-third of the costs of its kindergarten programs are covered by government subsidies, one-third by the local churches, and one-third by payments of parents.[83] There are no state-imposed limits on prayers, Bible stories, or other religious elements in the kindergarten programs.

In summary, based on the constitutionally enshrined concept of parental control over the religious upbringing of one's children, the norm of governmental neutrality in matters of religion, and the concept of positive religious freedom, Germany allows various forms of religion into its public schools as long as the principle of voluntary participation is respected. It also permits widespread public financial support for religious schools without interference with their religious missions, as long as the educational quality of the schools—as determined by the state governments—is assured. The sizable Muslim minority in Germany has been included in the system of public funding of private religious schools, but has experienced difficulties in breaking into the system of religious instruction in the public schools. Creating new forms and procedures to allow greater accommodation of its Muslim population in the public schools remains the biggest challenge in the area of religious freedom and education.

Church, State, and Nonprofit Service Organizations

Helmut Anheier of Johns Hopkins University has noted that "in Germany a highly developed nonprofit sector *and* a highly developed welfare state coexist. As the welfare state developed, the nonprofit sector in Germany expanded."[84] This is the case because the German government relies extensively on private nonprofit organizations to deliver most of the social services that are the hallmark of the German welfare state. The Catholic-inspired principle of subsidiarity plays a crucial role here.

> The doctrine of subsidiarity essentially holds that the responsibility for caring for individuals' needs should always be vested in the units of social life closest to the individual—the family, the parish, the community, the voluntary association—and that larger, or higher level, units should be enlisted only when a problem clearly exceeds the capabilities of these primary units. . . . What is more, the doctrine holds that the higher units have an obligation not only to avoid usurping the position of the lower units, but to help the lower units perform their role.[85]

Anheier and Wolfgang Seibel report: "The principle of subsidiarity of public welfare became the most influential ideological counterweight to state-centered ideas of welfare provision."[86] It has been explicitly incorporated into several laws that require the government not to take over and provide social services directly if there are private social service agencies able and willing to provide them. Section 4 of the Social Assistance Act states that "if assistance in individual cases is ensured by free welfare associations, the [public] social assistance bodies shall refrain from implementing their own measures."[87] The Youth Welfare Act contains the provision: "In so far as suitable establishments and arrangements provided by the free youth assistance associations are available or can be extended or provided, the [public] Youth Welfare Office shall not offer such establishments and arrangements on its own."[88] The theory of subsidiarity has resulted, in the words of Anheier, in "no less than a protected, state-financed system of private service and assistance delivery."[89]

The practice of relying extensively on nonprofit private associations for the provision of social services has a historical as well as theoretical basis. A host of associations emerged in Germany in the nineteenth century and "became the elementary form of political opposition against the state; after the failed revolution of 1848, they also became a surrogate for the democracy that had not been achieved within the state order itself."[90] As a result, associations playing an intermediate role between the individual and the government gained a certain legitimacy. Germany's experience under the Nazis worked to reinforce this legitimacy, with private associations coming to be seen as a way to avoid a dangerous, overcentralized, dominant government.

There are six main associations of social service and health care organizations that are referred to as the free welfare associations. They carry out most of these privately delivered services. These associations are Diakonisches Werk (the Evangelical Church's federation of social service and health agencies), Caritas (the Catholic counterpart to Diakonisches Werk), the Central Welfare Association for Jews in Germany (Zentralwohlfahrsstelle der Juden in Deutschland), the Workers' Welfare Association (Arbeiterwohlfahrt—an association of secular social agencies with ties to the Social Democratic Party), the German Equity Welfare Association (Deutscher Paritätischer Wohlfahrtsverband—an association of secular agencies not aligned with any political party), and the Red Cross (Deutsches Rotes Kreuz). These free welfare associations "provide 70 percent of all family services, 60 percent of all services for the elderly, 40 percent of all hospital beds, and 90 percent of all employment for the handicapped. The free welfare associations employ 548,420 full-time and 202,706 part-time staff. The number of volunteers is estimated at 1.5 million. . . ."[91] The first three of these free welfare associations are all religious in nature and two of them, Caritas and Diakonisches Werk, are by far the largest among the free welfare associations.

The religious associations share fully in the receipt of public funds. According to one estimate 25 to 40 percent of Caritas's funds come from public subsidies and 25 to 30 of Diakonisches Werk's funds do so.[92] These figures do not, of course, include funds originating in the church tax system, many of which find their way into the social welfare programs of the sponsoring churches. In response to a parliamentary question the finance minister reported that in 1995 the federal government granted the Catholic Church 227 million marks and the Evangelical church 177 million marks for a variety of social and research purposes (about $162 million and $126 million). For example, over 21 million marks was given to the Evangelical Church and almost 26 million marks to the Catholic Church for programs for families, seniors, and women and children.[93] When visiting a home for handicapped young people in Neukirchen sponsored by Diakonisches Werk we were told it is 100 percent funded by the government. Through the Central Welfare Association for Jews in Germany the small Jewish community shares in the receipt of public funds, especially for the resettlement of Jewish immigrants from eastern European countries.

There are very few nonprofit Muslim service organizations at the present time. One Muslim leader we interviewed had to think for several minutes before coming up with only two examples of such agencies: an agency in Munich where people can go for psychological help and a Muslim women's organization that has set up a telephone service for giving advice.[94] Those few Muslim social service organizations that do exist receive some funding from individual state and local governments, but they are not included in the cooperative funding schemes of the federal government. In theory they are eligible for such funding, but their very small numbers and the lack of an organized, centralized push for such funds have thus far prevented them from sharing in national funding schemes as do the two large Christian communities and the Jewish community.

Anheier and Seibel have made the additional important point that the nonprofit-government relationship goes beyond financial support by the government. "[A]s a result of both the principle of subsidiarity and the principle of self-governance, nonprofit organizations tend to be relatively well-integrated into the policy making function of government. In many areas of legislation, public authorities are required to consult nonprofit organizations in matters of economic, social and cultural policy."[95] There indeed is a nonprofit-government partnership in providing important social and health services, a partnership that includes the religiously based organizations as full partners.

The concept of church autonomy is important for understanding the degree of freedom religious nonprofit service organizations have in pursuing their religious missions, even when working as partners with the government in providing services. The concept of church autonomy includes religious service organizations. Robbers has made this point clearly:

> A church's right of self-determination is not restricted to a narrowly-drawn field of specifically "ecclesiastical" activities. The idea of freedom of religious practice extends to preserve the right of self-determination in other areas that are also based or founded upon religious objectives, such as the running of hospitals, kindergartens, retirement homes, private schools and universities.[96]

In an interview Robbers reemphasized this point. "Caritas, Diakonisches Werk, private schools, and kindergartens are a part of the church. They are ministries for the performance of persons' faith, for following Christ's example. They are the church being the church as much as saying prayers or lighting candles in a church. Therefore, the principle of self-determination applies to these ministries as fully as it does to the churches themselves."[97]

Article 137(3) of the Weimar Constitution, which was incorporated into Germany's current Constitution, reads in part: "Every religious community shall regulate and administer its affairs independently within the limits of the law valid for all." The significance of this provision, when combined with the previously made point that religiously based service organizations are considered an integral part of the church, can be seen in the 1983 Catholic Hospital Abortion Case. A Catholic hospital had dismissed a doctor after he had publicly stated he opposed the church's teaching on abortion. The Constitutional Court held that the hospital was an "affair" of the church and thus under church regulation.

> By laying down such duties of loyalty in a contract of employment, the ecclesiastical employer not only relies on the general freedom of contract, but he simultaneously makes use of his constitutional right to self-determination, [thus] permitting churches to shape [their social activity], even when regulated by contracts of employment according to a particular vision of Christian community service shared by their members.[98]

The Court went on to hold that, given the fact that Catholic canon law views abortion as the killing of innocent human life, to require the church to retain on staff a doctor who rejects this teaching would undermine the church's religious mission as it has defined it. Both the concept that a Catholic hospital is an integral part of the church and that under the Constitution the church has a right to self-determination entered into this decision.

There are still frequent struggles between the various religiously based service organizations and government regulators. But as seen in the Netherlands in chapter 3, most of the struggles revolve around the issue of the cutback of government funds in a time of retrenchment and issues related to professional performance standards, not issues of religion being integrated into the programs financed by the government. An official in the central office of Diakonisches Werk in Stuttgart told us: "We usually as a welfare organization really fight with different government departments in Bonn when they openly or covertly try to influence our autonomy. One is spiritual autonomy and the other is professional autonomy. In the case of spiritual standards they really do not interfere that much. But when it comes down to professional standards they try all the time."[99] This was a theme related to us by almost every person involved in religiously based service agencies that were receiving government funds. But we frequently were assured that when it comes to such questions as having salaried chaplains or pastors conducting religious services, requiring agency employees to be members of the sponsoring church and to meet expected behavior standards, and having devotional exercises as a part of their programs, they ran into no problems with government officials. One official in the central office of the Evangelical Church told us the big problem was not government interference, but finding enough young people with a deep religious life who wished to work for church social agencies.

In short, Germany has an extensive system of public funding of a wide variety of religiously based social service and health care associations. The strong German commitment to providing basic services, not through centralized bureaucracies but through private nonprofit associations, and its commitment to religious pluralism implied by the principles of neutrality and positive religious freedom, come together to support this system. The Evangelical and Catholic churches, with their large, well-established social and health ministries, share fully in this partnership, as do the Jewish and, to a lesser degree, the Muslim communities.

Concluding Observations

At the beginning of this chapter we suggested that the German system of church-state partnership and church autonomy has some important parallels with both the principled pluralism of the Netherlands and the partial establishment of England. We return to that observation.

Germany clearly does not have a formally established church as does England. Nevertheless, the underlying mindset that supports the concept of a church-state partnership has some similarities to the English mindset that supports its partial establishment, resulting in Germany's church-state relationship possessing some elements of the informal, multiple establishment model mentioned in chapter 1. Leopold Turowski, a Catholic Church representative in Bonn, has written that "religious and secular responsibilities are essentially aspects of a single common good, meant to fulfill the needs of one and the same human person in unified societal existence."[100] In so doing he has given expression to a concept at the heart of the German mindset as it addresses issues of church and state. Church and state—throne and altar—are seen as twin pillars on which rests a strong, prosperous German society. Throne and altar are in a partnership. This means that most Germans see religion as having an important public role to play as a unifying, inspiring, educating, critiquing force in society. As one American scholar has noted: "The deeply rooted German tendency to think of church and state as joint bearers of the public order has been an enduring feature of German *Staatskirchenrecht* [church-state law]. . . . [T]he notion that religion is an integral element of the public realm remains."[101]

As a result Germany supports a number of practices in which the state cooperates with, assists, and makes room for religion, such as the church tax and prayers of a broadly consensual nature in public schools. The formal ties between church and state such as those found in England are not present in Germany, but there are various informal means of church-state cooperation and support for consensual religious beliefs and practices, as there are in England. To the extent this constitutes an informal establishment, it is a multiple establishment, in that the cooperation and support extend to Protestants and Catholics alike and to smaller religious groups to some extent.

But this is not the full story. German church-state practice also has some important parallels with the principled pluralism of the Netherlands and its embrace of the pluralist church-state model. Germany places a strong emphasis on church autonomy and explicitly articulates principles such as state neutrality on matters of religion and freedom of religion as a positive right. These principles are similar to the principles of pluralism espoused by the Dutch and modify and qualify the German commitment to a church-state partnership. Germans see the partnership concept and the neutrality, autonomy, and positive religious freedom principles as complementing each other in such a way as to lead to greater religious freedom for all. Kommers has written that "the accommodationist stance of German constitutional law is often defended as a means of maintaining pluralism and diversity in the face of powerful secularizing trends toward social uniformity and moral rootlessness."[102] What many American observers would see as leftover elements of religious establishment that are subversive of religious pluralism and diversity, most Germans would insist are essential to religious pluralism and diversity.

The key to understanding these divergent perspectives is that the typical German observer has a concept of religious freedom as possessing both positive and negative aspects, while Americans tend to see religious freedom largely as a negative freedom. Rudolf Weth, the director of a federation of Evangelical social agencies in Neukirchen, referred, in an interview with us, to "positive religious neutrality."[103] This "positive religious neutrality" conceives of the state as not advancing any religious or philosophical viewpoint—it must be neutral. There was enough of that, he indicated, in the Nazi era and in the GDR. In that sense there is a separation of church and state. But, he argued, the state must also have a holistic view of human beings. People are religious, ideological beings. The state should not favor any one religion or ideology, but it must make room for the religious, ideological nature of humankind.

Under this perspective the state will be truly neutral only if it sometimes takes certain positive steps in order to make room for or to accommodate those who wish to live a religious life. Recall the Constitutional Court decision in the *Interdenominational School Case* that made the telling argument that "elimination of all ideological and religious references would not neutralize the existing ideological tensions and conflicts, but would disadvantage parents who desire a Christian education for their children. . . ."[104] A school that is made religiously "neutral" by removing all references to religion is neutral among contending religious traditions, but it is not neutral between religious and secular perspectives. Rather, it implicitly promotes a general secular "uniformity and moral rootlessness." German law—in contrast to American law—has recognized and sought to accommodate this perspective in its church-state stances.

There is a logic and an appeal to the German mindset on church and state and especially to the principles of neutrality and positive religious freedom that underlie them. Germany is clearly and appropriately committed to religious freedom and pluralism. It has largely been successful in giving due recognition to the importance of religion in the life of the nation and in the lives of many of its citizens, and at the same time has assured the freedom of those without religious faith. It has an expansive concept of the free exercise of religion. Its efforts to integrate both religion and secular ideologies into the public schools and to fund both religiously and secularly based social service agencies and private schools are fully in keeping with religious pluralism and state religious neutrality. One can always question whether in specific instances—such as consensual prayers and crucifixes in the public schools—the German Constitutional Court has reached the conclusion most in keeping with religious neutrality and freedom for all. But the German emphasis on an expansive concept of the free exercise of religion, the commitment to governmental neutrality on matters of religion, and the concept of positive religious rights have led the German courts—at the very least—to frame issues such as these appropriately and to ask the right questions.

All this is not to say that the German approach to church-state questions is without problems. Even if one takes the concept of positive religious freedom fully into account, the church tax seems to violate the norm of governmental neutrality. Although the church tax is imposed only on church members and the civil government is reimbursed for its expenses in collecting it, it nonetheless gives the three religious communities qualifying as public corporations an advantage over other religious communities and secular ideological organizations. Also, Germany is having difficulties fully integrating Muslims into the present system of religious freedom and church-state cooperation. Admittedly, Muslims have recently arisen as a religious minority and their organizational structures do not fit the prevailing German scene. But if Germany is to live up fully to its own norm of governmental neutrality, it will have to find ways, especially in the field of public education, to treat Muslims in a manner equivalent to the traditional, more established Christian communities. There may need to be compromise and flexibility on part of the civil authorities as well as the Muslim population and its leaders.

But these shortcomings ought not to deflect from the fact that Germany—building on the basic principles of neutrality, church autonomy, and positive religious rights and a strong emphasis on free exercise rights—has largely dealt successfully with issues of religious pluralism. It has done so while also paying deference to the traditional German sense of religion as a public force in society. It does not relegate religion to the private sphere as Enlightenment liberalism would do, but has created a public role, a public space for religion, and at the same time it allows for a plurality of religious and secular belief systems. This is what the now dominant liberal Enlightenment tradition in the United States has said cannot be done, which makes the fact that Germany has been largely successful in doing so all the more impressive.

Notes

1. Gerhard Robbers, "State and Church in Germany," in Gerhard Robbers, ed., *State and Church in the European Union* (Baden-Baden: Nomos Verlagsgesellschaft, 1996), 60.

2. Donald P. Kommers, *The Constitutional Jurisprudence of the Federal Republic of Germany,* 2nd ed. (Durham: Duke University Press, 1997), 461.

3. See Gerda Lederer, "Trends in Authoritarianism: A Study of Adolescents in West Germany and the United States since 1945," *Journal of Cross-Cultural Psychology,* 13 (1982), 299–314. Also see David P. Conradt, "From Output Orientation to Regime Support: Changing German Political Culture," in Ursula Hoffman-Lange, ed., *Social and Political Structures in West Germany: From Authoritarian to Postindustrial Democracy* (Boulder, Colo.: Westview, 1991), 127–42. Since these studies were completed before the 1990 unification of West and East Germany, the impact of the addition of the former East German population into the West German population is not taken into account by these studies.

4. See Robbers, "State and Church in Germany," 57.

5. The terminology used to refer to the Protestant Church in Germany can be confusing to Americans. The Evangelische Kirche in Deutschland (EKD) is usually translated the Evangelical Church, and we follow this customary practice in this book. But this term ought not to be confused with the way in which

"evangelical" is often used the in American and British contexts to refer to the more theologically conservative, biblically oriented wing of Protestantism.

6. Frederic Spotts, *The Churches and Politics in Germany* (Middletown, Conn.: Wesleyan University Press, 1973), 352.

7. *The Evangelical Church in Germany: An Introduction* (Hannover, Germany: Church Office of the Evangelical Church in Germany, 1987), section 2.

8. As reported by Spotts, *The Churches and Politics in Germany,* 6.

9. See "Religion in Society," *American Enterprise* (November/December 1992), 96.

10. On the Constitutional Court see Kommers, *The Constitutional Jurisprudence of the Federal Republic of Germany,* 3–29, and Donald P. Kommers, *The Federal Constitutional Court* (Washington, D.C.: Institute for Contemporary German Studies, 1994).

11. John S. Conway, "The Political Role of German Protestantism, 1870–1990," *Journal of Church and State* 34 (1992), 820. Also see Daniel R. Borg, "German National Protestantism as a Civil Religion," in Menachem Mor, ed., *International Perspectives on Church and State* (Omaha: Creighton University Press, 1993), 255–67.

12. Paul Banwell Means, *Things That Are Caesar's: The Genesis of the German Church Conflict* (New York: Round Table Press, 1935), 84.

13. Article 136. The outlawing of a state church was found in Article 137.

14. Spotts, *The Churches and Politics in Germany,* 9.

15. Spotts, *The Churches and Politics in Germany,* 9.

16. Quoted in Spotts, *The Churches and Politics in Germany,* 11. On this declaration also see Conway, "The Political Role of German Protestantism," 830–31.

17. Spotts, *The Churches and Politics in Germany,* 291.

18. The then-West German authorities insisted on calling the Constitution a "Basic Law" (*Grundgesetz*), since it was seen as being of a provisional nature because of the Soviet zone (soon to become the German Democratic Republic, or East Germany) not being included in the government that was being created. In this book we will use Basic Law and Constitution interchangeably, since the Basic Law functions exactly as a Constitution.

19. All quotations from the Basic Law are taken from the English translation published by the Press and Information Office of the Federal Republic of Germany (1994).

20. On the church in East Germany see Karl Cordell, "The Role of the Evangelical Church in the GDR," *Government and Opposition* 25 (1990), 48–59, and John P. Burgess, "Church-State Relations in East Germany: The Church as a 'Religious' and 'Political' Force," *Journal of Church and State* 32 (1990), 17–35.

21. Cordell, "The Role of the Evangelical Church in the GDR," 20.

22. Cordell, "The Role of the Evangelical Church in the GDR," 21.

23. See "Religion in Society," 94–97.

24. Interview with Axel von Campenhausen (February 13, 1996).

25. *Religious Oath Case* (1972), 33 BVerfGE 23. Reprinted and translated in Kommers, *The Constitutional Jurisprudence of the Federal Republic of Germany,* 454.

26. *School Prayer Case* (1979), 52 BVerfGE 223. Reprinted and translated in Kommers, *The Constitutional Jurisprudence of the Federal Republic of Germany,* 464–65.

27. *Rumpelkammer Case* (1968), 24 BVerfGE 236. Reprinted and translated in Kommers, *The Constitutional Jurisprudence of the Federal Republic of Germany*, 446–447.

28. *Rumpelkammer Case* (1968), 24 BVerfGE 236. Reprinted and translated in Kommers, *The Constitutional Jurisprudence of the Federal Republic of Germany*, 446.

29. *Religious Oath Case* (1972), 33 BVerfGE 23. Reprinted and translated in Kommers, *The Constitutional Jurisprudence of the Federal Republic of Germany*, 454.

30. *Religious Oath Case* (1972), 33 BVerfGE 23. Reprinted and translated in Kommers, *The Constitutional Jurisprudence of the Federal Republic of Germany*, 454–55.

31. Interview with Gerhard Robbers (February 23, 1996).

32. Quoted in Kommers, *The Constitutional Jurisprudence of the Federal Republic of Germany*, 494–95. The quotation is from the Catholic Hospital Abortion Case (1983), 70 BVerfGE 138.

33. Quoted in Kommers, *The Constitutional Jurisprudence of the Federal Republic of Germany*, 452. The quotation is from the Tobacco Atheist Case (1960), 12 BVerfGE 1.

34. Quoted in Kommers, *The Constitutional Jurisprudence of the Federal Republic of Germany*, 452–53. The quotation is from the Tobacco Atheist Case 12 BVerfGE 1 (1960).

35. Interview with Axel von Campenhausen (February 13, 1996).

36. Interview with Axel von Campenhausen (February 13, 1996).

37. *Blood Transfusion Case* (1971), 32 BVerfGE 98. Reprinted and translated in Kommers, *The Constitutional Jurisprudence of the Federal Republic of Germany*, 450.

38. *Blood Transfusion Case* (1971), 32 BVerfGE 98. Reprinted and translated in Kommers, *The Constitutional Jurisprudence of the Federal Republic of Germany*, 451.

39. *Blood Transfusion Case* (1971), 32 BVerfGE 98. Reprinted and translated in Kommers, *The Constitutional Jurisprudence of the Federal Republic of Germany*, 452.

40. Joseph Listl, "The Development of Civil Ecclesiastic Law in Germany 1994–1995," *European Journal for Church and State Research* 2 (1995), 17–18. The quotation is from an article by S. Muckel entitled "Muslimische Gemeinschaften als Körperschaften des Öffentlichen Rechts."

41. See Listl, "The Development of Civil Ecclesiastic Law in Germany 1994–1995," 15–16.

42. On this issue see Listl, "The Development of Civil Ecclesiastic Law in Germany 1994–1995," 19–21, Craig R. Whitney, "Scientology and Its German Foes: A Bitter Conflict," *New York Times* (November 7, 1994), A12, and Mary Williams Walsh and John-Thor Dahlburg, "Germany Versus Scientology," *Los Angeles Times* (February 6, 1997). A1 and A6.

43. Listl, "The Development of Civil Ecclesiastic Law in Germany 1994–1995," 20.

44. *The Evangelical Church in Germany: An Introduction*, para. 6.1.

45. Robbers, "State and Church in Germany," 66.

46. Interview with Gerhard Robbers (February 23, 1996).

47. See David P. Currie, *The Constitution of the Federal Republic of Germany* (Chicago: University of Chicago Press, 1994), 268.

48. Quoted by Currie, *The Constitution of the Federal Republic of Germany*, 268.

49. Interview with Axel von Campenhausen (February 13, 1996).

50. On the public corporation status of the three religious communities and its significance see Robbers, "State and Church in Germany," 61–62.

51. Interview with M. A. H. Hobohm (November 20, 1996).

52. On the church tax see Robbers, "State and Church in Germany," 68–70 and Kommers, *The Constitutional Jurisprudence of the Federal Republic of Germany*, 484–89.

53. Robbers, "State and Church in Germany," 69.

54. *Mixed-Marriage Church Tax Case I* (1965), 19 BVerfGE 226. Reprinted and translated in Kommers, *The Constitutional Jurisprudence of the Federal Republic of Germany*, 487.

55. Interview with Rüdiger Schloz (February 12, 1996). Also see "Notes on Church-State Affairs," *Journal of Church and State* 35 (1993), 440.

56. Robbers, "State and Church in Germany," 69–70.

57. See Charles L. Glenn, *Choice of Schools in Six Nations* (Washington, D.C.: U.S. Department of Education, 1989), 193–95.

58. Glenn, *Choice of Schools in Six Nations*, 195.

59. The writer was Alfred Rosenberg, quoted in J. S. Conway, *The Nazi Persecution of the Churches, 1933–1945* (New York: Basic Books, 1968), 182.

60. See Glenn, *Choice of Schools in Six Nations*, 197–201 and Spotts, *The Churches and Politics in Germany*, 212–19.

61. Spotts, *The Churches and Politics in Germany*, 219.

62. See Spotts, *The Churches and Politics in Germany*, 219–28.

63. *Interdenominational School Case* (1975), 41 BVerfGE 29. Reprinted and translated in Kommers, *The Constitutional Jurisprudence of the Federal Republic of Germany*, 469.

64. *Interdenominational School Case* (1975), 41 BVerfGE 29. Reprinted and translated in Kommers, *The Constitutional Jurisprudence of the Federal Republic of Germany*, 469.

65. *Interdenominational School Case* (1975), 41 BVerfGE 29. Reprinted and translated in Kommers, *The Constitutional Jurisprudence of the Federal Republic of Germany*, 470.

66. The decision was *McCollum v. Board of Education*, 333 U.S. 203 (1948).

67. Interview with Rüdiger Schloz (February 13, 1996).

68. Interview with M. A. H. Hobohm (November 20, 1996).

69. Inteview with Hans-Joachim Kiderlen (February 27, 1996).

70. Kommers, *The Constitutional Jurisprudence of the Federal Republic of Germany*, 472.

71. *Classroom Crucifix II Case* (1995), 93 BVerfGE 1. Reprinted and translated in Kommers, *The Constitutional Jurisprudence of the Federal Republic of Germany*, 474.

72. *Classroom Crucifix II Case* (1995), 93 BVerfGE 1. Reprinted and translated in Kommers, *The Constitutional Jurisprudence of the Federal Republic of Germany*, 478.

73. *Classroom Crucifix II Case* (1995), 93 BVerfGE 1. Reprinted and translated in Kommers, *The Constitutional Jurisprudence of the Federal Republic of Germany*, 478.

74. *Classroom Crucifix II Case* (1995), 93 BVerfGE 1. Reprinted and translated in Kommers, *The Constitutional Jurisprudence of the Federal Republic of Germany,* 481.

75. This statement, which appeared in the *Frankfurter Allgemeine Zeitung,* has been translated and reproduced in Kommers, *The Constitutional Jurisprudence of the Federal Republic of Germany,* 483–84.

76. On the Ten Commandments see *Stone v. Graham,* 449 U.S. 39 (1980), and on the cross see the 1996 Supreme Court denial of certiorari in a case in which the lower courts had ruled unconstitutional the incorporation of a cross in Edmond, Oklahoma's seal. See "Supreme Court Refuses Review of Oklahoma City Seal Cross Case," *Church and State* 49 (1996), 134.

77. Glenn, "Parental Choice in German Education," 203 and Manfred Weiss, "Financing Private Schools: The West German Case," in William Lowe Boyd and James G. Cibulka, eds., *Private Schools and Public Policy: International Perspectives* (London: Falmer Press, 1989), 193. This 5 percent figure and the ones given in the next sentence are based only on what was West Germany. The 1990 unification of Germany does not seem to have changed the situation greatly, however.

78. Weiss, "Financing Private Schools," 194.

79. Weiss, "Financing Private Schools," 199. Also see John E. Coons, "Educational Choice and the Courts: U.S. and Germany," *American Journal of Contemporary Law* 34 (1986), 5–7.

80. Quoted in Glenn, "Parental Choice in German Education," 204–5.

81. Interview with M. A. H. Hobohm (November 20, 1996).

82. Interview with Friedhelm Solms of Forschungsställe der Evangelischen Studiengemeinschaft (FEST) (Febraury 22, 1996).

83. Interview with Cornelia Marx-Coenen (February 14, 1996).

84. Helmut K. Anheier, "An Elaborate Network: Profiling the Third Sector in Germany," in Benjamin Gidron, Ralph M. Kramer, and Lester M. Salamon, eds., *Government and the Third Sector* (San Francisco: Jossey-Bass, 1992), 31. Anheier's emphasis.

85. "The Third Route: Subsidiarity, Third Party Government and the Provision of Social Services in the United States and Germany," in Organization for Economic Cooperation and Development, *Private Sector Involvement in the Delivery of Social Welfare Services: Mixed Models from OECD Countries* (Paris: OECD, 1994), 26.

86. Helmut K. Anheier and Wolfgang Seibel, "Defining the Nonprofit Sector: Germany," *Working Papers of the Johns Hopkins Comparative Nonprofit Sector Project,* no. 6 (Baltimore: Johns Hopkins Institute for Policy Studies, 1993), 7.

87. Quoted in Anheier, "An Elaborate Network," 38.

88. Quoted in Anheier, "An Elaborate Network," 38.

89. Anheier, "An Elaborate Network," 38–39.

90. Wolfgang Seibel, "Government-Nonprofit Relationships in a Comparative Perspective: The Cases of France and Germany," in Kathleen D. McCarthy, Virginia A. Hodgkinson, and Russy D. Sumariwalla, eds., *The Nonprofit Sector in the Global Community* (San Francisco: Jossey-Bass, 1992), 213. Anheier and Seibel have also written, "The early development of the modern German nonprofit sector happened in antithesis to an autocratic state." Anheier and Seibel, "Defining the Nonprofit Sector: Germany," 29.

91. Anheier, "An Elaborate Network," 41.

92. Anheier, "An Elaborate Network," 44. On the receipt of large amounts of government funding by Caritas and Diakonisches Werk as of 25 years ago see Spotts, *The Churches and Politics in Germany,* 201–3.

93. Geschäftsbereich des Bundesministeriums der Finanzen, "Antwort der Paarlamentarischen Staatssekretärin Irmgard Karwatzki" (May 3, 1995).

94. Interview with Halima Krausen of the Islamic Center in Hamburg (November 19, 1996).

95. Anheier and Seibel, "Defining the Nonprofit Sector: Germany," 30.

96. Robbers, "State and Church in Germany," 63.

97. Interview with Gerhard Robbers (February 23, 1996).

98. Quoted in Kommers, *The Constitutional Jurisprudence of the Federal Republic of Germany,* 494. The quotation is from the *Catholic Hospital Abortion Case* (1983), 70 BVerfGE 138.

99. Interview with Karl Dietrich Pfisterer (February 20, 1996).

100. Leopold A. W. Turowski, "The Church and The European Community: Developments and Prospects," *European Vision* 10 (1990), 15.

101. W. Cole Durham Jr., "Religion and the Public Schools: Constitutional Analysis in Germany and the United States" (paper given at the Western Association for German Studies, October 1977), 35.

102. Donald P. Kommers, "West German Constitutionalism and Church-State Relations," *German Politics and Society* 19 (Spring 1990), 11.

103. Interview with Rudolf Weth (February 14, 1996).

104. Interdenominational School Case (1975), 41 BVerfGE 29. Reprinted and translated in Kommers, *The Constitutional Jurisprudence of the Federal Republic of Germany,* 469.

Chapter 7

CHURCH AND STATE IN PLURALISTIC DEMOCRACIES

$\mathcal{J}$n the first chapter we said our goal in this study was to give new guidance to democracies, and to the United States in particular, in their attempts to relate church and state to each other in a manner that is supportive of their citizens' religious freedoms and the role religion plays in them. After having described the church-state principles and practices followed by the five democracies chosen for this study, we now seek to summarize the salient conclusions of the previous chapters and to consider what lessons and observations the experiences of these countries provide.

First, we summarize how each of the five countries has responded to the three questions we posed in our introduction.

- How far can a democratic polity go in permitting religiously motivated behavior that is contrary to societal welfare or norms?
- Should the state encourage and promote consensual religious beliefs and traditions in an attempt to support the common values and beliefs that bind a society together and make possible limited, democratic government?
- When religious groups and the state are both active in the same fields of endeavor, how can one ensure that the state does not advantage or disadvantage any one religious group or either religion or nonreligion over the other?

Second, we make five basic observations concerning what we believe can be gleaned from the experiences of the five countries whose church-state practices we have explored. Third, we respond to three objections that have sometimes been raised to religion playing a more fulsome role in the public life of nations.

A caveat is, however, in order. The material in our five country case studies shows that contemporary church-state practice has much to do with a nation's unique history and cultural assumptions. Practices that are largely unquestioned in one country, such as England's established church or Germany's church tax, are unimaginable in other countries, such as Australia and the United States. Having said that, we believe that countries can learn from each other and that the distinct church-state policy of these five countries is fertile and largely untapped soil for resolving what are persistent tensions between religious and political institutions.

Summary Conclusions

Free Exercise Rights

The religious free exercise rights of the five countries vary a good deal in theory, but not as much as one might expect in practice. The pattern that emerges from our review of these democracies is that each basically protects religious liberty (which is no small achievement), but struggles with how to interpret that right in specific instances.

There are three principal mechanisms by which these countries secure religious freedom: constitutional provision, legislation, and cultural attitudes and assumptions. With the exception of England, a basic right to the free exercise of one's religion is enshrined in the constitutions of each of the countries in our study. Our review of the practices of the remaining four countries has shown, however, that in many instances the courts do not consistently defend those rights. Cases from both the United States and Australia have established the precedent that constitutions do not always protect individuals and groups when their religious practice violates otherwise valid regulatory laws, irrespective of how important and deeply held are the religious beliefs that underlie their practice. The U. S. Supreme Court abandoned the compelling state interest test in its 1990 decision, *Employment Division v. Smith*, while the Australian High Court has never applied that standard in religious free exercise cases. The German Constitutional Court, by contrast, has been more aggressive in protecting religious liberty. While the Court does balance the religious rights of individuals and groups against the state's interest in public safety and health, it has been more likely than its judicial counterparts in Australia and the United States to overturn laws that conflict with religious belief and action.

Australia and the United States have gone the furthest with legislation to protect people against religious discrimination. Most of the Australian states have established antidiscrimination boards that defend people against religious discrimination; the United States also has a variety of laws against religious discrimination and the Religious Freedom Restoration Act requires the government to demonstrate that it has a compelling interest when it substantially burdens a person's exercise of religion, although it is not clear how the courts will interpret it. In England, there are fewer laws that specifically protect religious groups against discrimination.

Constitutional and legal rights are significant, to be sure, but public opinion and the cultural assumptions underlying it seem just as important a safeguard for religious liberty. England has neither a constitutional protection for religious liberty nor any law that specifically bars religious discrimination, but the nation's practice is not far different from that of the United States, which has both. The British protect religious liberty not so much because of the law, but because the British public culture values that right. Public attitudes in England have liberalized over the past century, and public policy has become more accommodating to the rights of religious minorities. The Netherlands also demonstrates the importance of cultural assumptions about religious freedom. The Dutch Constitution provides for religious liberty, but the judiciary does not have the power of judicial review over acts passed by the States-General. In theory, the States-General could pass laws that violate a person or group's right of religious free exercise, but in practice this rarely has happened because there is widespread public support for religious liberty and the Dutch may do a better job at securing religious rights than almost any other country in the world.

This is not to suggest that constitutional protections are meaningless. They provide the opportunity for religious groups to litigate when they believe that the state has violated their rights, as many have done in the United States, and in some cases the Supreme Court has used that litigation to extend religious free exercise rights. Much the same is true in Australia where the High Court has recently become more assertive in protecting constitutional rights against state action. Ideally, the courts would interpret a constitutional protection of religious rights as a mandate to defend minority religious groups whose views are unpopular and for whom the political process is not consistently a sufficient safeguard. Constitutional cases can provide the springboard for expanding free exercise rights, but a culture supportive of religious liberty has been as significant a force for extending religious rights in most of these countries.

The protection of free exercise rights, in whatever form it assumes, is an important expression of governmental neutrality on matters of religion. It sends a strong message that the government will not advantage or disadvantage people's religious choices by seeking to favor or burden any particular religion, but will instead ensure that there are no disabilities or advantages associated with adherence to any specific religion or secular belief system. This is particularly important for minority faiths whose religious free exercise rights the state might not otherwise secure.

There is one other significant pattern that emerges in these countries as it relates to free exercise rights. Germany and the Netherlands have a far more expansive and, we contend, appropriate understanding of religious liberty than England, the United States, or Australia. German practice recognizes that religious belief presupposes action based upon that belief; consequently the right to believe includes the right to act on one's beliefs. The German Constitutional Court explicitly acknowledged this point when it stated that religious freedom encompasses "the individual's right to align his behavior with the precepts of his faith and to act in accordance with his internal convictions."[1] In Australia and the United States, by contrast, the courts have adopted an Enlightenment liberal understanding of religion that views faith primarily as a private matter of individual conscience. Seen in this light, the state needs simply to protect an individual's right to believe what he or she will to secure religious liberty. The weakness of this idea is apparent in the failure of the U. S. Supreme Court to preserve the right of an Orthodox Jewish air force officer to wear a yarmulke as required by his faith, and the Australian High Court case that allowed the government to ban the Jehovah's Witnesses during World War II without any discussion of whether the church's teachings or practices threatened the state. Having abandoned or having never advocated a compelling state interest test, American and Australian courts lack a mechanism for discerning when people can legally *act* on the basis of their beliefs, which restricts religious free exercise rights for those people whose faith clashes with otherwise valid regulations.

The Dutch contribution to a more complete understanding of religious liberty is found in Article 6 of its Constitution which protects religious belief whether one exercises it as an individual or "in community with others." This communitarian emphasis contrasts with the Enlightenment liberal idea that protecting individuals' right to religious worship guarantees their religious liberty. In liberal theory, the state protects religious rights indirectly, by guaranteeing freedom of worship without fear of state discrimination. Communitarian theorists such as Michael Sandel, Alisdair MacIntyre, and Will Kymlicka have noted, however, that the modern individual is a creation of community.[2] Individuals do not choose or live a religion in isolation from others, so the liberal attempt to elucidate the right of religious liberty apart from the community is insufficient. As we have demonstrated in the country chapters, religion has a strong public facet to it and religious groups are actively involved in a wide variety of service activities. A more robust form of religious freedom requires the state to take positive measures aimed at protecting and promoting the religious expression of *groups* or *communities,* since people live out their religious life within faith communities and associations.

This is precisely what the Dutch model of pillarization historically recognized, with policies geared toward the main Catholic, Reformed, and secular groups in society. As we have noted, pillarization in the Netherlands has changed radically in recent decades, but in their public policy the Dutch have retained the idea that it is appropriate for the state to accommodate both secular and religious organizations because people naturally want to express their principles, secular or religious, within and through groups. The Dutch view the issues of public support for religious schools and organizations as matters of the right of religious free exercise, and not an establishment of religion, as would be the case in the United States. This results in a cooperative arrangement between church and state, but the Netherlands still maintains the idea of governmental neutrality. It does so not by equating neutrality with the government withdrawing all support for religion, but by equally accommodating and supporting all communities' desire for education and social services within their religious or secular traditions. The state is thereby neutral among all religions and between religious and secular systems of belief.

In theory and in practice, each of the five countries recognizes that there are some values that are so fundamental to human existence and democratic society that religious freedom cannot be the basis for their violation. Chief among them are the public health, safety, and social welfare of citizens. On these grounds, none of the countries would tolerate human sacrifice, child sexual abuse, or violence even if it was part of a group's religious beliefs. These easy cases belie how difficult it is to draw a precise boundary between free exercise rights and the state's various interests, particularly in those cases when a religious group's teaching or practice violates social values but endangers no one. It does, however, establish the appropriate precedent that there are times when the government legitimately may regulate and even outlaw religious practices because they undermine the social norms that are the basis for social unity and democratic governance. The debate about the need for a democratic society to invest its citizens with certain key values leads us directly to the second question in our discussion.

Consensual Values

There is a strong impulse in each of these countries to promote consensual values, even religious values, as a way of assimilating individuals and groups into democratic society. The norms often cited as being crucial for a democratic polity are tolerance, respect for the rule of law, and commitment to the democratic process. The institution that has historically had the key role as the incubator of these values in each country is the school. The contrast in the policy experience of the five countries is the extent to which this goal of cultural assimilation is the province of the *public* schools, as opposed to public and private schools, particularly religious ones. The United States is alone in providing virtually no aid to private religious schools, partly because of a belief that the common public schools should be the basic means by which children of all classes and religions are taught social and political values. There is a perception that private religious schools undermine this model because they segregate children on the basis of religion and allegedly on the basis of social class and race, and fail somehow to inculcate children with important democratic norms. A similar fear about the undemocratic character of Islamic schools has made it impossible for these schools to receive state aid in England, despite the fact that the state provides money for other private religious schools.

The issue is not whether the state should promote particular values. We believe that a democratic state must advance those norms that will help to sustain the polity. The question is what institution, or set of institutions, is best able to achieve that legitimate purpose. We contend that private religious schools and agencies are as capable of promoting key democratic values of tolerance, cohesion, respect for the rule of law, and commitment to the democratic process as are their public counterparts. The German approach to religious instruction is a good example of this. It is marked by representatives of the two main religious traditions in Germany developing their own religious instruction programs, which are then offered to the children from their own traditions in separate classes. Children of nonbelievers attend classes in secularly based ethical issues. There is no indication that the German released time practice or support of religiously based private schools and agencies harms the promotion of essential democratic norms.

There will be some cases of religious or secular groups that do not support basic democratic norms and they should properly be excluded from programs of public aid and participation in cooperative church-school released time programs. A private religious school that preaches hatred and violence toward others or does not provide an adequate education for children to function in the modern world has not signed on to the core consensual values of a democratic society and should not receive public support. The same is true for a religious counseling center that, for example, advises the female victims of violent domestic disputes to submit to the wishes of their abusive husbands. As a general rule, however, religious schools and agencies do not undermine democratic values, but support them.

Despite the concerns of liberals who stress the importance of the cultural assimilation of minority groups, there is very little evidence that religious schools or social service agencies fail to socialize citizens with the values necessary for life in a liberal democratic polity. The states that have gone the furthest to recognize group differences in their public policy—the Netherlands and Australia —seem not to have compromised their commitment to cultural assimilation or suffered any serious negative cultural effects for their policy.[3] There is not an inherent tension between the need for society to reach some consensus on key social values, with a public policy that accommodates group identities. As Michael Walzer notes, "ethnic citizens can be remarkably loyal to a state that protects and fosters private communal life, if that is seen to be equitably done."[4] The problem with some of these states is not so much that their public policies accommodate group differences, but that they fail to do so equitably. This is true in England, which does not fund Islamic schools; in Germany, which has not met the religious instruction needs of Muslim students to the same degree it has for Protestant and Catholic students; and in the United States, which restricts educational options to the state sector.

Having said that, we do not believe that the public schools can or should be the place for the inculcation of shared *religious* values. The experience of countries that include state-sponsored religious instruction and worship in public schools—as do England, Australia, and to a lesser degree, Germany—suggests that the pursuit of consensual religious beliefs in public institutions is doomed to failure. Each of these societies is religiously pluralistic and it is no longer possible, if it ever was, to discern consensual religious values that significant minorities of the population would not question. This is a myth fostered by nineteenth-century Enlightenment liberal educational reformers who mistakenly believed that one could suppress particularistic religious beliefs, but retain key values shared by all religious traditions. It is possible for a country to come up with guidelines for religious instruction and worship that satisfy the majority, of course, but this denies the rights of religious and secular minorities. The German Constitutional Court correctly recognized this fact in its 1995 decision that overturned a Bavarian law that required the display of a crucifix in every public school classroom, even when some students objected. Religious pluralism is a reality in each of the countries in our study, which makes it unfair for the state to promote a single religious worldview, and unlikely that it will succeed if it tries. A far better approach is for the state to allow separate religious education classes as the basic means for religious instruction, as both Germany and Australia do.

The debate in England, where the law not only permits but actually requires Christian religious instruction and worship, demonstrates the problems that come when public schools attempt to promote a single religious vision. The religious education curriculum in England focuses as much as possible on consensual religious values, but the results have dissatisfied non-Christians, nonbelievers, and many Christians as well. Non-Christians and nonbelievers fear that the schools will indoctrinate their children in the Christian religion, while many Christian groups contend that a focus on common religious values distorts and trivializes their faith. Not surprisingly, a majority of the schools have failed to meet the requirements of the Education Reform Act of 1988. The controversy illustrates that even when a majority of the people want religious instruction in the public schools, there is little agreement about what forms of religious worship and instruction the state should promote.

Public Aid to Religious Schools and Nonprofit Organizations

Religious organizations in each of the five countries in our study provide a wide variety of educational and social services to the public similar to those the five governments provide. Each state is committed to governmental neutrality on matters of religion, but they differ on what that means in terms of public financial support when religious groups and the state are active in the same field of endeavor. The issue that crystallized the tension between state and church authorities was state provision of education in the nineteenth century. Religious communities traditionally provided education for group members, but the distribution of that service was so uneven that the state gradually began to provide education for all its citizens. Educational reformers believed that the state should not provide aid to religious schools because they encouraged sectarian disputes and worked against the assimilationist goal of the public schools. Enlightenment liberal reformers in each nation saw particularistic religious beliefs as inherently dangerous, but they included in the public school curriculum what they considered to be "rational," consensual religious beliefs. This position engendered conflict from many church leaders, particularly Roman Catholics in each of the countries and conservative Protestants in the Netherlands, who argued that this state action threatened the power and autonomy of religious communities. This was not an unfounded fear. As Walzer has argued: "State welfare undercuts private philanthropy, much of which was organized within ethnic communities; it makes it harder to sustain private and parochial schools; it erodes the strength of cultural institutions."[5]

The reformist ideal never took hold in Germany where the government-sponsored schools originally were confessional in nature and most have gradually become schools that are broadly Christian in a nondenominational, nonsectarian sense. In the Netherlands and England church leaders secured state funding for denominational schools on an equal basis with state-supported schools. Church schools received little or no state aid in the United States and Australia, largely because the dominant Protestant groups joined forces with liberal reformers to stop money going to Roman Catholic schools. In the early 1960s, Australia dramatically changed its policy and began offering substantial support to church schools, while at the same time the U. S. Supreme Court was articulating a policy of strict church-state separation that ruled government could not provide funding to religious schools.

Neutrality in the United States has come to mean that the state withdraws its financial support for religious schools because of a concern that this aid would demonstrate a preference for a religious over against a nonreligious perspective. In the remaining four countries, by contrast, the justification for government support is that the state can only be truly neutral between secular and religious perspectives if it does not dominate the provision of so key a service as education, and makes it possible for people to exercise their right of religious expression within the context of public funding.

Denominational schools have thrived in those countries where state aid is available; a higher percentage of citizens attend religious schools in England, the Netherlands, and Australia than are members of a church.

The tension in those countries has come over the issue of which religious groups to include within the system. Australia and the Netherlands have gone the furthest to ensure that all religious groups are eligible for state aid, and there is a great diversity of religious as well as secular private schools in both countries. Because of its tradition of incorporating religious elements into public schools, Germany has relatively few religiously based private schools, but has provided state funding for those that exist and meet state standards. England has not provided support to those schools outside the current system—primarily Muslim and Christian fundamentalist—leading to a bias in favor of schools that have traditionally been within the system, usually Christian and Jewish.

There was less conflict between church and state when each of these governments began to expand its social welfare role in the twentieth century. The fact that Enlightenment liberal thinking did not place as great an importance on the services these agencies offered as it did on public education, which involved issues of national unity and the inculcation of democratic values, no doubt made it easier to adopt public policies that included religious associations. As a result, each of the five countries relies extensively on religious agencies to provide social welfare services. All five countries fund religious agencies and generally give them the autonomy to run their organizations as they see fit. This is not unexpected, since four of the five countries in our study also finance religiously based schools. What is somewhat surprising is that England has included Muslim agencies in this system, despite the fact that it does not provide money for Islamic schools, and that the United States funds religious agencies even though it does not fund religious schools. Because of the strict separation principles that led to the rejection of funding for religious schools, however, the religious autonomy of U. S. religious social service agencies is in more doubt in the United States than in the other countries.

Observations

We wish to make five observations that we believe are supported by the experiences of the democracies reviewed in this book. The basic norm of governmental neutrality on matters of religion we originally set out in the introductory chapter has been our guide in making these evaluative observations . This neutrality is substantive or positive in the sense of sometimes supporting positive governmental actions and sometimes governmental inaction. The basic, directing goal is that the state

should neither favor nor disfavor any particular religion or religious belief structures as a whole or secularly based belief structures as a whole.
Only in this way can the state ensure that people are neither advantaged
or disadvantaged by their adherence to their secular or faith-based tradition.

Government Neutrality and the Free Exercise of Religion

We are convinced that governmental neutrality is gained, first,
when free exercise rights are limited only because of compelling societal
interests. When government imposes certain burdens on religious practices—even when it does so in pursuit of what in most circumstances
are valid regulatory purposes—governmental policy disadvantages those
religions whose practices are being burdened. In the nineteenth century
U. S. laws against polygamy constricted the Mormons' free exercise of
their religious beliefs. Today, Dutch regulatory laws do not give Muslim
calls to prayers the same protections given the Christian ringing of
church bells. In England, the Netherlands, and Germany problems have
arisen over such issues as the right of Muslims to insist that their young
girls not be required to wear what they consider immodest clothing in
coeducation gym classes. Australia effectively banned Jehovah's Witnesses at the time of World War II, and Germany has not allowed the
Islamic ritual slaughter of animals or recognized Scientology as a religion.

We are not saying that neutrality demands that the claim of the
religious group must always trump the broader society's need for order
or other societal interests. What we do insist is that if governmental
religious neutrality is to be maintained, the state must only restrict the
practices of communities of religious or secular belief when there is a
compelling, significant societal purpose in doing so. We believe it is
more important that this be the standard that is fairly and honestly applied than any particular outcome in specific instances. Given the grave
danger from foreign invasion the Australians were facing in World War
II and given the clear antigovernment beliefs of the Jehovah's Witnesses
at that time, the government justifiably sought to protect itself against
organizations that actively sought to overthrow the state. A compelling
state interest of the highest order—survival of the state itself—was at
stake. Our problem with the action taken by the Australian High Court
related in chapter 4 lies in its failure to justify its decision on the basis of
whether or not the Jehovah's Witnesses did, in fact, threaten a vital state
interest. Similarly, our concern with the U. S. Supreme Court's decision

in regard to Mormon polygamy in the nineteenth century lies less in the outcome of the decision than in its basis (that the free exercise protection encompass only religious beliefs, not religiously inspired actions). Some limitations on the frequency and volume level of Muslim calls to prayer—as well as Christian practices that are public and intrusive into the lives of all citizens—can also be justified on the basis of a compelling state interest in public order and respect. As we noted in chapter 6, the German government could also justify its decision not to recognize Scientology as a religion on the basis of protecting the public from commercial fraud.

Our purpose is not to say how other countries—whose specific conditions and circumstances we can only know in general terms—should decide these sensitive, often difficult issues. We do, however, insist that they should not be decided on the basis of conventional, majoritarian practice or the political and social power of long dominant religious groups. They should be decided in a fair, honest attempt to allow the maximum amount of religious freedom congruent with societal order, health, and safety. Anything less would put the adherents of those religions at a disadvantage without there being a compensating societal advantage. In doing this, government's religious neutrality would be violated.

Government Neutrality and the Promotion of Consensual Religious Beliefs

Our second observation is that it is extremely difficult for states to promote consensual religious values and still maintain their religious neutrality. England and Germany have sought to do the most along these lines, and in the case of Germany it has self-consciously sought to do so in a manner respectful of differing religious traditions. Yet in reviewing their practices we came away convinced that their success in doing so, while maintaining governmental religious neutrality, is less than complete. Most efforts to inculcate consensual religious values have been directed at public elementary and secondary schoolchildren. (We are thinking here of religious or worship experiences that are made a part of the school day or—as is the case in some German schools—the presence of religious symbols in public school classrooms, not released time programs where schoolchildren receive religious instruction in the faith or secular beliefs of their families.) The fact that many British schools do not follow the clear legal mandate to include prayers and worship experiences of a "broadly Christian character" reveals the difficulty many school officials feel they have in doing so in a manner fair to all students in a society that is increasingly religiously pluralistic. The provisions that the German Constitutional Court has insisted upon for the right of children to be excused from public prayers in the schools or to insist that a crucifix be removed from their classroom have put a large burden on these children and their parents. Such children must choose between living in an atmosphere that goes against their religious beliefs and distinguishing themselves as being different from other students. Continuing British efforts to integrate the Church of England into public ceremonies and important state occasions also raise questions of state religious neutrality. The problem inherent in all such efforts is that religion and secular belief structures are particular and concrete in nature, not general or vague. It is simply not possible to find religious common ground that has enough content to be at all meaningful. Those who dissent from whatever religious common ground the state seeks to identify and then promote find themselves being put at a state-created disadvantage.

Government Neutrality and Church-State Separation

Our third observation is that efforts at the strict separation of church and state—in which the United States has engaged—also violate state religious neutrality. The state violates religious neutrality when under the auspices of strict separation public schools ban released time programs, schools sponsored by religious groups are denied funds, and religious social and health service agencies must downplay or put at risk their religious character in order to receive public funds all other agencies are receiving. Government is no longer treating religious and nonreligious viewpoints and groups in an evenhanded manner. It collects taxes from citizens who are adherents of a wide range of religious and secular viewpoints and from members of a wide range of religious communities (and, for some, secularly based communities of belief), and then distributes those tax funds in support of only some of them. Strict separation policies advantage those whose implicit or explicit beliefs lead them to be comfortable with public schools stripped of religion or with social service agencies whose religious character is left in question. But those who desire their children to receive religious instruction in keeping with their particularistic beliefs or wish to support or receive services from religiously based service agencies are put at a competitive disadvantage.

Strict separation was born in the context of eighteenth-century debates over the appropriateness of public funding for churches and their clergy. In that situation strict separation properly says the state should strictly separate itself from the church, not funding any or all churches.

Even funding all religions equally would still discriminate against or disadvantage those citizens who are adherents of no religious faith. In addition, when the issue is direct government funding of churches and clergy, for the government not to do so does not disadvantage religion generally, since the state would not be funding competing secular belief structures. The state is being neutral. That, however, is not the issue today. None of the five democracies included in this study directly funds churches or clergy to any significant extent. It is no longer even an issue.

Instead the issue has shifted to the arena of schools and social and health service organizations. Here the state, religiously based organizations, and secularly based organizations—all three—are providing the same services. Under strict separation the state may, of course, fund its own secularized services and presumably could fund and otherwise cooperate with private secularly based organizations, but could not fund or cooperate too closely with religiously based organizations (or at least could not fund them if they integrate their religious aspects into the services they render). But this is not neutrality. The state is favoring schools and organizations of a nonreligious nature over those of a religious nature. All of the democracies considered in this book except the United States have recognized this. Time and again in our interviews, and especially in the Netherlands, Australia, and Germany, people made reference to the fact that funding religiously based schools or social service agencies or making provision for released time religious classes in public schools constitutes an attempt at fairness or neutrality. In a statement quoted earlier, Sophie van Bijsterveld of the Netherlands made a key point that is widely recognized outside the United States—but often not recognized within it:

> There have also been court decisions [ruling] that government doesn't have to subsidize social work, charitable work, or youth work, but when it subsidizes this type of work it should make no discrimination on the basis of religion or belief. So if a "neutral" organization applies for this work it may receive it, but if a church or religious organization wants to carry out this work, it should not be excluded because that would not be equal treatment.[6]

Government Neutrality and Released Time Programs

A fourth observation relates closely to the point with which we closed our third observation. We would argue that public policies that provide for released time instruction in public schools or that provide equally for public funding of private religiously and secularly based schools and social service organizations are fully in keeping with state religiously neutrality, and may sometimes be required by the neutrality norm. This is a counterpart to the point we made in our first observation, dealing with free exercise protections. We argued there that if in the absence of a compelling societal interest the government were to limit the rights or practices of certain religious groups it would be putting them at a disadvantage in a way that other religious or nonreligious groups were not. Similarly, if government were to fund a variety of schools (either public or private) but not fund religious schools, it would be putting the religious schools at a state-created disadvantage. Or if government were to fund its own social and health services and private secular social and health services, but not fund religious social and health services, it would be putting those religious service organizations at a state-created disadvantage.

Not quite as clearly, if the public schools provide all sorts of secular instruction in a wide variety of fields, but make no allowance for the various religious groups to instruct the children of their members in their faith, one can argue that religion is being disadvantaged. Here there is, however, an easy counterargument in that the various religions could instruct their adherents' children during nonschool hours. That point can be countered, however, by the fact that the schools normally monopolize the prime morning and early afternoon hours outside of summer and holiday periods, leaving the religions with the leftover, less prime times. We do not need to take a stand on whether the lack of a released time program in government-sponsored schools violates state neutrality. What we do argue is that public policies that provide for released time programs for in-school religious instruction do not violate the norm of state religious neutrality. As long as schools provide classes for all or most of the religious groups represented among the students and alternative classes in secular values systems or other topics, government is being evenhanded. It is not favoring any particular religious or secular belief system.

Government Neutrality and Funding for Religious Schools and Service Organizations

Our fifth observation is that government funding of religious schools and organizations is not only in keeping with the norm of state religious neutrality, but that it also actively promotes three key values often associated with liberal democracy: choice, social pluralism, and participatory democracy. We want to elaborate at some length on how state aid promotes these social norms.

Public funding makes religious education more affordable for low- and middle-income parents who choose to exercise that option. Parents who want a religious education for their children have more choice in Australia, the Netherlands, England, and Germany than in the United States. Similarly, without public finance of religious social service organizations there would be less diversity in those services. Citizens in each nation have access to services that have a specific philosophical basis in such key areas as mental health, drug and alcohol rehabilitation, residential aged care, and marriage services. The current policy encourages greater citizen choice and is neutral among religions and between a religious and a nonreligious perspective. To the extent that choice is a value (and we do not suggest that it is the only value in a liberal democracy) public funding of religious schools and agencies is preferable.

Genuine choice is only possible, however, if the state grants nongovernment schools and welfare organizations a significant degree of autonomy. We believe that nongovernment organizations should be accountable to the government for the funds they receive and that they must meet standards in the services they offer, but nongovernment organizations must also have freedom in how they operate. There are limits to that freedom. The state should not allow religious or secular associations to engage in or advocate illegal actions that would undermine public order, health, and safety. Nor should they be allowed to foment hatred and the violation of norms of civility and respect for the rights of others. The government should not, however, seek to impose a standardized model into which Muslim, Catholic, Jewish, and secular child care or marital counseling services would be forced. The imposition of common rules and standardized services to such agencies would threaten the diversity that is a virtue of the contemporary policy. To the extent that there are groups of citizens who want services tailored to a specific value system, schools and agencies must be free to retain their specific character with policies on hiring, admissions, and service delivery.

State funding for religious schools and service agencies also promotes social pluralism and cultural identity. Religious schools enable groups to maintain and instill the tenets of their faith and relate them to the contemporary world. This is particularly true for immigrants who do not necessarily support a policy of assimilation with its tacit contention that new groups should be absorbed into the dominant values and ethos of that society. Since government schools and agencies typically support consensual religious or secularized perspectives, people who belong to religious communities with distinctive, nonmajoritarian religious beliefs will tend to find themselves put under significant disadvantages. Pluralism asserts that the state should tolerate competing educational and social service ideas because the diverse religious and secular communities that make up a nation have a right to exist in the context of freedom to live out their beliefs uncoerced by the state. Pluralism challenges the idea that the intent of public education or social services is to unify a diverse polity by supplanting particularistic identities through cultural assimilation.[7]

As each of these societies becomes more pluralistic, the demand for particularistic services grows and the issue becomes whether or not each state will accommodate group differences through public finance of religious schools and social service organizations. So long as there is a clear demand for services to be organized through ethnic and religious communities, we believe that it makes sense for the state to finance those organizations. Public aid reinforces group identities, which gives greater recognition to the fact that religious and ethnic life is lived out through community organizations like the school. While we recognize that the state has an interest in assuring that these organizations meet certain minimal levels of service by establishing uniform standards, centralized service provision is economically inefficient and potentially dangerous, particularly for those groups that want to retain a distinctive perspective. We argue that genuine pluralism is preferable because it demonstrates public recognition and support of the religious group differences that are a part of each of these societies.

Public aid to religious schools and welfare organizations also strengthens participatory democracy and localized decision making. Public aid to religious schools and agencies empowers groups at local levels to participate in the decisions that are most important to them. It reinforces what Paul Hirst describes as "associative democracy."[8] Associationalism claims that "individual liberty and human welfare are both best served when as many of the affairs of society as possible are managed by voluntary and democratically self-governing associations."[9] In an associational democracy, the state provides the finance for public goods, such as education or social welfare, but allows local associations to administer them. These groups are accountable to the government for use of the funds, but are more responsive to those for whom the service is provided.

Hirst and other communitarian theorists have made a case for the notion of group rights. The idea is that the state encourages groups to organize themselves by assigning to them rights and political power. The

Dutch corporatist arrangement is the clearest indication of this policy in practice. We do not suggest that corporatism is the appropriate model for any one of these states, but we do believe that there are legitimate ways for the state to step in to structure and encourage religious group life. With the exception of the United States, the countries in our study have taken positive and, we believe, legitimate steps to ensure that religious groups can live out their faith in what is probably the most important public institution, the school. Each of the states has allowed group life to flourish in social welfare services, although the autonomy and status of those organizations are in some question in the United States. England has followed a restricted form of pluralism in its educational system because of its failure to aid newly emerging religious groups outside the current system, and Germany has also done so by its failure to incorporate religious instruction for Muslim children into the public school system. We believe that governmental neutrality demands public finance for all religious groups. We also contend that state aid promotes the socially beneficial goals of choice, social pluralism, and participatory democracy.

Two Objections

In this book we have made clear the extent to which the U. S. church-state practices, especially as they relate to establishment of religion issues such as state funding of religious schools and social and health service organizations, differ from those followed in the other democracies considered here. We have also argued that this strict separationist approach of the United States to these establishment issues has led it to violate the norm of state neutrality toward religion. Clearly, we believe the other democracies considered here—especially the Netherlands and Australia—have done a better job of meeting the norm of state religious neutrality and thereby of assuring the full religious freedom of all than has the United States.

It is appropriate for us to close this book by briefly considering two objections often raised in the United States to the practices and principles followed by other democracies and advocated by us. One key point that opponents of public funds going to religious schools and service organizations often make is that doing so leads to invidious distinctions in society along religious lines and undermines key goals of a liberal polity, including societal unity and tolerance.[10] According to this argument it is a mistake to recognize and accommodate group differences, and especially religious group differences, because doing so leads to dangerous divisions in society and encourages the kinds of social demarcations that are unhealthy for democracy. A successful democracy assumes a minimum of consensus that a truly pluralistic society cannot achieve. A policy of public funding for the educational and social service efforts of separate religious groups is unacceptable because doing so reinforces the tendency of people to separate along ethnic, class, and religious lines. Sectarian conflict such as what Northern Ireland and the lands of the former Yugoslavia are experiencing today and the horrors of religious wars in Europe of the seventeenth century illustrate the dangers one courts when religion and politics are allowed to mix. What is preferable is a model of strict church-state separation, in which religion is privatized, and liberal individualism that evaluates people on the basis of their individual achievements, and not according to their membership in groups. A commitment to these liberal values provides the common bond for the nation's citizens and overcomes the problems inherent in a more pluralistic system.

This is a powerful and, in some cases, persuasive argument. Northern Ireland and the former Yugoslavia are indeed terrifying examples of what can happen when a polity makes invidious distinctions between people based solely upon their group membership. Liberal individualism rightly calls attention to the horrors that can result when the notion of group identity gets out of hand. We recognize the grave dangers in a rigid, extreme form of separatism that elevates group loyalty—whether based on religion, ethnicity, language or other considerations—to a position of preeminence over all other loyalties. Loyalty to one's religious or other group then becomes all-consuming and is not balanced by loyalties to the nation-state, community, and other forces present in a pluralistic society. Separatism of such a nature is not the democratic ideal, either for society as a whole or for the minority groups in question.

Two facts need to be recognized, however. One is that religion does not pose a unique danger of being the source of an extreme separatism that threatens societal unity. One has only to think of the American Civil War, the tragic fighting that Guatemala experienced in recent years, the breakup of the Soviet Union, and the ongoing, sometimes violent struggle of the Kurds in Iraq and Turkey for a separate nation-state to realize that many forces other than religion can lie behind societal disunity and actual or threatened civil war. Religion does not pose a uniquely dangerous source of societal division.

A second fact in need of recognition is that historically religion has become a dangerous, divisive force in society when one or more religious groups asserted monopolistic claims. It is when religion asserts the right to monopolize state or societal power and force its will on the rest of society or to claim prerogatives or advantages denied other religious groups that tensions and possibly violent conflict arise. This was true in the case of Europe's religious wars in the seventeenth century and the civil war in Bosnia–Herzegovina in the 1990s. Similarly erring are those people and groups in the United States who today advocate a constitutional amendment that would declare the United States a Christian nation or who seek to reinstate organized prayer in the public schools. The problem in these cases lay with the idea that the government should promote or endorse a particular faith over other religious and secular worldviews. This naturally leads to bitter social and political disputes among people who are not of the preferred faith.

Thus the key question becomes whether a likely effect of aid to religious schools and social service agencies, and perhaps other positive actions to recognize or accommodate the whole range of religious and secular belief structures, is to intensify cultural differences in unhealthy ways that breed an extreme separatism that will place loyalty to one's religious groups above all other loyalties and will lead to attempts to assert monopolistic claims. We believe that the answer to this question is clearly no. We can think of no instance when a genuine pluralism accompanied by mutual respect and freedom for all religious groups led to dangerous societal divisions.

The countries in our study with the most pluralistic system of state aid to religious schools and organizations—the Netherlands and Australia—have witnessed less conflict among religious groups and fewer problems of social divisiveness than countries with less extensive systems of support, notably England and the United States. What is remarkable from the Dutch and Australian experience is the extent to which a political coalition among the various faiths—Catholic, Protestant, Jewish, Islamic—has formed to protect their shared status. The pluralistic policy of aid to all religious schools and organizations gives them a common stake in the political system, which has helped to domesticate religious disputes in those two countries. This is no small accomplishment. By contrast, there are persistent disputes in England among Muslims and fundamentalist Christians who understandably feel discriminated against because the state provides aid to some religious schools but not to theirs. Similarly, religious tensions are high in the United States because many religious groups contend, with some justification, that the state disadvantages them with its policy of strict church-state separation.

We argue, further, that state aid to religious and ethnic organizations' educational or social efforts can promote the state's goal of integrating immigrant groups into society while at the same time encouraging social pluralism.[11] Surveys of Jewish and Muslim communities in Australia, for example, indicate that involvement with ethnic or religious organizations has helped, not restricted, the assimilation process for immigrant groups. According to one report, involvement with Jewish organizations provides new immigrants "with important avenues for acculturation that eventually allow them to broaden the areas of social interaction with the host society."[12]

We are well aware of the potential dangers to democratic stability of the politicization of religious disputes, therefore, but we conclude that those problems inhere in countries that provide aid in a discriminatory manner, either to one or a small number of religious groups or only to secular perspectives. A pluralistic policy of funding for religious schools and social agencies has not intensified social divisiveness in those countries that have adopted this policy, and there is no reason to believe that it would engender greater conflict among religious groups if the United States followed this example.

A second basic concern often expressed by American strict separationists is that a strict separation, no-aid-to-religion approach is necessary to safeguard the welfare of religion. The argument is that state support for religion—even its educational and social service activities— inevitably leads to a weakening of religion as government imposes regulations along with its support and religion becomes fat and complacent. In fact, American strict separationists often point to the experience of European countries such as England, Germany, and the Netherlands to make their case. The argument is that in these countries religion receives much public aid of one type or another and the churches are moribund; in the United States religion does not receive public aid and the churches are alive and active. Works by Roger Finke, Rodney Stark, and Laurence Iannoccone that have applied a supply side economic theory to religious activism *seem* to make the same point.[13] They account for variations in religious participation rates among nations on the basis of the degree of state regulation for religion. They argue that an unregulated religious economy increases the overall levels of religious commitment and participation as churches appeal to specific segments of the religious market in order to survive. A highly regulated economy, by contrast, creates an unnatural religious monopoly that depresses competition among the churches and decreases religious activism and vitality. That public support for religion is bad is suggested by the secularization of Europe, where the state provides aid to religious organizations, and the lack of a corresponding secularization movement in the United States, where aid is not as available to religious organizations.

We would make two responses to these suggestions. One is that the key to church vitality in the United States according to Finke, Stark, and Iannoccone has been competition among the churches, and not the American model of church-state separation per se. This model has allowed for the formation of a genuine religious pluralism in America, but there are other church-state models that would encourage this type of competitive struggle just as well. We believe that the state can provide funds to religious schools and social agencies without inhibiting competition among the churches. Our policy of state neutrality among the churches and between religious and secular perspectives would arguably enhance religious competition. A closer look at church activism in these countries will show that the issue is not so much the presence or absence of a strict church-state separation, as some suggest, as with public policies that inhibit competition among the churches.

American religion acquired a uniquely entrepreneurial tone or spirit because of the extreme religious diversity found in the United States and the unsettled, changing social conditions of a new, rapidly expanding nation. The fact that the state did not generally restrict religious competition provided a better atmosphere for new, upstart religious movements that formed to appeal to the common people, responded to their needs and desires, and lured members away from the more "respectable" established churches ("established" in a social not political sense). In the early United States the Presbyterians, Baptists, and Methodists challenged the more established Anglicans and Congregationalists. Now they are the respected mainline churches and have been losing members to the newer Assemblies of God, evangelical "megachurches," and other charismatic or evangelical groups. All this means churches in the United States have to be entrepreneurial—they must compete for new members and hold their present members by responding to the needs of their members and potential members. If they do not, there will always be other churches who will be willing to do so. The absence of a state-imposed religious monopoly gave new religious movements the freedom to form and made American churches populist and sensitive to the desires of their adherents and potential adherents, thereby increasing church attendance and other measures of religious commitment. This is in stark contrast with England and Germany, where the state historically regulated the religious economy in such a way to inhibit the development of religious pluralism and vitality. Church-state policies of both countries restricted access to the religious market for new churches and gave the established church or churches built-in advantages. Church activism suffered as the established churches did not have to be sensitive to religious market demands in order to survive. The fact that even today the German church tax continues to be collected by the state may mean that clerics still feel less pressure to recruit a congregation or tailor their "product" to meet specialized religious market demands (in the terms of Finke, Stark, and Iannoccone).

The important difference between the United States and Europe according to this account is the presence or absence of a pluralistic and highly competitive religious scene: "a set of specialized firms will, together, be able to appeal to a far greater proportion of consumers than can be the case when only one faith is available without risk or sanctions. . . . Competition creates vigorous organizations."[14] While we are not prepared to say that this is the only reason for the different levels of religious commitment in the countries considered here, and there has been much debate about the utility of the Finke, Stark, and Iannoccone thesis, it is likely a reason.[15] A church-state policy that restricts competition among the churches, such as a religious establishment, is unhealthy for religion.

We see no reason to conclude, however, that a policy of strict church-state separation is the only one that would facilitate competition among the churches. Our proposal would not inhibit competition or make America more like its European counterparts in terms of religious vitality. Our policy calls for the elimination of any state-imposed monopoly—religious or secular—that is discriminatory among ideological perspectives and leads to the kinds of market failures highlighted by Finke, Stark, and Iannoccone. The key point that American discussions of church-state issues often miss is that church-state separation is *not* neutral among ideological perspectives, but advantages secular ones. Government assistance that is genuinely neutral can increase the pluralism that seems a natural state of a religious economy and is so important for religious vitality. Government aid to religious schools and agencies in the Netherlands and Australia did not restrict competition but enhanced it as new religious organizations formed to represent their distinctive perspectives. We believe that much the same thing would occur if England extended its system of aid to Muslim and evangelical Christian schools, and if the United States allowed public money to go to religious schools.

Our second response to the argument that a neutral governmental policy of aiding religious and secular schools and social agencies weakens religion is that there is almost no evidence linking the secularization—or diminishing church activism—of the British, Australian, Dutch, and

German societies with state aid to religious schools and organizations. In the Netherlands, for example, there was a clear secularization trend that swept through Dutch society in the 1960s and 1970s.[16] If government funding of religious schools and social service organizations caused this trend, however, it was a long time coming, since there had been significant public funding of such organizations since the end of the nineteenth century. In addition, the Dutch secularization trend started not so much in the schools and religious social service agencies, but in the churches themselves. And the churches receive no governmental support or aid. If government support and recognition of religion is a causative factor in the secularization of Dutch society, one would expect it to be most advanced where the most aid is found—the schools and social service organizations—and the least advanced in the churches themselves who do not receive aid. This relationship does not, however, hold up. Similar points can be made in regard to all four of the countries studied where the state has made public provision of funds available to religious schools and social service agencies. In all four of these countries, for example, we interviewed people from religious schools and social service organizations whose religious commitments were strong, vigorous, and up-front. Yet they all also received public funding. At the very least this demonstrates that there is not a necessary causative link between public funds and the atrophy of distinctive religious commitments.

At the close of this book we return to the theme of religious freedom for all—the freedom to believe and follow the eternal truths one's conscience dictates without the involvement of government either to favor or to hinder. This becomes an ever more elusive goal in an era marked by increasing levels of religious pluralism, and with the growth of the modern welfare state that involves the government in almost all aspects of society. There is much that liberal democracies can learn from each other. We are convinced there is especially much to be learned from those practices rooted in an acceptance and even celebration of religious diversity. Those practices seek to attain religious neutrality, not by a blanket, no-aid-to-religion standard nor by seeking and supporting consensual religious beliefs, but by treating all faiths and secular systems of belief in a manner that accepts them for what they are, protects them to the extent vital societal interests allow, and in programs of governmental support and cooperation, treats them in an evenhanded manner. There is much wisdom in such a course.

Notes

1. *Religious Oath Case* (1972), 33 BVergGE 23. Reprinted and translated in Donald P. Kommers, *The Constitutional Jurisprudence of the Federal Republic of Germany,* 2nd ed. (Durham: Duke University Press, 1997), 454.

2. Michael Sandel, *Liberalism and the Limits of Justice* (Cambridge: Cambridge University Press, 1982), Alisdair MacIntyre, *After Virtue: A Study of Moral Theory* (Notre Dame: University of Notre Dame Press, 1984), and Will Kymlicka, *Liberalism, Community, and Culture* (Oxford: Clarendon Press, 1989).

3. See Arend Lijpart, "Self-Determination versus Pre-Determination of Ethnic Minorities in Power Sharing Systems," in Will Kymlicka, ed., *The Rights of Minority Cultures* (Oxford: Oxford University Press, 1995), 275–87.

4. Michael Walzer, "Pluralism: A Political Perspective," in Kymlicka, ed., *The Rights of Minority Cultures*, 153.

5. Walzer, "Pluralism: A Political Perspective."

6. Interview with Sophie C. van Bijsterveld (February 9, 1996).

7. James C. Cibulka, "Rationales for Private Schools," in William Lowe Boyd and James C. Cibulka, eds., *Private Schools and Public Policy* (London: Falmer Press, 1989), 91–104.

8. Paul Hirst, *Associative Democracy: New Forms of Economic and Social Governance* (Amherst: University of Massachusetts Press, 1994).

9. Hirst, *Associative Democracy*, 19.

10. Stephen Macedo, "Transformative Constitutionalism and the Case of Religion: Defending the Moderate Hegemony of Liberal Constitutional Values," (paper presented at the 1995 Annual Meeting of the American Political Science Association).

11. For a good analysis of this position, see Iris Marion Young, "Together in Difference: Transforming the Logic of Group Political Conflict," in Kymlicka, ed., *The Rights of Minority Cultures*, 155–78.

12. John Goldlust, *The Melbourne Jewish Community: A Needs Assessment* (Canberra: Australian Government Publishing Service, 1993), 85.

13. Roger Finke and Rodney Stark, *The Churching of America, 1776–1990* (New Brunswick: Rutgers University Press, 1992), and Rodney Stark and Laurence R. Iannoccone, "A Supply-Side Reinterpretation of the 'Secularization' of Europe," *Journal for the Social Scientific Study of Religion* 33 (1994), 230–52.

14. Stark and Iannoccone, "A Supply-Side Reinterpretation of the 'Secularization' of Europe," 233.

15. A number of scholars have challenged the Stark, Finke, and Iannoccone argument. See, for example, Steve Bruce, "The Truth About Religion in Britain," *Journal for the Social Scientific Study of Religion* 34 (1995), 417–30, and Frank J. Lechner, "Secularization in the Netherlands?" *Journal for the Social Scientific Study of Religion*, 35 (1996), 252–64.

16. One historian who has carefully studied the Dutch secularization trend of the 1960s sees the chief causative factor lying not in the Dutch pluralistic system of recognition of and aid to religious and secular schools and social agencies, but in the religious, political, and social elites' response to the cultural changes moving through western societies in the 1960s. That response emphasized accommodating and accepting rather than resisting these changes. See James C. Kennedy, *Building New Babylon: Cultural Change in the Netherlands During the 1960s* (Ph.D. dissertation, University of Iowa, 1995).

Index

About the Authors

Stephen V. Monsma is professor of political science and chair of the social science division at Pepperdine University in Malibu, California. A widely published scholar in the area of religion and politics, his books include *Positive Neutrality: Letting Religious Freedom Ring* (Greenwood Press, 1993) and *When Sacred and Secular Mix: Religious Nonprofit Organization and Public Money* (Rowman & Littlefield, 1996).

J. Christopher Soper is an associate professor of political science at Pepperdine University. He has written numerous articles on religion and politics and is the author of *Religious Beliefs and Political Choices: Evangelical Christianity in the United States and Great Britain* (New York University Press, 1994).